Other books by Roger E. Herman

Keeping Good People: Strategies for Solving the #1 Problem Facing Business Today
(in English, Spanish, Portuguese, and German)

The Process of Excelling *(enriched edition)*
(in English and Portuguese)

Turbulence! Challenges & Opportunities in the World of Work
(in English and Spanish)

Disaster Planning for Local Governments

Emergency Operations Plan

Other learning tools to help you create a meaningful organization include a six-cassette audiotape album, entitled **Keeping Good People** *(not a reading of the book's text), and a multimedia training package, called* **Keeping Winners***, for organizations large and small. Both products are available from The Herman Group.*

Both Roger Herman, and his co-author, Joyce Gioia, are available for consultations and speaking engagements. Contact them at:

The Herman Group
3400 Willow Grove Court
Greensboro, North Carolina 27410
(336) 282-9370
www.herman.net

Lean & Meaningful

A New Culture for Corporate America

S̓uccessful business has often been described as

"lean and mean."

S̓uccessful business in the future will be

"lean and meaningful."

Lean & Meaningful

A New Culture for Corporate America

Roger E. Herman
&
Joyce L. Gioia

Oakhill Press

This publication is designed to provide accurate and authoritative information in regard to the subject matter covered. It is sold with the understanding that the publisher is not engaged in rendering legal, accounting, or other professional service. If legal advice or other expert assistance is required, the services of a competent professional person should be sought. *From a Declaration of Principles jointly adopted by a committee of the American Bar Association and a committee of Publishers.*

10   9   8   7   6   5   4   3   2

Library of Congress Cataloging in Publication Data

Herman, Roger E., 1943–
　　Lean & Meaningful : a New Culture for Corporate America / Roger E. Herman and Joyce L. Gioia
　　　p. cm.
　　Includes bibliographical references and index.
　　ISBN 1-886939-07-1 (alk. paper)
　　1. Corporate culture. 2. Cost control. 3. Downsizing. 4. Social responsibility of business. I. Gioia, Joyce L., 1947–
　　II. Title.
HD58.7.H463   1998
658.4—dc21   98-13258
                                                                              CIP

Dedication

This book is dedicated to the thousands of men and women who have pioneered in the field of meaningfulness in the ever-changing and sometimes complicated world of corporate work. In a wide range of organizations in the public, private, and not-for-profit sectors, they've broken new ground and blazed new trails. We salute their creativity, their foresightedness, their bravery.

In addition, we dedicate this book to our fathers, who were pioneers in *their* fields, Dr. Carlton M. Herman and Dr. Murrel H. Kaplan. This work is also dedicated to our mothers, Estelle Herman and Louise May Kaplan, who provided immeasurable support to their husbands and to us.

Thank you . . . for making a positive difference.

Roger Herman and Joyce Gioia

Contents

Preface

Every organization has a unique culture that influences the way it functions. Culture guides the organization's relations with employees, customers, stockholders, suppliers, regulatory agencies, the media, and the community at large. To a large extent, culture—attitudes, protocols, beliefs, and values—determines how successful a corporation will be in interactions with all its stakeholders.

Prospective (and current) employees, customers, suppliers, and others use their perception of a company's culture to determine whether they even want a relationship with the company . . . or how deep that relationship might be. Individuals and organizations (collections of individuals) evaluate corporations, their products, and their services based on these cultural issues.

Corporate culture has evolved along a continuum for several generations in America. We've moved from a collaborative design during the cottage industry period through benevolent dictator, autocratic, democratic, participatory, and team-based phases as companies, their leaders, and their people sought the best way(s) to work with each other. Culture is a people thing—it's the way people work together in organizations. Management gurus have made small fortunes promoting new ideas about the "right" culture for corporate success. We've seen everything from scientific approaches to reengineering efforts applied in search of the ideal solution.

Culture is unique to each organization. It's inspired and reinforced by leaders, guided by managers, and implemented by all the people who are *members* of the organization. Yes, corporations have "members"—people who subscribe to the values and behaviors that are part of the cultural "script." Those people who don't subscribe, who don't demonstrate their support, are deemed to be rebels, outcasts, misfits, or loners. Today's organizations, highly concerned about having everyone "on-board" and concentrating on the same results, are less tolerant of nonmembers on the payroll. And people who don't sense a good fit with their employers are increasingly likely to leave in search of a better home.

Factors outside the corporation can drive various aspects of a company's culture. We see those influence(s) today as employers become more sensitive to economic trends, labor shortages, technological developments, and competitive challenges. Corporate leaders seek ways to do more with less, to concentrate on their core business, and to position themselves for a rapidly changing future. To respond with agility and speed to emerging marketplace opportunities, companies must shed their redundancies and extra weight. They must recruit, optimize, and retain top talent to serve their customers, design new products and services, maximize productivity, and maintain a high level of competitiveness.

Based on outside factors, as well as internal desires to do things differently (often directed by a strong, fresh emphasis on values), companies are deliberately and energetically changing the ways they do business. They're becoming more lean, flexible, and responsive. The drive to "get lean" means streamlining both the size and the operating processes of the company; it's a deep, philosophical shift that reaches into every nook and cranny of the organization. This leanness is viewed, understandably, as a threat by some; most view the new orientation as long overdue. As we move into the years

ahead, practically every organization—corporate, governmental, and not-for-profit, will move in the lean direction.

To achieve their objectives, these lean organizations need
people. Not just any people, but competent, dedicated, high
performers. Those special people are in relatively short supply. Every employer wants them . . . and there simply aren't
enough to go around. As a consequence, the desired workers
(and there are a lot of them!) have plenty of choices about
where they work. They'll now *choose* their employers; we've
entered a sellers' market in labor. Employers no longer have
a large pool of qualified applicants to choose from. With
choices, workers are developing a new set of criteria to *select*
their employers.

The workers of today and tomorrow want to work for a
company with a culture that's compatible with their own values and beliefs. These cultural criteria override the financial
issues; people want more "compensation" than just a fat paycheck or a cushy benefit plan. They want meaningfulness in
their employment experience.

Meaningfulness? Yes. Today—and even more so tomorrow—people want meaning and balance in their lives.
They've been through a lot in the past decade or so in the
work environment. It's time for a change. Enlightened
employers have sensed this feeling, and many of them have
begun to do things in their organizations to make a difference
in the areas we describe as "meaningful." Workers will
demand these new approaches, expressing themselves by
selecting employers who build more meaningfulness into the
way they do business.

As Strategic Business Futurists watching trends, and as
Certified Management Consultants watching what's actually
happening in organizations, we see the next generation of
corporate culture as a design we describe as "lean and meaningful." In this book, we'll explain the shift, the transition to
this emerging culture. We'll show the kinds of things that can
be done to bring a higher level of meaningfulness into the

work environment, illustrating the opportunities with examples of what some enlightened companies are already doing.

Writing this book was an exciting project. Every day we saw confirmation of our forecasts about the changing corporate culture. We talked to many people—in all walks of life—who validated our perspectives. Learning about what companies were already doing was fun: many of them are very enthusiastic! Even with all the companies we've cited, we know the examples are by no means complete. Hundreds of other employers are doing wonderful things to become lean in a positive way and to add meaningfulness to work life.

This book was written to provide you with the insights and role models, or at least road signs to assist you in your transition. The road to becoming a lean and meaningful organization may not be smooth. Change is never comfortable. However, we promise that your sincere efforts *will* be rewarded.

Roger E. Herman, CSP, CMC   Joyce L. Gioia, CMC
roger@herman.net   joyce@herman.net

Acknowledgments

Putting together a book like this is a demanding project. Months of designing and writing were preceded (and accompanied!) by over a year of research. This is not something that is done by just one or two people.

Noal Hebert was a major contributor to pulling all the research together with us—to make sense of everything we were observing as futurists and consultants. We thank her for helping to craft the presentation of the trends, concepts, and ideas you'll read in the pages that follow.

When Roger's first book was written in 1980, the technology of a correcting IBM Selectric typewriter was still sufficient to produce a good manuscript. We've come a long way! Now we sit at our Compaq notebook computers using sophisticated word processing programs and e-mail. What a difference! Thanks to all who made this technological transition possible, especially Scott Herman, owner of PC Plumbers, Buffalo, New York. We never realized how much our computers could do for us.

We thank our kids, especially Samantha, for putting up with our concentrating on research or the manuscript when they would have preferred a little more attention or a fancier dinner. Our fine team at The Herman Group provided wonderful support, giving us "space" to write, rewrite, redesign, and critique.

A special thanks to our editor, Estelle Herman. Even with all the computerized spelling and grammar checks, she still found ways to improve this book for you, our appreciated reader. A salute to Ed Helvey, Paula Gould, and Craig Hines. What a team!

Finally, a note of gratitude to our clients. Your feedback and the laboratories you provided for our work have made this book all the more "real" and practical.

Roger Herman and Joyce Gioia

Disclaimer

In preparing a book like this, it is impossible to cover everything. We are undoubtedly guilty of omissions—both intentional and unintentional. Within the constraints of knowledge, time, and space, we have presented what we believe to be an appropriate volume and breadth of information to address the topic.

Lean & Meaningful will remain a "work-in-progress." We welcome your input to expand our knowledge and perspective. If you have some ideas for strategies or tactics we haven't included in this volume, please tell us about them. If your company—or one you know about—is doing great things that would be of value to others, pass the information along.

Recognizing that we'll hear about lots of new ideas after *Lean & Meaningful* is published, we've decided to continue collecting and sharing what companies are doing. As we gather information and ideas, we'll make our new knowledge available through a web site and in a subscription e-mail newsletter. You'll be able to subscribe right on the web site. For details, visit www.LeanandMeaningful.com (not case-sensitive) or call our office at (336) 282-9370.

Feel free to contact us directly by phone, fax, or e-mail. We're eager to learn more as we study the transformation of corporate culture to the new design described in this book.

Here's our obligatory word about gender. While we have indulged in a few "he/she" utterances in this book, we find the form unwieldy. Having no better alternative, we have resorted to the use of "he" to represent both genders. Wherever you read "he," please accept that "she" would fit just as nicely (unless, of course, we're referring to a particular male person who would rather be described as "he"). Whew!

Nothing in this book should be construed as offering legal advice. We are not attorneys. Legal matters should, of course, be referred to your attorney. In accounting matters, we suggest you contact your Certified Public Accountant. If you'd like to explore consulting issues, we are both Certified Management Consultants and invite you to call us.

Roger E. Herman, CSP, CMC   Joyce L. Gioia, CMC
roger@herman.net   joyce@herman.net

The Herman Group
3400 Willow Grove Court
Greensboro, North Carolina 27410-8600
(336) 282-9370
FAX 282-2003
www.herman.net

1

The Shift to
Lean & Meaningful

As futurists concentrating on workforce and workplace issues, we study trends and forecast what we expect to see in the years ahead. Most of our work involves speaking at conventions and consulting for corporate executives. In our work, we have had the pleasure, excitement, inspiration, and advantage of interacting with thousands of leaders.

We have talked and exchanged ideas and perspectives with company presidents, political leaders, executives of nonprofit organizations, and educators.

Most discussions have been provocative. Thought-provoking, insightful, stimulating conversations have revealed significant similarities in the challenges we all face as we move at a too-rapid speed into the future. Exploring issues of importance with these leaders, we've learned about the principal concerns shared by practically everyone: workforce preparedness, technological development and application, resource allocation, optimal corporate design, and account-ability to stakeholders.

Savvy corporate leaders are keenly interested in what their companies will look like. After all, a critical part of their responsibility is to develop the strategies that will posi-tion their companies for future success—in their own right, as well as competitively in the global marketplace.

Each company will confront specific challenges in its industry. Technologies differ, but practically every organiza-tion will engage in vigorous upgrading of current technolo-gies, while looking for new technologies to apply to achieve their specific results. Robotics, materials, market penetra-tion, creative capitalization, and information management will dominate our research and development landscape as we seek better ways to generate our desired results. "Better ways to generate desired results." What does that mean?

Essentially, enlightened, forward-thinking companies will aggressively pursue strategic approaches to minimize their costs while maximizing their return. At the same time, they'll drive to attract and hold top talent for as long as pos-sible, managing to produce the greatest possible return on their investment in their human resources. For most compa-nies, their employees, their people, will be their most volatile resource. The people element will be the most critical, the most sensitive, and the most expensive resource . . . and in many ways, the most difficult to manage.

Based on these core assumptions, we focus on corporate success being driven by efficiency and good people. Those are the key components for high achievement. Those are the principal factors for the productivity that will satisfy accountability to stakeholders.

So, what's the design that will increase our efficiency? How will we attract and hold the high-performing people we need to get the job done?

The Lean Organization

Transforming a present-day organization into a lean organization is first a philosophical shift. Before anything can be accomplished strategically, there needs to be a serious change of thinking—at the top of the company, especially—and at all other levels as well.

The corporation of the future will look dramatically different than today's concept—structurally and conceptually.

For generations corporate leaders have endeavored to build their companies into large, powerful machines . . . omnipotent and far-reaching. Size has been equated with power, performance, influence, and results. Even though the opposite is actually the case, corporate moguls continue to build up and out. These large organizations have become complicated, political bureaucracies, populated by clever opportunists and work-avoiding drones whose personal missions are to block progress, destroy other people's initiatives, or protect their own positions. These motivations do not contribute to the company's success.

Other cases of corporate molasses are less insidious, but potentially just as damaging. Over the years, for various reasons, many companies have built redundancies, detours, or ad hoc "expediencies" that are no longer needed. Efforts to eliminate departments, people, functions, or processes in environments driven by growth, expansion, and more-more-more often fall on deaf ears. Growing smaller or taking something away is so dramatically counter-culture that popular resistance will impede any serious attempts to "downsize." In the face of reduction efforts, a vast protection network spreads like a web woven by a spider on steroids! Overt and covert methods are used to hinder and deflect people, organizations, or campaigns that might threaten the well-preserved status quo.

The human and systematic bureaucratic energies have

been so focused on defending traditions, penetrating the solid wall of resistance becomes a serious challenge. Tuned-in leaders are highly sensitive to these challenges. They know that their most vital responsibility will be to change the way people look at corporate strength. Resistance to stream-lining must be neutralized if progress is to be made.

The extra burden carried by today's organizations is described as "fat." Companies are loaded with waste—wasteful processes, facilities they don't need, departments that no longer function, and people who should have left years ago. The recession in the late 1980s and early 1990s provided a wonderful opportunity to get rid of some of the fat, and many employers took advantage of it. Unfortunately, too many limited their efforts to removing people and ignored the other fat that was inhibiting their agility.

The surgical downsizing must continue, but the cutting and redesign should reach into all areas of organizational design, staffing, operations, and performance. The much-touted "reengineering" is, again, another important step, but there's more to be done. Every aspect of the company must be examined, explored, justified, and reconnected based on the contribution made to the company's desired results. It's time to declare that "Nothing is sacred!" Anything that doesn't work must be made to work or be removed.

The People Factor

As we explore the differentiating factors that determine business success, it's clear that a company's people are often the enterprise's most valuable asset. Yes, people make the difference. As old as that cliché may be, employers went through an interesting transition as we passed through the late 1980s and 1990s.

During the recession-inspired (or -justified) downsizings, many employers removed older workers from their payroll. Through layoffs, reductions in force, and early retirements, companies jettisoned older workers who, while being paid more, held valuable knowledge, insights, wisdom, and maturity. Eventually, many employers realized their error and brought back the experienced people they had let go—often under substantially higher contractual arrangements or consulting relationships. Employers paid dearly for their haste, but regained the benefit of the knowledge they needed.

Yet older workers don't have all the answers, creativity, or energy/motivation to do everything that needs to be done today . . . and tomorrow. New blood is needed. Young people, workers from other companies, and people already in the organization are needed to redesign and reenergize the company to respond to our changing business environment. There is no question that employers need top talent.

The people companies need are becoming more discriminating about where they work. They're very much aware that they have some valuable leverage in the existing sellers' market. With a wide range of choices available to them, *they* will choose where they work. Their attitudes and interests— values-driven—will determine which recruiters will have an opportunity to interview—and persuade—them regarding joining their organizations.

Money is, of course, somewhat important to these workers, as it will continue to be in the future. Young people also know that they belong to the first generation that will not enjoy a standard of living higher than the one enjoyed by their parents. Understandably, they're not too excited about that prospect. Removing money drivers from the center of their lives, values take on a greater relevance.

Today's (and tomorrow's) workers are rather strongly motivated by their values and will make their employment decisions with values more clearly in focus. Money is no longer the overpowering deciding factor in the way people design their careers and their lives.

The movement toward values-based decision making is most strong among people in their twenties. Various influences during their growing-up years have inspired these young people to have some different attitudes toward work in their lives. Different than most of their predecessors, they work to live rather than live to work. Work is not the central purpose or focus of their lives.

Twenty-somethings have been barraged with information, more than any previous generation. Their world is much smaller and much faster-moving than anything experienced—or even imagined—by people in their thirties and forties, let alone older folks. With all the knowledge and choices before them, decisions are sometimes more difficult to make; the overload of input can be overwhelming. To aid their decision making and life management, young people have built sets of values to use as criteria. While each of these people is certainly an individual, we can see a strong commonality of thinking.

Meaningfulness

The increasing velocity of life today moves people of all ages to proclaim, "Stop the world! I want to get off!" The pace of life does seem much too fast. What's it all about? There must be some meaning, some significance, to all this activity, we muse. So, in our uneasiness in a world of uncertainty, we search for meaningfulness.

The search for meaningfulness permeates every aspect of our lives, including our work lives. Meaningfulness in work? Are these two concepts that don't even fit together? Our experience suggests that most people have looked outside work to find meaning in their lives. Some have found it; others are still searching . . . but getting closer as society moves more into values-inspired behaviors. An increasing proportion of workers have found meaning and have subscribed a set of values. While there's a sense of spirituality about all this growth, the values we're exploring are not religiously based.

As people search for meaning in their lives, family issues often surface as their most intense concern. Attention is given to living conditions, healthy neighborhood environments, education, time together, and care of children when the parents may not be directly available. People are more concerned about their communities; volunteerism and activism are on the rise. They're worried about their environment—taking personal responsibility for recycling and similar actions instead of just waiting for the government to do something. With an awareness that they'll probably live longer, people are devoting more time, money, and attention to physical fitness, wellness, and nutrition. To keep up in a fast-moving world, people are reading more and taking classes to sharpen their skills.

Values shared by a growing and influential majority of workers are based on shared perspectives of what life should include. Now, with employers changing the way they do business, corporate leaders are examining company values. Is bigger better? Are people expendable or to be valued? Is downsizing and streamlining the company consistent with current and future values? Are the company's values and sense of meaning congruent with the feelings and attitudes of the people who work for the company today . . . and those who may work for the company in the future?

Perspective

The intensifying relationship between a mobile and volatile workforce and employers in values transition is complicated. We know that companies must shed their fat to become more effective and efficient. We know that they will need people, the right people, to serve internal and external customers.

Employers need a stable workforce to build the kind of continuity that assures productivity and delighted customers. People want to work where they can find meaning in their work and in their work environment. Their decisions about where they'll work will be influenced by different factors than we've seen before. Their criteria will be very different and may not even be well-articulated by most applicants and recruiters.

Are these values compatible? Is it possible to have a lean, streamlined company and still have meaningfulness for employees? Can employees searching for meaningfulness and fulfillment find it in a lean company?

We not only believe that leanness and meaningfulness are compatible; we believe they are congruent and mutually supportive. As we look at the corporation of the future, we see these two concepts very closely linked in the most successful organizations. Our forecast is that employers will become more lean and more meaningful, but that most owners, executives, and managers will have some difficulty with this transition. The transformation will be confusing, threatening, unsettling, exciting, and rewarding—all at the same time.

The balance of this book is devoted to educating, enlightening, counseling, and comforting employers and employees as we move through the transition. We'll explain concepts and their application, giving lots of examples of what some companies are already doing. While few, if any, employers are doing everything they could (there may not yet be a pure lean and meaningful company), a surprising number of companies are doing some things that move them farther along the path to meaningfulness.

We're careful to counsel that there is no one right way to be meaningful. There is no ideal way to get lean. We'll share our perspectives, ideas, and advice. We'll tell you a lot of what we've learned about what others are doing, how, and why. But the decisions you make about what you will do with your new knowledge and insight are yours alone. Learn from the examples, adapt them to your work environment, and consciously strive to make a positive difference.

Design and implement changes as rapidly as your company's culture allows. Be sensitive to the fact that you'll be changing your culture as you move into a new mode. Be careful, move deliberately, and keep everyone involved. Remember that each company is a manifestation of its people, not of its brick and mortar.

The organizational culture of tomorrow's successful organizations will be lean and meaningful. This emerging culture is obvious to those analytically watching trends in the corporate world. How fast will your company move into this new set of relationships and protocols? The speed will be determined by your organization's openness to change. Your speed and sincerity will influence how well you will be able to attract, optimize, and retain the talent you will need to carry your company comfortably and profitably into the future.

As we begin to look at where we are going, let's look at where we are today. It's always smart to understand the starting points as we move into the future.

2

Corporation of the Present

Over the years, many American corporations have gotten fat. They've become sluggish, inwardly centered, profit-driven, and—in the opinion of a lot of workers—not such nice places to work. The phrase "lean and mean" is used in a positive, almost complimentary manner to describe the powerful corporations that seem to dominate our business landscape. Too many companies are still "fat."

What is a "fat" company? What does this mean? Let's use this concept as a platform to look at today's corporations to learn what the problems are.

A fat company consists of people and a corporate culture that uses too many resources and employs unnecessary, redundant, excessive, or obsolete business processes. As a result, it will ultimately fail to provide sustained value to its customers. The fat company unwittingly places employees' and owners' wealth, security, ego satisfaction, personal growth, and other benefits at risk.

While the company's leaders, managers, and other workers create fat through wasted activities and spending, they can also create a more subtle form of fat. Potentially even more dangerous, this form of fat can be found in a company's attitudes, capabilities, and motivation. An organization that strives to be "good" will never be "excellent." Leaders who surround themselves with people who are weak or who rarely challenge them will never achieve excellence. Too many senior leaders, protective of their own egos, have followed this ill-advised path.

Managers who seek power and influence become involved in empire building. We've seen it happen too many times. What's really dangerous is when incompetent managers insulate themselves from discovery—and reality—by building layers of subordinates around them. "Make work" becomes a way of life, an expensive way of life, to protect job security.

Processes

Processes sometimes become inefficient when they have too strong a champion or too many people insist on being involved. The extra steps in such processes are clearly wasteful. If people have to waste valuable time getting approvals from too many people, the whole system bogs down.

Even if things are working well, the risk of fat accumulation is present. When favorable environments persist for sustained periods of time, the company enjoys significant opportunities to succeed. But success may hold the seeds of its own undoing, including the opportunity to get fat. Yesterday's rewards become tomorrow's expectations. Entitlement creeps into the company's culture. The culture develops an entitlement momentum that is powerful enough to carry along all the company's people. People create and sustain fat cultures when they choose easy work. The principle of entitlement suggests that once fat takes hold of a culture, its impact accelerates.

If people become complacent in a fat company, they lose the edge and sense of urgency born of hunger for success. They make investments because the money is available, not because the projects add value. They do things because they've always done them that way. Thinking gets fuzzy.

Fat companies become internally focused. Complex processes and systems are created to support other internal processes and systems. It takes a while for the financial results to catch up to the realities of undisciplined fat behavior. Even when the news does come, there is usually denial and anger before the acceptance of reality.

A process may not have sufficient output. It may be sufficient, but lack quality. Or it may not be relevant or meaningful, such as a product that no one wants. Process output can be low simply because the company set its goals too low.

Sometimes people create nonessential or unnecessary processes. When this happens, they have created fat for the life of the process. Process measurement enhances process awareness. Processes that are appropriate for one time and place can become obsolete in the face of a changing environment. Technology can make processes obsolete.

The company's people and culture sustain fat processes. The process owners may not be aware that their process is fat. They may not *want* to improve an ineffective process. The company's culture may accept or even nourish mediocre processes. Things are going fine. The company is achieving its objectives. Why change anything?

Leadership

A company with poor leadership stumbles along. Leaders who have no vision, an ambiguous vision, or a flawed vision cannot develop a successful strategy for the company or a subgroup within the company. People will not align with such a leader and the company is left floundering. The pattern has been memorialized in Scott Adams' Dilbert® cartoons.

A good leader needs both internal and external knowledge to set direction. Externally, he must be very familiar with the dynamics of the industry, the needs of customers, the environment, economic trends, competition, technology trends, and innovative management practices. Internally, the leader must know his people and the strengths and weaknesses of the company as well as the key business processes.

Leaders need the skill to absorb, distill, and integrate signals from the team and the environment. Without this ability, the vision and strategy for the company may be totally disconnected from the actual work performed by employees. Lacking a good knowledge of the company's core competencies, the leader may try to implement initiatives that are not feasible. Wrong direction. Bad use of resources. Fat.

Individuals who manage are charged with achieving the company's objectives through the efforts of others. The successful manager forms the right team, builds its competencies, and makes sure that the company's objectives are achieved. Individuals who manage poorly increase the fat in a company. Not only are they ineffective themselves, but the entire team becomes ineffective as well. Unfortunately, many of our corporations are led and managed by people who lack training, experience, and perspective to avoid fat.

Selection, role definition, and people development are all components of success when it comes to assembling a team. Selecting inappropriate or incompetent team members is the sign of a poor manager. Defining the wrong role for a team is a form of fat. Keeping incapable people too long reduces productivity as well. An amazing number of employers simply hire "warm bodies" because they need people to get the job done . . . or to "fill slots" on the organizational chart. Their ignorance expands the fat.

Too few managers have been trained, tasked, or reinforced to really build the competence and performance of their people. They should challenge team members, encourage self-development, train, coach, counsel, provide feedback, measure progress, and support their team members. Most managers don't perform these duties well, if at all. The result is that their skills atrophy over time.

Individuals tend to be poor managers when they micromanage, try to do everything themselves, behave inconsistently, or are indecisive. We hear these complaints all the time. Most managers, promoted too quickly with inadequate preparation, don't know how to do their jobs. Few know how to establish good working relationships with team members. They must learn how to be open, listen well, and engage in professional discussions with their teams.

The company's culture consists of its values and is reflected in its workstyle. Culture is communicated through the company's heroes, legends, celebrations, and rewards. When a company celebrates and/or rewards an innovation, it makes a statement about what it values. Even with this knowledge, leaders shy away from discussing values (that "soft" stuff), the very core beliefs that are so important to their people.

Fat companies fail to empower workers, keeping decisions at too high a level. Result: people are underutilized, feel little control over their work, believe their capabilities are not valued . . . and that, as individuals, they are not valued. This attitude eventually leads to stagnation, weakened people, and a depreciated organization.

The company's environment dictates the extent to which fat can enter a culture. It is difficult to get fat in an unfavorable environment, whereas a favorable environment encourages the growth of fat. Cultures often stay fat because the company is not aware that it even *has* a fat culture. The company is doing well. It's complacent. It is not measuring its vital signs; there is no external benchmark indicating how well it *could* be doing. This lethargy can also happen because the company is aware that it has a fat culture, but the employees are enjoying its benefits. They prefer to maintain the status quo.

The company's culture is the DNA of the company. It specifies the unwritten rules that help the company define itself. It clarifies the importance of such dimensions as customer satisfaction, integrity, competition, corporate politics, fads, hard work, cost control, short-term financial focus, risk aversion, and teamwork. The company's priorities are summarized by the company's values and workstyle. Inappropriate values and workstyle create a fat culture.

A fat culture is not easy to change because it guides company-wide behavior and influences choices of new hires. It has an inertia of its own that can only be affected by the people of the company. This cycle—the culture influencing the company's employees and the employees affecting the culture of the company—places the company's people in a position of determining whether the culture will be fit or fat in the future. People have the power, but someone has to take the initiative to begin the "diet." This role is difficult to assume in an environment of complacency.

As departments become invested in their own growth, a lack of coordination within and between departments creates waste and fat. The silo effect comes into play when interactions have to travel up one department's chain of command and down through another department's organization before anything can get done. More activity does not always produce proportionately more output. Eventually, additional activity can actually diminish output. Project overstaffing is one example of this phenomenon.

To cover themselves and register some forward movement, fat corporations push. They push their people, push the market, push for results. There's a lack of creativity, of excitement. It's the same thing every day; there's no fun. No meaning.

Stop Pushing

In the recent past, we've seen an increasing resistance to being pushed. Employees, customers, suppliers, investors, communities, regulators, and other stakeholders have cried "Enough!" This business style isn't working. There must be a better way.

Companies began to look more carefully at themselves. They wanted to find and eliminate their problems, to "tight-size," to reduce the fat. Regrettably, culture fat can be difficult to spot, especially by the people within the culture. Leaders of fat corporations are usually reluctant to admit their problems and seek outside help, so they spend a lot of time either making excuses or trying to make improvements. Eventually, they realize that they really do need professional assistance.

Sure enough, a myriad of consultants, gurus, and authors has risen to the challenge. In the past decade, businesses of all sizes have been bashed, thrashed, rebuilt, demolished, and reinvented. Corporate leaders and analysts examined internal concerns and external factors. Surprise! The world has changed! Thousands of companies discovered to their horror and chagrin that major changes had occurred—almost overnight.

Companies that had continued to grow for years now faced new competition from Europe, Asia, and Latin America. Companies from around the world could do things faster and cheaper. Profits dipped, then slipped, then went on the skids. American companies scrambled to figure out ways to regain their profits and market share. Dependable, qualified workers who used to be in abundant supply were suddenly much more difficult to attract . . . and hold. The stability of continuity was being replaced by the trauma of constant change.

Corporations with long histories discovered that during the "good" years, they'd gotten fat—fat around the middle management area. So they went on a diet . . . a crash diet. Hundreds of thousands of middle managers found themselves out on the street. Line employees were replaced by cheaper labor in other countries. Senior management was able to show a quick profit by cutting all those employee costs. Then there were mergers and acquisitions. Profits grew as companies reduced redundancy. With leveraged buyouts, whole divisions of conglomerates were sold off to service the debt. Downsizing worked: short-term profits looked good enough to satisfy investors.

Okay, now we've gotten rid of the deadwood, what's next? We need to be rightsized. Just enough people to do the job, to be lean and mean. To be competitive, companies had to meet the needs of their customers quickly. Flexibility to respond to changing market trends was essential if companies were going to stay afloat. Well, there certainly weren't too many employees, but the old hierarchical structure just wasn't responsive enough. Decisions took too long. Changes were difficult to implement. So the structure was reengineered.

The old organizational chart was out; horizontal organizations were in. Cross-functional teams were formed to handle special projects. Decision making was pushed farther down in the organization so that the company could respond to customer needs more quickly. Corporations raced to embrace the efficiencies of Dr. Edwards Deming's Total Quality Management . . . sometimes successfully, most times not.

Employees were expected to give 110 percent so that companies could grow, even though constant change and insecurity left them uneasy and empty. Technology made it possible for one employee to do the work of the three who were required before the downsizing. Long hours and extra days were expected.

While companies were busy trying to meet the demands

of the marketplace, what's happened to employees? All these changes and struggles caused a breach of the unspoken contract between workers and employers—the contract that said that if you worked hard and were loyal, you would have job security. The economic challenges of the early 1990s, and corporate reaction to them, destroyed forever the idea that an employee would spend a whole career with one company. Just when companies needed more from workers, employees felt less desire and commitment.

This new contract seemed to say that the company would offer no job security, but would keep employees who provided value to the company. Employees are expected to figure out what that value is and how they can contribute. Employees could expect the company to provide them with interesting and challenging work, give them resources and training to perform their jobs, and give them opportunities to increase their employability.[1]

The result was a mixed bag. Although employees lost job security, they often gained more freedom in performing their work. The new horizontal organizations gave workers the opportunity to experience more variety in their work, which could make them more employable if the company changed its core business. What companies lost was the loyalty of employees. Now workers felt no compunction about moving on to a more attractive offer or refusing a relocation assignment.

Workforce Demographics

And through all these changes, the demographics of the workforce were changing. There are more women in the workforce—an increasing proportion looking for career opportunities, not just a job. Young people are entering the workforce, individually and independently driven to rise quickly in their chosen occupations—which change frequently. They challenge more set-in-their-ways managers unaccustomed to such demanding employees. These population groups and others are challenging the fat companies. Employees don't want to work or stay where things aren't happening. They want a dynamic work life, not a stagnant and boring existence. If they don't find what they want, these energetic people simply leave to try another position. Quality of work life has become an equal concern to quality of personal life.

A few years ago, *Working Woman* Magazine did a poll of 502 top female executives. Of the respondents, 56 percent said they knew of female executives that left the company because of the corporate culture. Failure to recognize family needs was the reason for leaving, according to 31 percent of the respondents. In some cases, twice as many female executives were leaving companies as their male counterparts. With fewer job opportunities and unfriendly corporate cultures, these well-trained executives were opting out of the corporate world. Some would return home to care for children; others would start their own businesses or return to school. Not only did companies lose highly skilled, knowledgeable employees, but the employers discovered that it was costing up to 150 times these executive women's salaries to replace them.[2]

Single parents have even greater challenges, particularly when children are ill or have special needs. People become single parents in several ways. Some parents become divorced. In other cases a spouse dies. In some situations, the spouse is still alive and even present in the home, but may be incapable physically or mentally of assuming parental responsibilities. Births to mothers who are not married represent over 20 percent of children born each year. Many mothers are well-employed (not on welfare), but just don't want a husband around. Each one of these constituent groups faces different challenges.

The aging population impacts the workforce in two ways. The first is the workers themselves. Employees who had been part of the old systems now faced a whole new set of rules. Companies will need to motivate these people who have years of experience and a wealth of knowledge. To facilitate learning for this generation of workers, companies will need to create a safe and secure environment. These workers still want to contribute, but may be more risk-averse because they have more at stake near the end of their careers.

The other significant impact the aging of the population has on the workforce is the increasing need for employees to care for their aging relatives. Today about 25 to 30 percent of employees are concerned about eldercare. In the next decade the number of people over 65 is expected to increase as nine million will need assistance. For many families the burdens of elder care will fall during a time when they still have children at home or are just getting them off to college. The financial and emotional strains for the "sandwich generation" of balancing both will be significant.

Generation X gets a lot of attention. These people, born between 1964 and 1985, are much more independent than the Boomer (1946–1964) or the Parent (pre-1946) generations. [They're also known as "Baby Busters" and "The 13th Generation."] Thirty-somethings view work in an entirely different way than their Baby Boomer parents. Because they never bought into the old employment contract (loyalty equals job security), they expect more flexibility in work and balance in their lives.

These workers don't respond to the competition that motivated their parents, but will step up to support a mission. They want to know their work is meaningful. They are open to working on teams and learning opportunities, seeing their resumés, not their employers, as the keys to their success. They will change jobs every 2 to 4 years, seeking fulfillment, variety, growth, and interesting opportunities to make a difference. It is these workers who will drive the changes in our corporate cultures in the next 10 to 15 years. Forget tradition with these folks—they'll blaze their own trails.

Bottom Line

Today's corporation, while productive and relatively progressive, has some problems. Particularly in the eyes of the younger workers, who are desperately needed by so many employers, these companies are dysfunctional. They've gotten fat, things move too slowly, and they're not really attuned to what employees want from their workplace today.

Workers want meaningful work. They struggle with their balance between family and career. Some highly skilled employees are opting out of the system and, in some cases, actually competing in the marketplace by establishing their own smaller companies. An increasing number of employees are parents or taking care of elderly relatives. A large part of the workforce is preparing for retirement. Most of their careers were spent under the traditional, hierarchical corporate structures. Now they are learning to adapt to a new set of rules.

The newer members in the workplace community come to it with entirely different motivators and expectations. Competition to attract good, qualified workers remains fierce. Success means keeping costs low and market share high. For companies to succeed in the future, they will need to address some significant issues. Among those issues, none will be more significant than the relationship they have with their employees. Recognizing the significance of this relationship, conscious employers are sensitive to their risk— they consistently rate employee issues such as finding and keeping good people at the top of the list of what keeps them awake at night.

Surveys continue to show that over 50 percent of employers are understaffed. The understaffing causes missed deadlines, poor customer service, higher stress, and increased employee turnover. Organizations, like Olsten Forum, keep tabs on these numbers and report that the problem is intensifying. Do we have too few people, too many positions to fill, or both?

Corporate leaders are only now beginning to look carefully at how their companies are organized and staffed to meet tightly focused objectives. It's a frustratingly slow process, especially when executives and managers are afraid to reduce staffing because doing so may erode their political power and career progression.

The future cannot be like the past. The corporate world is in the midst of a substantial transformation. Leaders in every industry are challenged with uncertainty, confusion, and ignorance about what really needs to be done. Some of these leaders are rising above the clamor and becoming more visionary. They're looking into the future with excitement and a serious commitment to change their cultures—to change the way they do business. Others concentrate their view on what's around them—and they often can't see or understand the fat that inhibits their progress into the exciting years ahead.

What's fascinating is that in every competitive marketplace we have a range of companies, each at a different level of evolution in the transformation process—becoming lean and meaningful. Some will win, some will lose as we move through the coming years. And in almost every case, the choice is theirs.

Becoming lean isn't easy. All sorts of factors need to be considered—from financial issues to human resources to production processes and distribution systems. Becoming meaningful won't be sufficient. To successfully compete—for business and for workers—your company must also become more lean. Let's explore this concept in the next chapter.

Endnotes

1. Wyatt, John, *Fortune*, June 13, 1994.
2. Lawlor, Julia, *Working Woman*, November 1994.

3

Becoming Lean

L ean is an attitude. It's a philosophy, an approach, a workstyle. Leanness is a culture, inspired, led, and reinforced by a dedicated leader and his followers. It's a way of managing an enterprise that continually reduces operating costs while maximizing return. It's a methodology that selects and applies resources in ways that achieve consistently high levels of efficiency and effectiveness.

Any kind of organization can operate with a lean orientation. Manufacturing organizations have been targets for lean designs as factories strive to optimize their production processes. Administrative environments have sought to reduce their fat through computer technology and shifting human resources (clerical support pools instead of personal secretaries). Retailers watch their inventory and use Electronic Data Interface (EDI) to order only what they need, when they need it. Healthcare organizations have become more lean in response to rigid scrutiny from the managed care movement. Governmental entities, faced with citizens who resist more taxes, are finding ways to better manage their resources. Trade and professional associations are challenged to provide more services with fewer dues dollars. The list goes on. No organization is immune.

The movement to become more lean has begun. Reengineering, zero-based budgeting, total quality management, and statistical process control are familiar terms to many who have already wrestled with the universal effort to do more with less. Even with the work that has already been done, some with a relatively high profile, most companies have yet to be as serious as they could be with the tightening-up process.

We saw a lot of downsizing in recent years, but that effort was only part of the answer. The answer lies not in merely downsizing, but in what we call "tightsizing." This term implies tightening up everywhere in the organization, not just in the personnel count.

Options for Becoming More Lean

Notice the heading of this section. We're talking about becoming *more* lean. Regardless of where you are in your tightening-up process, you will probably have to go farther. It's an ongoing, continuous process. Open up your creativity. Look for innovative ways to make a difference. Think positively; look for innovative solutions that will enable you to perform better with fewer resources, rather than cutting costs indiscriminately. Our concern in this process is not just to reduce costs, but to minimize costs relative to results achieved. It's a matter of gaining the greatest return on your investment, no matter what specific resources you're investing in.

There are a number of options for changing the way we do business in a cost-effective and positive way. Let's explore some of them.

Reduction of Current Operating Costs

This technique had to come first. It's the most obvious. Where can you remove fat from your current operation? Can you do the same, maybe even more, or comfortably *less* with fewer people? Yes, even less production may be acceptable . . . especially if you're producing over capacity now. You may be considerably more cost-efficient (read: profitable) operating at a slightly lower level. Explore and analyze the alternatives.

Examine carefully everything you do in your enterprise. Can you spot some duplicated or redundant effort that isn't needed? Are you handling papers or product too many times?

Do things take too long to get finished? Why? Does inventory sit on the floor too long between processes? Is there too much inventory on hand? Do customers wait too long to be served? Is your cash flow limited by your billing process? Are you targeting the right prospects or wasting resources with aggressive marketing to prospects who will never buy from you? Are you losing qualified applicants because you don't respond to their applications fast enough? Is data transfer jamming your systems because your computers aren't fast enough? How many unnecessary reports are you preparing because "we've always prepared that report"? Or, worse, how much is done "because we've always done it that way"?

When looking for opportunities for improvement, nothing is sacred. Challenge everything. Involve your dedicated people on "the front line" of your business. They know what's not working, and probably how to fix most of the problems. If given the freedom and encouragement, they could make your operation run a lot more smoothly.

Improved Resource Utilization

Over the years we have acquired a variety of resources that seemed necessary at the time. Those same resources may not be needed today. Resources cost money. Extra resources cost a lot of money—the funds to maintain them and the cost of the opportunities lost because the funds weren't available for a higher and better use.

Begin with your physical plant. Do you need the facilities you have now? Are you in the best location for your business? Are your facilities organized in the best way for you to optimize your results? Does your communications system support your full use of your company's facilities? Have you properly allocated the space used by each component of your enterprise? How about the flow of material, information, or product through your facilities? Is your lighting consistent with needs?

Analyze the hours you operate in your facilities. Are your operating hours standardized to the rest of the world (i.e., 9 to 5) or are they matched to customer service, human resource availability, or the flow of product and services? Do your outside lights operate by timer—set to Daylight Standard Time when it's Daylight Savings Time?

How effective is your communications system? Are your telephones equipped with the latest or most appropriate technology? Do you have the right number of internal and external lines? How about your paging system? Should you be using two-way paging technology? Do you have an intranet? Is your web site, if you have one, serving your complete needs, and when was it last updated? If you don't have a web site, you're probably missing opportunities for costs savings and revenue. How well do your people use e-mail to build communications efficiency—with customers, suppliers, and fellow employees?

Building Human Resources Capacity

If your company has just the right number of people and they're all working up to 100 percent of their capacity with high morale and great results, skip the rest of this section.

You're still reading?

Why aren't you getting the maximum return on your investment in human resources? Do you have the right kind of people working with you? Are your recruiters and employment specialists bringing in applicants that meet your current—and future—needs? How effective is your orientation process in building understandings of your culture and your focus on results? Do your training and education programs adequately prepare your workers for the jobs they must do today . . . and tomorrow? Are your leadership and management styles consistent with your culture and compatible with your workers' needs and expectations?

Are the right people working in the right jobs? Are they working to their full potential? Are you using available technology to optimally schedule people in order to best utilize their competencies wherever they're needed? Is your succession plan in place, with ongoing development of successors to be sure they're ready? Are you benefiting from a myriad of ideas for improvement suggested by your people?

Combining Operations

When was the last time you looked at each of the various functions and departments of your enterprise? Are you wasting management and other resources by maintaining an organizational design that is too splintered? Can you combine some operations, some departments, some work groups to achieve greater efficiency and effectiveness?

How about combining people and departments? As an example, let's say you produce widgets during an assembly line process each day. During the early part of the day you need extra help in the departments that pull inventory and stock the lines for the day's production. During the day, you need as much help as you can get on the assembly line, putting everything together and getting your product ready to be shipped. As the end of the workday nears, finished product is piling up in the shipping area. More help is needed there so you can get the merchandise out the door. You could float people from stocking to assembly to shipping, staffing each area as needed without having to overstaff any department when the people would be underutilized.

Analyze each operation, function, and process in your business. If you were to design your company "from scratch" today, would you organize it the way you have it today? What would you do differently? Why? Look carefully, take time to think. Rather than rushing in, consider your alternatives and justify how they would be better than the current arrangement. Sometimes misorganization is the result of adding tasks or responsibilities incrementally over time, but some misorganization also results from hasty attacks on pressing problems. Don't allow yourself to make things worse by hurrying; evaluate your alternatives in view of your objectives.

Explore centralizing or decentralizing multilocation operations. Challenge each aspect of the way you're doing business. Look at who is doing the work. Is each task assigned to the right person, team, or department? Along the way, confirm that the tasks really need to be done.

Streamlining Operations

People working on the "front line" in any company have the greatest potential of making things run more smoothly and efficiently. In an energetic effort to simplify procedures for employees and customers, Advantage Rent-A-Car, San Antonio, Texas, enlisted all its employees as "idea people." Their "Making It Easy" campaign, complete with incentives for participating employees, helped the company make its processes more lean. Management listened carefully to employee ideas and took necessary steps to accomplish significant improvements.

Telecommuters

Not all of your employees need to work in your facilities all the time. Part or all of their time can be spent in their homes or at satellite locations. An increasing number of workers are telecommuting—in a wide variety of industries. Why endure the expenses of office space, telephones, utilities, parking space, and similar costs to support workers who could (more effectively) operate from their homes?

With advances in modern technology, people can work from home and still be very well connected to their employers, suppliers, colleagues, and customers. The telephone is an obvious link, but the communication capabilities are considerably greater than merely having a single- or multiline telephone to use at home. With emerging technology, employees can be directly linked with employer site(s). With highly sophisticated call routing systems, people who are widely dispersed geographically may even function in a call center environment.

The telephone lines also give us full access to facsimile communication, electronic mail, and the full power of the internet. Video communication is now possible, with technology advanced to the point that you can be "on the phone" visually and orally at the same time—sharing all kinds of information on the computer screen. There is no longer any reason to believe that telecommuters disappear into some black hole to surface only to cash their paychecks. (In fact, payroll can be managed with direct deposit, entirely avoiding paychecks)!

Research shows that teleworkers are considerably more productive than their counterparts who commute to a congregate workplace every day. With [totally] flexible hours, they report actually working *more* hours at home than they did/would at the office! Managing these remote workers is often a challenge for supervisors who have always had hands-on, proximity-based relationships. Attack and conquer the problems and you'll discover that more tasks than you imagined can be performed in the home environment.

There are a couple of other advantages of teleworking to consider. One is that employers are no longer constrained by geographic distance in recruiting and hiring. Teleworkers do not need to be physically close to the congregate work site to be high performers. At the same time, workers now have a much wider range of where they can sell their services to employers. The playing field is very different!

Outsourcing Captive Departments

As you evaluate your company, be alert for departments that are needed, but not at their current levels. You may not be able to reduce the number of employees because the fluctuation of work loads requires that you have the capacity available. If that is the case, can the excess capacity be sold to other companies? Will such a strategy strengthen the return on your investment in this department? Note the concept of developing a bottom-line orientation for every one of the company's departments.

If you still need the department as part of your organization, but don't need its services full-time, consider spinning off the department to create a separate company. The new company will continue to operate in its space (or maybe you'll do some reorganizing) and will serve your company as its primary customer. You can arrange for the new company to pay for rent, utilities, and other services . . . as well as to charge you for services performed. It's sort of like having an arm's length relationship while still holding hands!

The company can sell its services to other noncompetitive client companies, increasing its revenue.

To really make things interesting, you might even have the new company bid on work for you—against other companies interested in providing the service. They'll have to stay competitive to keep your business!

External Outsourcing

Outside companies, which may or may not have ever had an affiliation with your company, can often provide goods and services more cheaply than you can produce them yourself. Or, even with a higher cost, they may be able to produce them faster, cleaner, or closer than you can. There is a variety of criteria you can use to determine whether it's better to have various functions performed in-house or by an outside resource.

An effective way to move toward a more lean organization is to arrange to have work done by outside organizations instead of company departments. Savings can be realized in overhead costs, personnel costs (such as recruiting, training, and retention—let alone payroll costs), space, scheduling, material/inventory costs, and management.

Usually outsourcing is done with companies that will serve you over a relatively long period of time. A relationship builds between your people and theirs that is remarkably similar to the relationship enjoyed by people who work for the same employer. You may even create partnering mission statements and provide special services, like training, to keep everyone synchronized in their work.

Quite often repetitive support functions are outsourced. Examples include operation of a mail room, photocopying, shipping, and payroll.

Contract Firms

When the work to be done is of a more short-term or more defined nature, you may contract with one or more other companies to provide certain goods or services. The parameters and criteria are similar to those involved with an outsourced firm, but may be more specific.

A company might contract with a supplier to produce parts, deliver components or finished goods, or provide cleaning services. The relationship is more "distant," without the closer relationship intimated in the outsourcing approach.

Shedding Nonrelevant Operations

Are you wasting resources doing things that have nothing to do with your core business?

Over a period of time, companies have a tendency to add product lines, services, locations, people, etc. that are incongruent with the reason the company's in business.

There's a magnetic factor, a force field, that just seems to attract all this extra load. It's fat. Just like the stuff that accumulates in your body when you take in too much of the wrong food. And, just like the fat on your body, it goes on a lot easier than it comes off! To streamline your company, you'll have to go on a corporate diet. "It's time to learn a new lifestyle." Everyone who has ever been on a serious diet has heard these dreaded words. "Change your eating habits, get exercise, think thin." As we write this, we're highly conscious of being less than entirely effective in our dieting and lifestyle management. It's not easy. Not for humans, not for companies.

One advantage with corporate dieting is that you can build some really wonderful support groups. Of course, there will also be the chorus of voices that tell you it's all right to eat just one cookie! Expect the political consciences to wrestle with every decision you make about shedding nonrelevant operations. One division will be someone's baby. Another will have corporate history implications. You'll have to be tough, just like human dieters.

Look carefully at each of your business ventures. If they aren't helping you move forward in your core business, if they don't support fulfillment of your mission, seriously consider eliminating them. One venture may be sold—to the employees, to an investment group, or perhaps to a competitor or company in a relevant field. Another venture may be spun off as a separate company through an outsourcing process. Yet another may simply be closed.

You may sever the relationship with one entity, but stay

close to another through some sort of strategic alliance or joint venture.

As you move through this process, consider carefully what resources you need to achieve the objectives of the core business. You may be sharing some resources now. To maintain your strength, you may need to realign, reassign, or make other organizational changes to assure you have what you need for the success of the core business. Phrased colloquially, "don't throw the baby out with the bath water."

Moving Accountability Lower

A disarmingly simple method of improving the utilization of your resources is to push accountability down in your organization. Too many companies become bogged down because most of the decisions are made at the top of the organizational chart. Some champions of this practice justify this high-level control by arguing that the people at the top get paid the big bucks for making those decisions.

In reality, the people lower in the organization can make the same decisions. These workers are good people with plenty of experience and sharp business sense. They are often as underutilized as the top people are overpaid. And, being closer to the reasons for the decisions, they often have a much better sensitivity for what choices are most appropriate.

An astonishing number of businesses do not fully utilize their employees who have answers, ideas, and solutions. In our years of experience as Certified Management Consultants, we have been amazed numerous times as we encountered corporate cultures or political systems that have kept decisions and control jealously guarded at the highest levels. We have shaken our heads, too, when the corporate leaders complained that their subordinates wouldn't make decisions on their own. They've been trained not to make decisions, not to take risks, not to assume control—and those behaviors are (unwittingly) reinforced by senior leadership almost every day.

If you could break through this antiquated system, think about how your company could achieve so much more with the same or fewer people. Some of those highly paid executives could move on to other work—or other companies—if more of their work can be done by lower-paid people who are closer to the problems. By placing more responsibility and accountability on managers, front-line supervisors, and hourly workers, you'd also be gaining a substantially higher return on your investment in these valuable people.

As a side note, there's a restlessness in the workforce and workplace today. With a strong economy generating an abundance of jobs, workers who are not happy are more prone to leave than ever before in our history. They want meaningful work—and they'll change jobs to find it. If you shift responsibility and accountability to the people who really should be doing the jobs, they'll feel a greater sense of influence, ownership, and accomplishment. This pride and power is what they're looking for, so they'll stay longer. The lower turnover will save the company a lot of money, thereby increasing profits in the lean and meaningful organization.

Contract Workers

Not all your workers will be actual employees of your company. Some will be contract workers, independent people engaged to perform specific tasks under a relatively formal agreement. They will be paid for the specific work they do. When the work is completed, their compensation stops and so does their relationship with the employer. There is no further obligation. Contract workers do not receive benefits, privileges, or deductions from their checks. They are regarded as vendors, not employees.

When you don't need people on a full-time or regular part-time basis, contracting may be the answer. With the growth in numbers of people who want to control their own career destiny, plenty of qualified workers will be available for assignments. Many contract employees will be engaged for projects. Examples will range from production or assembly work, auditing, marketing, property maintenance, engineering, and other tasks of a clearly defined and often short-term nature.

In most cases, the relationship between the company and the contract worker will be direct, but we do foresee a network of brokers developing in the not-too-distant future. Brokers will maintain a list of qualified contractual workers, all independent performers and usually specialists in some area or another. Companies will go to brokers to find the people they need, much like staffing agencies function today. The broker will collect a percentage of the money paid to the contractor.

To control labor costs as a lean company, you can use defined term/defined project contract workers to accomplish work now assigned to regular employees. This strategy will allow you to reduce your payroll (and taxes) or shift valuable people to other, more pressing work. Explore how this approach might work for your company. It has worked well for us.

Contingent Workers

While contract workers are engaged for projects or term assignments, contingent workers are employed to perform shorter-term work details. In one sense, these engagements have been described as "day work" or "day labor." People are hired, as needed, to perform certain tasks, usually unskilled or semiskilled, that don't need regular employees assigned.

The term "contingent workers" has been used to describe temporary help, contractors, and others who are hired (usually through agencies) when needed. There is no other relationship with the company. When the contingent worker has finished work for the day, there may or may not ever be a callback for that person to work for the company in the future.

A less expensive alternative applied by many catalogers and fulfillment operations is to have your *own* list of contingent workers. Find those people—"trained" in various skilled, unskilled, or clerical positions—who do not want to work full-time, but welcome the opportunity to work on a part-time or temporary basis when needed.

Certain aspects of your company's operation may lend themselves to use of contingent workers. Unskilled labor needs, clerical vacation fill-ins, small projects, and skilled worker fill-in due to turnover are examples of how these people will be used. You can use these contingent resources to help balance the load during peaks and valleys of labor demands.

Getting Started, Making It Work

Realistically, shifting to a more lean operation won't be as easy as it sounds. Even with champions in your company, it will be challenging. Many people within your organization may have their own agendas that could conflict with your desire to run a tighter ship. Be very candid in your discussions about your transformation. Invite objections and concerns. Get them on the table so you have more open communication and can deal with the issues.

Of course, encouraging high involvement and open communication doesn't mean you'll get full cooperation. Stay focused. Stay clear about what you're doing and why.

You may need outside help. Consultants can help you stay on track, suggest ways to approach and manage change, and help you through the process. As Certified Management Consultants who have been through a number of corporate visioning, restructuring, and reorganization experiences, we recommend that you not ask or allow the consultant to drive the process. Placing authority in the hands of a consultant (or interim executive) places outsider(s) in a "hatchet" role.

Employees at all levels are understandably reluctant to cooperate with cost-cutters for fear they may be the next target.

Consultants can be tremendously valuable assets in helping you design and implement the process. But the responsibility and the accountability for actually doing what must be done should stay in the hands of the leaders, executives, and managers of the company. After all, it is your company, not the consultants'.

Your work to become more lean is only one part of the story. Looking at the big picture, we know that you're moving deliberately to position your company for future success. Let's explore what the corporation of the future will look like.

4

Corporation
of the Future

What will the corporation of the future look like? How will the corporation of the future differ from what we've seen in the past and what we experience today? How will it be structured? What kind of a workforce will we need to staff the corporation of the future, and how will people work together?

These are all valid questions. And they're just the start of the inquiry into how we might expect corporate life to be in the years ahead. Anyone who is a leader in business, government, education, or a not-for-profit organization must be concerned about what the work environment will be in the future. Aspiring leaders have the same concerns—what are they working for, what will they inherit?

When we have a clear view of the future—one design or alternative scenarios—we can better manage today. How we manage today will influence what our tomorrows will be. These are strategic issues—on an organizational level and also on a personal one. What role do we see ourselves playing in our future work environment? How can we best prepare for the future we want for ourselves, our families, our colleagues, our enterprise?

Futurists

As futurists, we observe trends and consider what scenarios may develop in the foreseeable future. It's fascinating work, particularly when you let your mind stretch to imagine possibilities that are "on the fringe" of what we see in today's world. In the past few years, we've seen a considerable amount of progress—moving us dramatically into a different kind of world. The velocity of change is increasing at a rapid rate. We're all having difficulty keeping up.

To do a thorough job as a futurist, it's necessary to watch the trends in a wide range of arenas. These trends interact with each other, causing reactions that are sometimes clearly predictable . . . and sometimes more elusive. Since most of our work as consultants, writers, and speakers revolves around the corporate world, we pay careful attention to trends that influence the continuing evolution of corporate structures, cultures, strategies, people, operating systems, relationships, and environments.

A Transformation

The corporation of the future will be substantially different from the corporation of today. Trends in organizational structure, operating technology, workforce availability, strategic relationships, and economic development suggest that tomorrow's company will be much more streamlined and simplified. Leaders will concentrate on the entity's core business, valuing characteristics such as agility, nimbleness, responsiveness, and flexibility. They will have a tighter structure, emphasize efficiency, and build strength through outsourcing, contracting, alliances, and creative approaches. A nucleus of collaborators will drive the corporation's success, drawing in outside resources as needed to accomplish work for customers.

This new design, this new organizational culture can best be described as "lean and meaningful." The driving strategies will be to do more with less—and to have the work done by highly productive employees who are all well qualified, find meaning in their balanced lives, and genuinely enjoy their work.

Counterbalancing the streamlining will be a new focus on building the meaningfulness of work and the work environment. The future corporation will be concerned with providing meaningful work, offering a meaningful career characterized by personal control, an enhanced sense of family centeredness, dedication to community involvement, social consciousness, environmental awareness, spirituality, and similar issues.

Leaders will be both forced and motivated to create new, more meaningful cultures to attract and hold quality employees. This organizational design will be easy for some employers, almost impossible for others. The future of our corporations and what is described as "corporate life" could easily be threatened by the influence of social and financial trends. The key today is not just how people treat each other, but whether there is enough inherent strength in the organization to sustain it through the inevitable shift to the corporate design of the future.

Where We're Heading

Corporations will not change dramatically overnight. The move into the future is an *evolutionary* process, not a *revolutionary* one. The shift will be gradual.

The transformation to a lean and meaningful culture will be led from the top of the organization in almost every case. People at lower levels will be understandably reluctant to rock the boat of tradition. Inertia will be overcome only through the enlightened, assertive, and visionary leadership of company owners and senior executives who know how to think and lead far past the bottom line at the end of the next reporting period.

Lean Machine

We know the corporation of the future will be lean. The movement toward reducing fat, streamlining operations, concentrating on core businesses, and achieving strong results for stockholders in a turbulent world are "given," to use a term from geometry.

The effort to tighten up is a driving force in the business world, as well as in government and nonprofit organizations. The evolution is marked by what seemed—at the time—to be revolutionary events. Processes are improved. Facilities are reduced. Workforces are downsized. Product lines are limited. Inefficient operations are closed or sold. Expenses are controlled. While it is dangerous to go too far with cost-cutting measures, there's plenty of fat to be trimmed in most enterprises.

As this crusade continues, executives will redesign, reengineer, reshape their companies to do more with fewer resources. In recent years, we've seen some dramatic examples of such campaigns. Practically every corporate leader in America is familiar with "Chainsaw Al" Dunlap and his board-applauded reputation for slashing costs. That's lean—no question. But it's also *mean*, in the eyes of most people in management and nonmanagement positions. Many people agree that cuts have to be made; the issue is *how* the cuts will be made and who they will affect.

Less Hierarchical

Multilevel corporate hierarchies will experience a dramatic metamorphosis. With apologies to Max Weber, the father of bureaucracy, intricate bureaucracies will become creatures of the past. They'll be replaced with matrix organizations that are not just flatter, but multidimensional in their multiple connections with collaborative work groups both inside and outside the company.

Much more responsibility will be placed on each member of the corporate team. We'll see considerably more autonomy for employees. Each work group will have more opportunity to have an impact on the decision making of the organization, more authority to implement decisions, and more opportunities for learning and personal growth.

Self-directed work teams, ad hoc task forces, and all sorts of new designs will emerge as people work with a higher focus on achieving desired results . . . then moving on to the next thing to be done. No longer will we see people sitting around waiting for their next assignment. Everyone will be a lot more tuned in to what's happening . . . in the whole organization.

Performance-Driven

Performance of the organization will be tied to the performance of the employees. Employees will understand how their jobs and responsibilities fit in attaining corporate goals and be rewarded based on their contribution to the success of the company. No longer will employees be put in dead-end jobs that have no value to the organization just because of longevity. Employees will need to demonstrate how they enhance the profitability of the organization. And if the organization is to enlist the support of these highly mobile employees, it will need to provide a clear set of goals that support a strong mission.

Agility

The competition will demand that organizations be agile and flexible, able to switch markets or make design changes to meet customers' needs in days, if not hours. To keep this agility, organizations will need to optimize the collective intellectual capital of their employees. Companies will need to include employees from all levels in decision-making roles, using the collective knowledge to remain competitive. Only when employees have a meaningful role in the organization will they be optimally productive.

Customer Focus

Not only is the workforce changing, but customers are making decisions based on more than successful advertising campaigns. Customers are becoming more sophisticated in the methods they use to determine which product to buy. They now take into account the way a company responds to the local and global environment; the relationship of the company to the community and to its employees; the values the company stands for and how it demonstrates those values publicly.

Successful companies know that to compete in the current marketplace they must be customer-focused. They must be able to respond quickly with a quality product or service. Companies are also learning that the lynchpins to this customer-driven cycle are employees. The people who provide the services, build the parts, answer the phones, send the invoices, etc., are, individually and collectively, the keys to the success or failure of the business. And that is precisely why, after all the chaos of the past decade, companies must change their relationships with their employees. Finding, keeping, and motivating good employees is the key to a successful business future.

Stable Workforce

One of the lessons learned after all the downsizing was

that customers value stability in the workforce of the companies they do business with. As we've seen in banking over the past few years, customers are becoming increasingly dissatisfied by the lack of service. Dissatisfied customers soon leave a bank, profitability declines, and investors are less interested in the company. The impact of employee turnover is particularly evident with companies that have significant customer contact, but even in a manufacturing environment, absenteeism and turnover will always impact product quality. Poor quality always impacts customer satisfaction. The cycle is the same.

A recent study of 275 portfolio managers by Ernst & Young's Center for Business Innovation showed that 35 percent of investor decisions were driven by nonfinancial information. The ability to attract and retain talented employees ranked high on the list of factors to be considered when making investments. Investors are increasingly including employee stability and motivation as part of the analysis process.[1]

As the workforce becomes more fluid, companies will be increasingly concerned about recruiting and retaining good employees. Not only will companies need the knowledge and expertise of these employees, but they will also need to keep close tabs on the costs associated with employee turnover. Recruiting and hiring costs can amount to as much as two to seven times the annual salary of the employee being replaced.[2]

In our changing global economy, which is becoming more competitive every day, companies have recognized that their employees are the key element in overall profitability. So how's a company going to develop a loyal, stable workforce under this new "employment contract"? The first step is to understand what employees want and need. The second step is to design programs to meet those needs. Let's examine some of the most important issues for workers in the corporation of the future.

Meaningful Work

Employees want to know that what they are doing is meaningful—to the organization and/or to the world at large. There's a strong sense of personal and corporate responsibility rising—a drive to do something to make a positive difference . . . something beyond self, beyond profit. Wise employers in the future will emphasize the intrinsic value of the company's work for the various stakeholder groups who benefit.

More than just a paycheck, employees in the future will want a stake in the success of the employer organization. They'll look for reward through stock options, incentives, training, perks, and bonuses. Few employees will remain in dead-end jobs without significant potential for personal growth or contributions to the betterment of our planet. This expectation will present some serious challenges for a lot of employers in the years ahead. Too many of today's companies simply don't think in these terms.

Career Security

Employees also want to develop a meaningful career path that makes them more marketable both internally and externally. To accomplish this self-development, they want opportunities to learn, to increase their responsibility, and to create and implement solutions. Learning opportunities include both academic and experiential methods and apply to both work and personal skills. They also want health care and retirement benefits to be portable, so that they can care for their families now and in the future, regardless of where they work.

Tomorrow's employees will assume responsibility for managing their own careers. In so doing, they'll deliberately seek opportunities to strengthen their knowledge, experience, and marketability.

A Values-Based Organization

Employees want to know that they are working for an ethical company with a mission and a clear set of values they can believe in. Workers are more likely to leave an incompatible work environment than ever before. Generation X workers are much more motivated to support the mission more than the process.

To keep these employees of the future, a company will need to stand for something more than a profit. Generation X employees are more interested in the mission of the company than the stock prices. Older employees have put in their time under the pressures of the old system and the overwhelming changes of the past two decades. They are more cynical and less inclined to give their all to a company they instinctively mistrust. To keep good employees in the future, companies will need to maintain a values-based culture. How a company is perceived by society will have an impact on its ability to find and keep good employees.

Balance Between Work and Family

Employees are looking for balance in their lives. The quality of their work and family lives is becoming more important. Child and eldercare issues are not just women's issues any longer. Increasingly, men are making career decisions based on family matters.

What employers have to gain by addressing these issues is a motivated, stable, productive workforce. To remain competitive in the marketplace, companies cannot afford to ignore these needs and expectations.

Companies will need to demonstrate that they understand the work *and* personal needs of the employees and be willing to act on that understanding. Employees are increasingly concerned about quality of life issues. The need to find a balance between work and family is a prime motivator for many workers. The companies who fail to take this into account will lose the best and brightest, either to another company that meets those needs or because employees are willing to downsize their lifestyle to achieve balance.

As we look at how some companies are meeting the diverse needs of their employees, it will become obvious that the cost/benefit analysis produces a favorable outcome. In many cases, the family-centered programs adopted by companies, both large and small, return benefits far in excess of the cost.

The Relationship Between
the Company and Its Employees

The expectations of employee populations will be big challenges for employers. If companies are to be successful, they will need to create an environment that will attract and keep good employees. Concepts like "It's just a job" or "It's a paycheck" will no longer suffice to keep employees motivated and productive. Meeting the needs of the "internal" customers, the employees who *are* the company, will be the only way to succeed in meeting the needs of the marketplace.

The Relationship of the Company to the Environment

The level of environmental awareness is a growing influence on a corporation's image. Whether the company uses environmental considerations in the planning stages or ignores the issues unless it gets caught can make a difference in the loyalty and marketability of the organization. A company that is aware of environmental issues and takes an active role in protecting the environment, either through its own product or through community involvement, will have a stronger position with its constituencies.

The Relationship to Society, Both Locally and Globally

Companies are judged on their actions in the community at large. Customers and employees prefer companies that look beyond today's profits to opportunities for giving something back. The process is similar to the agricultural investment in crop rotation.

Workers and consumers seek companies that have a demonstrated commitment to the future of society, not just to market share. How an organization invests its time, its people, and its resources in activities that impact the greater good of society will be an important factor in the future.

Companies will become more involved in their host communities, making a positive difference for their surroundings and for their employees. Enlightened companies will contribute resources to support activities in which their employees are involved. This tactic supports the community *and* the employees—attracting and holding workers who are involved in local activities (community leaders who can also assume greater leadership at work).

Moving Toward a Different Design

How companies operate relates in large part to the way people are treated in the corporate environment. They can go along with the "lean," but resist the "mean" aspects of the "lean and mean" company. The emphasis—based on attitudes in corporate America, societal trends, expectations of the workforce, and a shifting work environment—clearly indicates a rising demand for more meaningfulness in work—and other aspects of our lives. We'll talk a lot more about the various aspects of meaningfulness in this book, but let's explore other descriptors of how we see the corporation of the future.

The corporation of the future will be laser-focused on its core business. Any services, functions, divisions, or structures not purely invested in fulfillment of the company's tight mission will not be part of the core corporation. To use scientific terms, the corporation of the future will be a nucleus. That's all. No extraneous or support organizations . . . just the nucleus. The people who work in the nucleus corporation will coordinate and manage the acquisition and application of outside resources to accomplish the work of the company. The focus will be very tight, with high levels of accountability accepted by each member of the team.

With this very clear understanding of the company's

business focus, resources available, and results expected, there will be minimal need for a deep hierarchical structure of management. A very flat organization of collaborators will manage the work. These key people, each strongly empowered, will work closely together to guide both internal and external resources. The organization will be strongly decentralized, using technology-enhanced networking systems to communicate and share vital information.

With this kind of arrangement, employers will have a critical need to attract, optimize, and retain top talent. The kinds of people it will take to run tomorrow's businesses will be in short supply and high demand. This circumstance makes it vitally important to create, maintain, and promote a corporate culture that is highly supportive of high-quality workers. With the intensity of the work to be done, much like the intensity we identify with the New York Stock Exchange trading floor, it is essential that obstacles to high performance be removed. The lean nature of the future corporation addresses this issue. And, under this kind of pressure, caring sincerely for the people who work with the company will be fundamental. Leaders will aggressively destroy obstacles and shred red tape wherever they find anything getting in the way of success. They'll encourage people to work *with* the company, not just *for* the company.

Resource Management

The team members of the nucleus corporation will manage a variety of resources to fulfill the company's mission. Probably the most critical—and volatile—resource will be the human resource. For many companies, the majority of people who work for the company will not be traditional full-time employees. They certainly will not be employees who expect to work their entire careers at that company to earn the gold watch and a rocking chair to see them through their final days.

The corporation of the future will be staffed with several categories of contingent workers: part-time employees, directly contracted individuals, people contracted through brokers, and temporary workers. Some of the so-called permanent workers will be leased employees, not even on the company's payroll. The variety of human resources suggests that nucleus corporation managers will be juggling options to connect the right type of resource to the right type of work.

Some workers will be engaged directly, some through various kinds of agencies—some of which will provide full benefit packages and maintain close relationships with their people. The workers' length and type of attachment to the core corporation will depend on the kind of work they do and the company's needs at the time. These relationships will be ever-changing in a flexible and responsive system that utilizes resources only when they are needed.

The corporation of the future will be heavily invested in the use of outsourced companies and services. Tasks and functions that are commonly regarded as part of the corporate structure today will not be part of the core, or nucleus, of tomorrow. They will gradually be spun off into outsource organizations, some actually operating within the environment of the host company. Others will be nearby, some may be across the country or on another continent, and some will be connected only through virtual relationships via the internet or some evolution thereof.

Close relationships will develop between host (core) entities and their outsource networks.

Long-term agreements may guide their interactions, but we'll also see a lot of competitive bidding for work. The more solid alliances will be based on capacity and performance issues, of course. Beyond operational issues, shared values will increasingly determine which companies will work best together. Criteria used to select suppliers—and customers—will be some of the same qualities we relate as "meaningful" for employees in this book.

Strategic alliances will become increasingly important for the corporation of the future. These alliances will link vertical supply and demand chains, as well as reach into horizontal marketing machines. Organizations will seek—and find—all sorts of ways to build symbiotic relationships to maximize the utilization of resources and accumulated goodwill, while minimizing their own investment in any resources they don't need or use directly. Imagine the complicated webs that companies will weave to best share scarce resources.

The Culture

The culture of the successful corporation of the future will be exciting, fast-moving, and challenging. There will be an openness that fosters a high sense of camaraderie that will make work truly enjoyable. Attitudes will be positive, strongly influenced by enthusiastic leaders with a very clear sense of where they're going and how they'll get there. People will *want* to work for these leaders and these companies!

Risk taking will be encouraged to respond to the ever-changing environments in which the company operates. And people working for core organizations will be cross-trained to handle a wide range of tasks inside and outside of their areas of specialty. Everyone will be concerned with the company's environments: market, supply, financial, labor, regulatory, and operations.

Life in the corporation of the future will be largely experiential. Depending on lessons learned in the past might be dangerous in the face of constant and rapid change. Whether operating in a local or global arena, every entity will build a heightened sensitivity to factors influencing the way they do business. The old adage of the butterfly flapping its wings in China affecting life on the other side of the world will be a reality.

Everyone working in the corporation of the future will be continually learning. Traditional training classes will be supplemented by on-the-job training, college and university education at undergraduate, graduate, and executive development levels, and ongoing research into what "the other guys" are doing. Given our freedom of communication and instantaneous media, most corporations will be like an open book. Secrets about how they're doing business—structure, relationships, and more—will be relatively common knowledge . . . or at least readily available with a little bit of exploration.

The key to greatness will be how all the knowledge about what everyone else is doing is gathered, assimilated, and applied in each company. No one company cited in this book, for instance, is doing everything well. Each one does one thing or some things very well, but may not do other things as well as a company across town or across the country. We'll learn from each other, then create our own unique mix of how we will do things. That "mix" will determine our success in all the various arenas in which we operate.

Skills for the Future

We are often asked what skills will be most valuable— most needed—in the corporation of the future. Our answer includes noting the importance of all the skills we possess today. Technical and technological skills, in particular, will take on greater importance. We'll see growing needs for people who can understand and fix systems—from computer systems to product distribution systems to plumbing systems.

Visionary skills will be in demand. The ability to gather and absorb a wide range of input, then use that knowledge, understanding, and perspective to guide organizations into the future will be vital. Some will develop this capacity on a relatively short-term scale; others will look far ahead. Practically every company will have to move away from today's obsession with the next financial reporting period. Numbers and measurement will be important, of course, but smoothing the flow from month to month, from quarter to quarter, will be essential for highly profitable long-term performance.

The ability to organize will definitely be important in the corporation of the future. Everywhere you look there will be a need to organize something. Resources, work flow, marketing mix, financial opportunities, and much more will demand high levels of organization . . . and reorganization.

Persuasive skills will be used in all facets of the operation of the corporation of the future, internally and externally. Knowing how to present information and ideas in a way that others can understand and support a particular position will enable people to be considerably more effective. Salesmanship skills will be essential in many more interactions than we consider today, especially within the organization.

We hesitate to list "communication" skills. We hear that word so much from our corporate clients that we often call "communication" the "c" word. However, the skills of listening, writing, reading, speaking, and describing will be invaluable. There will be precious little time to be misunderstood, only to have to make corrections later. Tight margins may well make miscommunication a fatal corporate disease. Human interaction will be significant, so the skills to enhance related activities will be central to the strength of the corporation of the future.

The ability to learn will empower people to grow in effectiveness, helping their companies achieve desired objectives. Some of this skill is innate, but many people will acquire the ability to learn—and relate aspects of learning—in college and university environments. We believe the liberal arts education experience will prove to be the most valuable type of education for tomorrow's leaders.

The employees of the corporation of the future will be flexible, creative, and stimulated to make a positive difference in the world. They will seek balance, growth, and fulfillment in both life- and work styles. The corporation of the future must respond to those needs and desires, or they will find themselves hampered by a lack of qualified people to accomplish the organization's work.

Our next chapter begins our learning about the various aspects of meaningfulness that will be so important to employees of corporations in the future.

KEY CONCEPTS

▶ Demographics of the workforce and the world are changing.

▶ Employees are more mobile than ever and require different things to be productive and stay motivated.

▶ Customers, shareholders, and investors are basing decisions on the relationship of the company to its employees, the environment, and the community, both locally and globally.

▶ The corporation of the future will be substantially more flexible, responsive, and focused.

▶ People will work much differently in companies in the future.

ACTION PLAN

Ask the hard questions:

• What does your company stand for?

• What is your company doing or not doing in relation to the employees, the environment, and society?

• Where does your company need to improve now? In the future? How will the transformation be designed and managed?

• Why do people work for employers today? How will that change tomorrow when people have even more choices about where they work?

Endnotes

1. Shellenbarger, Sue, "Work & Family," *The Wall Street Journal*, March 19, 1997.
2. Herman, Roger E., "The Cost of Turnover." A White Paper published by the Workforce Stability Institute, Greensboro, North Carolina, 1997.

5

Meaningful Work
& Career

How can a company create a meaningful environment that will make it possible to recruit and retain the kind of employees essential to its success? As the labor market becomes tighter and companies compete for valuable workers, entire corporate cultures will need to change.

Today's worker is no longer willing to work in an environment that is authoritarian and dehumanizing. Workers want meaning in their work and balance in their lives. Given the amount of time people spend at work, it is essential that their jobs be more than just taking home paychecks. Workers want opportunities to contribute and to know how their work contributes to the organization. They also want to be acknowledged as individuals with goals and aspirations, not just replaceable drones in the hive.

The very nature of organizations can make the change

more difficult than it sounds. Every organization has reasons for its existence. Essentially, a corporation is a structured environment with a purpose . . . a business purpose. It is not a natural human social environment. It's an abnormal environment established to create wealth. Our challenge is how to build human relationships in nonhuman environments.

The foundation for creating these human relationships is a mutual respect for both what the employee contributes to the organization and for the individuals themselves. As James Autry, long-time magazine editor and author, so eloquently put it at the Annual Indiana University Business Conference, what we deserve from our work is "dignity, nobility, meaning and purpose."[1]

The underlying tenet of meaningful work must be a culture that values and respects the individual. Using this foundation, companies will be able to find and keep the kinds of employees they need to be successful. The evolution to this new, meaningful corporate culture will encompass many things. Not only will the design of work and compensation change, but organizational culture will include quality of life, environmental accountability, and social responsibility, and acknowledgment of the human spirit.

Creating Meaningful Work

The first step on this evolutionary path is to redefine work. What is the nature of work? How do employees want to relate with the work they do? Do they really want to be "engaged" in the work, or simply put in their time? Research shows that people want to do more than simply "attend" work.

A recent survey by Response Analysis, in Princeton, New Jersey, identified employees' top three most important aspects of work. Of the 1,600 people responding, 52 percent of them wanted to be responsible for their work and the results it produced; 42 percent wanted acknowledgment for their contributions; and 39 percent wanted their tasks matched to their strengths.[2]

People want to be responsible for their work and the results it produces! That's a far cry from the organization of the past, where workers were thought to be interested only in doing as little as possible. Today, companies that want to attract and motivate enthusiastic and dedicated employees will demonstrate their sensitivity to the level of responsibility workers want. They will design work so that employees can take responsibility and be rewarded appropriately. In doing so, these organizations will take a big step toward making work meaningful. What else does it take to make work meaningful for employees? Here are some key elements for redesigning work.

Valued Part of the Whole

To take responsibility for their work and its outcome, employees must see how their work fits into the organization as a whole. Repetitive factory work is no longer viable, nor is office work that simply moves paper from the in-box to the out-box. These kinds of mindless tasks destroy motivation and productivity. Workers want to know that their work is important and how it fits into the corporate strategy. For this transition to be made smoothly, organizations must share more information with more people than ever before. Remember, employees want to be responsible for results. They must have access to information to fulfill that responsibility.

Making an Impact

Employees need to know not only how the work they do affects others and the organization's strategic goals, but how they—as individuals—can make an impact. Who knows better how to improve the processes and environment than the people involved on a daily basis? This ability to improve the process is part of the intellectual capital of employees. Successful organizations understand and appreciate the intellectual capital of their employees, that is, what employees know is more valuable than what they do.

Workers can provide the organization a wealth of information through their knowledge and experience that cannot be acquired elsewhere. In order for this intellectual capital to be tapped, the organization will need to create a culture that encourages and supports collaboration. The enthusiastic contribution of this knowledge by the employees comes only in a corporate culture that values the individual.

Responsibility for Outcomes

Having the responsibility and authority to make decisions increases the meaning of work. Being able to recommend and implement improvements allows individuals to see their influence on the organization. Employees respond positively when they are given clear goals and the authority to make it happen.

This kind of exchange can only survive in a culture built on mutual trust. The organization must trust that employees are capable of making the right decisions. Employees, on the other hand, must trust that it is safe to take the risk of making decisions. This evolved process doesn't take away accountability. It does, however, focus evaluations on objective results and create an environment for continuous feedback and improvement.

Measuring Results

For workers to be responsible and find their work meaningful, they need direct and timely feedback. Making changes and improving performance comes from an ongoing evaluation process. Energy is created when workers are actively involved in improving their performance and meeting goals and objectives. When workers gain feedback from the customer (internal or external), it reinforces the importance of their job in the organization. They can gauge their influence in making things happen, solving company problems, and making appropriate decisions.

To assure a continuous flow of valuable feedback, establish systems for customers to evaluate service performance. Provide coaching for every employee on an ongoing basis. Involve employees in their performance rating, encouraging them to take initiative in improving their work and their results.

Every employee's work can be measured in some way. Develop those measurements, assure the flow of information needed to assess progress, and facilitate the evaluative process. Without measurements, employees will have a feeling akin to bowling in the dark. They'll put out lots of energy . . . with no sense of return. Tomorrow's employees—and many of today's workers—won't tolerate that ignorance, that vacuum.

Meaningful Rewards

The profitability of a company is directly related to the quality and efforts of the workers. A direct relationship between their performance and rewards makes work more meaningful.

Compaq Computers enjoys an unusually low turnover rate among its employees. The culture, typical of many companies in the computer field, expects people to work long and hard to achieve big results quickly. In some companies, this kind of constant push would inspire people to seek employment with less pressure.

Instead, high-quality people stay with Compaq. This company's culture emphasizes a tremendous sense of individual responsibility for results. There is a high respect for individuals—from the top of the organization down. It's modeled by management in all sorts of interactions, including providing access to information, resources, and higher management. Both company and employees benefit from creating opportunities for every employee to self-actualize . . . and be rewarded for the achievement. Compaq measures performance to assure that contributions are rewarded proportionately. At

Compaq, the empowerment concept reaches its full potential.

To keep employees involved and loyal to the organization they must share in the profits they create. Workers are reluctant to give 110 percent—only to discover that executive salaries skyrocket, while their own incomes barely keep pace with inflation.

Rewards (financial and other) for a job well done acknowledge the contribution of the individual. Not only are these incentives motivational; they underscore the importance of the individual within the organization. Enlightened companies are redesigning compensation to reflect this connection. The new performance-based compensation packages can help keep payroll costs low while keeping valuable employees motivated.

Putting It All Together

The Ritz Carlton hotel and resort company has always been at the forefront of customer service. After winning the Malcolm Baldrige National Quality Award in 1992, Ritz Carlton people continued their pursuit of quality. They established a pilot project of self-directed work teams that embodied many of the components of meaningful work. The pilot was so successful that, by 1995, there were 30 more Ritz Carlton Hotels and Resorts using the same self-directed work team concept.

These teams have the responsibility for management and leadership functions, work process improvement, developing team goals and missions, scheduling and payroll, team performance reviews, coaching and feedback, and purchasing and maintaining supply inventories. The Ritz Carlton uses these teams to allow people who are working on the front lines to have the authority and responsibility to deliver the quality their customers demand. By giving these front-line workers control over the process and outcomes of their jobs, management taps into employees' problem-solving skills and reinforces their commitment to high-level customer service.

With self-directed work teams of line employees in control of daily activities, managers have time to provide vision and direction. The Ritz Carlton has experienced an increase in satisfaction from the owners, the guests, and the employees. Additionally, the team environment allows employees to gain experience in a broad range of activities. This experience is valuable in recruiting and retaining good employees, since it allows employees to increase their skill levels and become more marketable to both the Ritz Carlton group and to other organizations in the hospitality industry.

Even with the focus on individual accomplishment, there is a powerful sense of team-ness at Compaq Computers. Every employee is expected to support everyone else to serve the customer. The worldwide profit-sharing plan reflects this togetherness: distribution is based on a balanced formula of customer satisfaction and return on invested capital. All employees benefit from this program—with the emphasis on employee collaboration.

Creating a Meaningful Organization

Once the process of work is redesigned to encourage collaboration, responsibility, and appropriate compensation for performance, then it's time to look at the surrounding corporate culture. The culture serves as the foundation for how an organization functions—at all levels.

Meaningful work is just a part of what it will take for companies to maintain the high-performance workforce necessary to remain competitive in the marketplace. Both employees and customers are more discriminating in their decisions. Enlightened companies know that their responsibilities extend beyond their own front door.

Workers will choose their employers based on how they perceive the organization. They'll be looking for the meaningfulness qualities we've explored in this book. Their choices will be deliberate, and they'll quickly and comfortably leave employment that isn't "right" for them.

Balance Between Work and Family

Employees seek balance in their lives. The quality of life, both inside and outside the organization, is more important to today's workers than ever before. Parents, both women and men, struggle to balance the requirements of the workplace and the needs of their children and extended families. Some workers care for both children and elderly members of their families. Employees without those responsibilities want time to pursue personal interests. Enlightened companies are finding ways to facilitate a balance between the work and personal lives of their employees. By addressing these issues, employers support a motivated, stable, productive workforce.

To remain competitive in the marketplace, companies must be highly sensitive to employee needs and expectations in the area of work/personal/family balance. It makes sense—on several levels—to make a significant investment in personal/professional balance. Cost/benefit analysis, when performed, reveals a favorable return on such an investment. In many cases, programs adopted by companies—both large and small—return benefits far in excess of the cost. Companies that demonstrate an understanding of quality of life issues can create a meaningful environment that is conducive to building a stable, productive workforce. The companies that fail to address quality of life needs will lose the best and brightest. Employees will either seek out other companies that offer quality of life programs or will downsize their lifestyles to make the balance.

Personal and Professional Growth

Employees also want to develop a meaningful career path that makes them more marketable both internally and externally. To accomplish this self-development, they want opportunities to learn, to increase their responsibility, and to implement solutions. Learning opportunities include both academic and experiential methods and apply to both work and personal skills.

People are highly energized when they are learning. Companies always benefit from workers who are actively engaged in improving their skills or knowledge. Professional development adds meaning to work; personal development adds meaning to the individual, both creating more self-confidence and self-esteem. Knowledgeable, confident workers are essential for the lean and meaningful companies of the future.

Most workers don't want to stay in the same job forever. They want to try new kinds of work to grow, expand their capabilities, and avoid boredom. If people don't have an opportunity to try different types of jobs with their current employer, they'll change jobs to find something new. So, wherever possible, give people a chance to experiment. Cross-training and cross-experience build skills and the employer's capacity to assign people where they're most needed.

Workers are skittish about changing jobs to try something new, if there is not a safety net in the event they don't like the new work. Can they say, "no thanks," and return to their former assignments? Land's End, Dodgeville, Wisconsin, responds to this uncertainty with something they call "job enrolling." Employees can try out a new job without even transferring out of their current position. If they like the new work, they can request an official transfer.[3]

The Relationship of the Company and Its Employees

The ways companies handle diversity, harassment, hiring and firing, profit sharing, and any number of other employee issues are used as criteria by consumers, prospective employees, and investors. A number of companies recently in the news can vouch for the impact of their internal decisions on their image.

AT&T lost huge image points when it laid off thousands of workers in a year of profits; Texaco's failure to handle discrimination within its own ranks will remain in the public consciousness for years to come. Prospective employees will not be interested in signing on with a company that has a history of treating its people badly—not to mention, the loss of current employees to companies with better track records. Investors are also watching companies carefully because the connections between employee retention and profitability have been made quite clear.

Diversity is a major concern in corporate America, and it will continue to occupy a place of significant importance for years to come. Diversity is much more than a racial issue. Emphasis is now on celebrating the differences between people and taking advantage of the varied perspectives that people bring to the workplace. The shift in relationships with employees will move us from mass considerations to individual interactions.

The Hearst Corporation celebrates the unique talents and contributions of each person working for the company. Whether the employees are high-profile reporters, secretaries, or little-seen printing press operators, their achievements are celebrated. When someone does something worthy of recognition, flowers are sent—to the employee's spouse. Really special situations call for a small gift from Tiffany's. Receipt of the gifts at home brings the family into the celebration, connecting the spirit of the family with the spirit of work.

Social Responsibility

Employees want to know that they are working for an ethical company with a mission and a clear set of values they can believe in. Workers are more likely to leave an incompatible work environment than ever before. Generation X employees are more interested in the mission of the company than the stock prices. Older employees have put in their time under the pressures of the old system and the overwhelming changes of the past two decades. They are more cynical and less inclined to give their all to a company they instinctively mistrust.

To win these valuable workers over, companies will need to live their mission statements. Employees and customers are aware of what organizations are willing to give back to the community. In a tight labor market, prospective employees will include a company's social report card as part of the decision process. How a company is perceived by society will have an impact on its ability to find and keep good employees.

Customers, shareholders, and other stakeholders are looking for more than just profitability. Companies are being held increasingly accountable for being good corporate citizens. Whether purchasing a consumer product or investing in stock, customers are choosing to make themselves aware of the company's policies and standards and voting with their pocketbooks.

The Relationship of the Company to the Environment

The commitment to environmental awareness is a growing factor for a corporation's image. Whether the company uses environmental considerations in the planning stages or ignores the issues unless it gets caught, can make a difference in the loyalty and marketability of the organization. A company that is aware of environmental issues and takes an active role in protecting the environment, either through its own product or through community involvement, will have a stronger position with its constituencies.

Spirituality in the Workplace

The human spirit, at the core of every being, where hopes, dreams, and aspirations lie, has previously been banished from the workplace. Yet there can be no meaning in either work or life when this aspect of human beings is ignored. An enlightened and meaningful corporate culture makes a place for the spiritual side of its people. For people to be their best, they must be able to express their values, to share their hopes, to tap into their creativity in the workplace. This expression can happen in many different ways, resulting in benefits ranging from better internal communication to new product design.

Evolving into a meaningful organization presents some big challenges. This new, meaningful culture takes into account all the areas we've discussed. Some aspects will be easy for companies to adopt; others will be less comfortable. Almost every company will have some meaningfulness—the issue will be the extent . . . and the *motivation* behind the shift. Sensitivity to the human spirit—in the work environment—will drive the most sincere, longest-lasting, and most effective movements into true meaningfulness.

Organizations must be mindful of all their relationships and act with integrity at all times. But the core relationship is between the company and its employees. The ability to build strong, collaborative relationships with employees will determine whether a business evolves into the future or is lost along the way.

As you read on, you'll find a number of ways that other organizations have made work and working meaningful. Your organization is unique, but you will be able to find opportunities to incorporate some of these ideas. With the imperative to find and keep good employees in a shrinking labor market, the efforts made to positively change the relationship of employees, their work, and the organization will be the defining factor in the successful corporation of the future.

One of the most important ways that employers can make work meaningful is to inspire employees to collaborate, to work together toward shared objectives. In the next chapter, you'll discover how to build this feeling in your organization.

KEY CONCEPTS

▸ To recruit and retain good employees, help applicants see that their work has meaning in the organization.

▸ Employees want to have an impact on the organization.

▸ Employees want to have decision-making responsibility.

▸ Compensation needs to reflect the contributions of the individual.

▸ Employees, customers, and investors are basing their respective decisions on the relationships of the company to its employees, the environment, and the community, both locally and globally.

ACTION PLAN

- Review your corporate communication systems. Do employees know how their jobs fit into the big picture?
- Review how job descriptions and responsibilities are aligned. Do people have an opportunity to contribute their intellectual capital?
- Review your performance evaluation process. Do employees receive timely feedback, goal setting, and compensation to support meaningful work?

Ask the hard questions:

- Why are we in business?
- What does the company stand for?
- Does the company demonstrate its values, or are they just words on paper?
- What is the company doing or not doing in relation to the employees, the environment, and society?
- Where does the company need to improve now? In the future?

Read on for ideas about how to make your company lean and meaningful!

Endnotes

1. Key, Peter, *Indianapolis Star & News* Business Column, March 6, 1996.
2. *Performance Strategies*, June 1996.
3. *PBS Nightly News*, January 27, 1998.

6

Collaboration

For companies to be viable in the future, they must demonstrate the idea that the whole is greater than the sum of its parts. Employees in the future will not be mere cogs in the machine, but rather the fuel that drives the engine.

Evolving corporations already know that the intellectual capital of their employees is their most valuable asset. For employees, the opportunity to share their knowledge and contribute to the overall success of the organization is part of what makes work meaningful. This new kind of partnership between employees and employers is the key to moving successfully into the future.

Corporate Democracy

Some enlightened companies have created a complete democracy at work, where the employees have decision-making power throughout the organization. In an age where workers are better educated, well informed, and more connected with what's happening, we can expect them to have a greater capacity to become involved and make intelligent decisions. Given the velocity of life, sharing decision making is a wise strategy.

Ann Price is CEO of Motek, a small software company in Beverly Hills, California, which has created a new paradigm for the relationship between the organization and its employees. Price not only changed how employee benefits are handled, but redefined them altogether. At her company, the core value that defines how everything in the company operates is "succeeding on our own terms." Many people, even though they are successful in their organizations, feel that they must relinquish their own values to the company.

Price has recruited high-quality people from around the world to work with her firm, because they have chosen to have their work reflect a different set of values. The corporate culture at Motek is different in the way it defines the relationships employees have with each other, including the CEO. The talented people employed there have left the corporate world to invent their careers by their own rules, on their own terms.

The Motek culture is democratic. Employees vote on everything from benefits to salaries. The idea is for the organization to be self-governing, not to be a monarchy. The people in this organization collectively take care of each other, including CEO Price, who considers herself as *taken care of* by her employees. There is an abiding belief in the value of the individual that flows through every aspect of the company.

In celebration of the individual, Price gives each employee two clocks, one runs on the time where the employee was born and the other runs on the time that the employee considers his dream city. Price believes fervently that time is precious and so it should be invested following our dreams. "You can only be 27 and on the beach in Hawaii once," she says. "You can be on the same beach when you are 40 but the experience will be different." Each day is unique and special—*"carpe diem"* (seize the day) has real significance.

The benefits that the company offers are a reflection of this belief. Employees are given one month off—with pay—each year. They also receive $5,000 with the stipulation that it can only be used for airlines, cruises, hotels, and other travel expenses. Employees are expected to take time to refresh and rejuvenate, to really experience the meaningfulness the culture emphasizes.

When an employee decides to make a change to another company, Price will help that employee find an appropriate new position. Every employee who has gone to another organization has stayed in touch. One former employee took time off from his current job to come back to Motek to help out on a special project. This level of loyalty could only happen in an organizational culture that honestly respects and honors the individual.

In the beginning, Price embraced the hot new idea of telecommuting. When she hired people she provided a big cart of equipment, told them to take it home and start working. Only a few people, including Price, came into the office on a daily basis. Because most of the employees were telecommuting, the office space was small and used as a hub and a location for a monthly meeting.

However, Price wanted all telecommuters to have their own desks whenever they needed to be in the office. When Price visited employees in their home offices, she often found pictures of other office workers. Within the year, all but two employees had relocated closer to the office and were coming in on a daily basis. This change was not the result of a corporate edict, but simply the evolution of employees wanting to work in the office environment and closely with each other.

For companies that are considering starting a telecommuting program, Price recommends that they spend time openly discussing all the details. She has never had a situation where telecommuters were not working hard and pulling their weight. As a matter of fact, she has had concerns that the telecommuters were working too much and not taking time for their personal lives.

The corporate culture at Motek flies in the face of the Los Angeles freeway lifestyle and suggests that it is a good thing to be able to walk to work. One woman, who used to commute at least two hours on the freeway each day, now lives a block from the office and walks to work. She says that the quality of her life is substantially improved. The company also helps find housing for any employee who wants to abandon the Los Angeles freeways and walk to work.

Price has found that when the quality of life increases, the hours in the office decrease. Her desire is not that employees work long hours and weekends. The closeness of the Motek team is not meant to be a replacement for a family or personal life. Team members encourage each other to have full and satisfying lives outside the workplace.

Joining the Motek team is a very selective process. The company will not hire people it doesn't intend to keep. Only job candidates who are sponsored by a current employee are considered for employment, and the company will create positions for great people. When an employee sponsors a new hire, that employee is responsible for the success of the new team member for the first year. If the new employee is having trouble with a deadline, the sponsoring employee is expected to pitch in to assure that the project is done correctly and on time.

One of the goals at Motek is to provide a professional environment that facilitates growth and learning. In this culture, the individual's growth and learning are very important. For one employee, growth might mean a significant increase in skill level, while for another employee, it might mean having a safe place to "hang out" and work during a difficult time in life.

Price expects her company to double in size in the next year. To keep the corporate culture from changing, she is considering dividing the company into smaller, tight units. Each of these units would continue to function as the company functions now; that is, governing itself. Motek is an experiment in growing a company and keeping a successful corporate culture alive. But Price knows that corporate culture is always evolving and is defined by the employees. As the leader of the company, she does not see herself in control of the culture. "Leaders need to be brave enough to let go," she says.

She challenges other leaders to substitute the word "inspire" for "empower"; rather than empower employees, leaders should seek to inspire them. Price believes that leaders are responsible for the environment and the success of their people. Leaders should ask themselves what they could do to create an environment where employees are happy to come to work. Motek invests every day in the mental health of its employees by helping them follow their dreams, develop professionally and personally, and have a voice in the evolution of their corporate culture and careers.

Open Book Management

If you want to incorporate all the elements of meaningful work into one sweeping cultural change, consider the concept of "open book management." With open book management all of the employees are made aware of the company's financials. From CEO to janitor, every employee knows how the company is doing—all the time. They also know what the expenses and profits are for their respective areas. All employees are expected to participate in decisions regarding costs, production, expenditures, and scheduling. And, they are all keenly aware of how what they do makes a difference in the overall success of the organization.

John Case writes in his book, *Open Book Management*, the idea is "helping them (employees) to think and act like business people rather than like hired hands."[1] An extraordinary example of this kind of management philosophy was demonstrated by Ricardo Semler at Semco, his manufacturing plant in Brazil. In 1980, when Semler took over the company that was founded by his father 53 years earlier, it was facing disaster. With 100 employees, the company generated $4 million producing hydraulic pumps for ships. They needed bank loans and struggled to find the paperwork for contracts that had been made by former executives.

Under Semler's leadership, supported by diligent efforts of other managers, they began to turn the company around. He brought in new managers and used expensive short-term financing for mergers and acquisitions. In 1988 the company had 800 employees and earned a 10 percent profit margin on sales of $37 million.

Semler acknowledges the hard work and good luck that played a part in the turnaround, but credits most of the success to the complete change in their management concept. Semler manages his company on three tenets: democracy, which lets all employees set and monitor their own working conditions; profit sharing, which rewards all of them when the whole company is doing well; and access to information, all information, so that everyone knows how well the organization is doing. These are the guiding principles for all activities at Semco.

Semler learned that in order for employees to work well together, groups should be small and management layers must be minimized. In their food service equipment division, they divided the facility of 300 employees into three separate units to maintain strategic agility. Initially costs rose, but within a year, sales doubled, inventories dropped, and eight new products were introduced. The previous layers of management that had prevented workers from getting these things done in the past were now gone. The company thrived.

The new organizational design let workers take control of the processes of the plants. Decision making at Semco is done collaboratively, even down to choosing and designing a new building location. When workers chose a site Semler had doubts about, democracy ruled and the company moved in. Workers designed the layout and hired a well-known Brazilian artist to paint the whole facility, including the machinery. Despite the initial misgivings, profits more than tripled and market share increased 14 percent in the first year at the new location, and it continues to rise.

Having access to information, particularly financial information, means that everyone must be able to understand what the numbers are all about. Through the union, Semco has all employees attend classes to learn how to read the financials. Now, everyone knows everything about the finances of the company, including executive salaries. For Semler, "if executives are embarrassed about their salaries, it probably means they aren't earning them."[2]

At Semco, accountability is pushed down to the lowest levels of the organization. Workers know how their jobs impact the profitability of the company and hold each other accountable. When problems arise, the workers themselves find the solutions. They set their own schedules, even on the factory floor; *subordinates* interview and accept or reject people prior to promotion; employees set goals for production; and workers use their own judgment on expenses when traveling for the company. Employees are invested in the company, because they actively participate in all decision making.

Even when it comes to profit sharing, Semco uses democratic principles. Profit sharing is based on the results of each individual division. Twice annually a calculation of 23 percent of after-tax profit is made on divisional income. The money is pooled until the division employees can vote on how they want it distributed. Often the cash distribution is divided equally. That means that everyone gets the same— from the janitor to the division head. Profit sharing works because every employee can see exactly where the numbers come from, how the profit is divided, and how their own work is related to the whole.

Empowering Workers Corporate-Wide

Empowering workers at all levels to make decisions is more common in the U.S. than other parts of the world. Ricardo Semler was able to do it in Brazil, but can a global company apply the same concepts around the world?

AES Corporation, an independent producer of electrical power, says yes! Dennis Bakke and Roger Sant, co-founders of AES, believe in the abilities of their employees to make decisions. This trust allows them to respond to opportunities much faster than their competition. AES grew from $200 million in revenues in 1990 to $835 million in 1996; from one power plant in 1986 to 82 in 1998.

It is not unusual at AES for employees who are young and new to the company to find themselves negotiating million-dollar acquisition deals or running power plants around the world. Wherever in the world AES goes, it takes its corporate culture. It is not always easy to transplant, but the bottom-up management style ultimately proves to be the best, most profitable model.

This culture is working in power plants in Argentina, Hungary, China, Kazakhstan, Pakistan, and Ireland. It's not always easy to change how things work in other countries, but as Oscar Prieto, the director of an affiliate in Brazil, says, "If you treat human beings fairly, they will respond as adults. It's a matter of believing in people." Prieto, by the way, was relatively new to AES in 1996, when he agreed to meet with a group discussing the privatization of a public utility in Brazil. Eighteen months later, Prieto oversees hundreds of millions of dollars in construction and is an integral part of the expansion of AES into South America.

AES looks for well-rounded people who are willing to learn, make decisions, and have fun. Bakke and Sant know that employees have fun when they are growing, achieving, and being challenged. Headquarters for the multimillion-dollar organization has a staff of about 30 people. The company functions without the usual departments for human resources, finance, legal affairs, or operations. Responsibility for making the company work is in the hands of individuals and teams around the world. People are encouraged to ask questions of anyone, including the co-founders, but ultimately the decisions are up to the individual employee.[3]

Committees for Participatory Problem Solving

Decisions are more effective when workers have an impact on the outcome. In a team environment, employee committees that represent workers from all team levels can be very effective in problem solving. Everyone benefits from the wide ranges of experiences and perspectives.

The Donnelly Corporation, based in Holland, Michigan, an auto parts maker, has been operating with democratic committee principles since the mid-1940s. At Donnelly all employees belong to teams. These teams elect members to "equity committees" that handle disputes and interpret personnel policies. Representatives are elected from the equity committees to participate in "The Donnelly Committee," which makes recommendations to the board on wages and benefits. Employees from the rank-and-file to top management are represented on both the equity committees and "The Donnelly Committee."

When Donnelly found itself falling behind in the marketplace, the company went to the equity committees and asked for help. The committees came up with cost-cutting measures that included pay cuts for employees making $40,000 and up.[4] When the tide turned six months later, the salaries were reinstated. This kind of cost cutting was successful because the decision came directly from employees. It demonstrates the level of commitment employees are willing to give an organization when they know that their input and labor are valued.

The more input employees have in the workplace, the more productive they will be. This change from a relatively dictatorial arrangement can be uncomfortable for managers from the old school. More traditional managers, who are accustomed to one-way communication with workers, often find it difficult to be receptive to input from subordinates. Soliciting that input is even more of a stretch, but the benefits make it very worthwhile.

Workers Set Their Own Schedule

Traditionally, managers have been solely responsible for creating and implementing solutions to problems, without input from the workers. The overall result was seldom as effective as managers hoped, because the affected workers had no part in the problem-solving and decision-making process. When managers and workers collaborate in problem solving, the results often exceed expectations. Workers bring valuable information to the problem-solving process. When they participate in developing the solution, they will support the decision.

In the past, it would have been heresy for workers to set their own schedules at J.W. Pepper & Son, a Philadelphia-based sheet music distributor. But when the company did allow workers that autonomy, the result was positive in every way.

CEO Ron Rowe was concerned. Although sales were increasing, profits were not. When a company survey indicated that employees felt that 30 to 50 percent of their time was wasted, Rowe went straight to front-line supervisors for a solution. Over the next year, he met on a weekly basis with the supervisors over brown bag lunches. What resulted from the meetings was nothing Rowe would have imagined.

Pepper's customers are schools and orchestras. The work is cyclical with very busy periods occurring just before school opens in the fall. Other times during the year the work schedule can be tediously slow.

The solution to wasted time was that during the 29 weeks when business is slow, workers work four 7.5-hour days and get paid for five. The extra 29 days are in addition to regularly accrued vacation days. When it's busy, they go back to the five-day week. The extra 29 days off were still less than the amount of wasted time reported in the survey and employees were more productive and motivated when they were at work.

The success at J.W. Pepper was not only due to the change in schedule, but also to increased employee training. Employees are now trained in multiple tasks, so they can do whatever work needs to be done, rather than focus on a single aspect of the process. In this way "crunch" times are covered, and there is no down time. Where shipping used to take days, it now takes minutes.

Like the employees at Semco, J.W. Pepper employees are in charge of themselves. Instead of being monitored by a supervisor, employees are now accountable to *each other* for time away from work. There is no paid sick leave. If an employee needs to be away, he must make arrangements with co-workers to get the job done. Because workers were part of the solution to the problem, the outcome has been very effective. Profits are up; absenteeism is down. Rowe feels good about the increased time off and the cross-training because of the change in perspective of the employees. As a result of their involvement, employees treat the company as their own, not just a place to work.

For Rowe, it was a personal challenge to change his leadership style. Moving from the old autocratic methods to a democratic system was quite a transition, but he says, "The fact of the matter is that if you want true quality, you can't rule it, dictate it, or policy it. It only happens when people are involved."[5]

Work Teams for
Performance Improvement

In large organizations, a team approach to improving performance is an effective model. In this model, small groups of employees in teams are responsible for setting goals, solving problems, and improving performance. The closer workers are to the process, the more significant the effect is in improving performance. Work is more meaningful when workers can make decisions and see the results immediately.

GE Fanuc Automation North America, Inc. in Charlottesville, Virginia, created a formalized method of employee involvement called High Involvement Work Force (HIWF). In 1990, the entire workforce of 1,500 employees made the transition to this model. At Fanuc they understood that the people best suited to make changes and improvements were the people closest to the process. Their HIWF program decreased the layers of management and created 40 work teams. These teams are responsible for setting their own goals and measurements within the framework of the overall corporate strategy.

To keep the teams functioning at the optimum level, they meet once a week, off-site, to evaluate current performance and brainstorm improvements. To make the transition to this new work structure easier, employees received 100 hours of training. Employees needed support in learning new ways to communicate and participate in decision making for this cultural change to be successful. To reassure employees of the company's commitments to dramatic change, Fanuc guaranteed workers that no one would lose a job due to the new HIWF programs. Reinforcing the systemic change, managers' evaluations were based on their support of the team process and their encouragement of employees to move within various teams.[6]

The way Fanuc developed their HIWF program is a good example of the evolution of the corporate culture that is essential if such programs are to be successful. The company's concept of teams would not have been successful without the cultural change that was supported by refocusing managers' evaluations and making the employees feel secure in their jobs.

For Fanuc, the change to an involved workforce created a number of benefits for the organization and its people. The organization got a more productive workforce and the employees had the opportunity to see how their work had a direct impact on the organization's success. That involvement keeps work meaningful for Fanuc employees. The ability to move freely among the teams gives employees more marketability because of their broader skill base. By creating an environment where workers can continually increase their knowledge and skills, the organization gains an edge in recruiting employees.

One Big Family

When discussing how people work in a company, we describe the relationship as being like a family. In addition to addressing interactions between workers in similar terms to how family members get along, we also emphasize family values. To an extent, the cohesive values and bonding that occur in a family environment can be replicated in the corporate world.

Here's a company that prepared for the competition of the future, by applying the values of the past. Rosenbluth International, a $2.5 billion travel service business, is run like a family farm. Yes, a family farm. The family farm can be a very good model for the current business climate. A farm is always running on close margins, subject to the total unpredictability of the weather and selling a product that is exactly like its competitors'. Furthermore, everyone on the farm must be ready to work and be able to do a number of different jobs. Every member of the family must rely on the others to make the venture a success. The core value at Rosenbluth is "treat your employees well and everything else will fall into place." Through thick and thin, CEO Hal Rosenbluth has kept that value alive.

The Rosenbluth "farm" includes 3,500 employees spread over 1,000 offices in 41 countries. So instead of one big farm, Rosenbluth makes each office a farm unit and relies on high tech to keep them connected. The corporate culture is designed around friendship. Employees treat each other like friends and, as such, work hard to support each other.[7]

Cardinal Meat Specialists, Mississauga, Ontario, encourages collaboration among all employees . . . and a true family feeling. The company bestows "E Awards" ("E" for effort) to individuals or teams that have demonstrated exceptional effort. The recognition is presented at the company's annual dinner dance. That event is almost as much fun as the annual family day at a local theme park.

HA-LO Industries, Inc., the largest firm in the marketing and promotion field, employs 3,400 people in 50 countries. Based in Chicago, the company enjoys an extremely low employee turnover rate. Strong emphasis is placed on hiring very carefully, seeking people who will be happy with each other. With the right people being hired, management has a responsibility to create the best opportunity and environment to inspire those good people to stay. They don't even require noncompete contracts from their salespeople; they don't expect them to leave!

The people employed by HA-LO become good friends as they work together over the years. They enjoy a lot of good times together, along with the highly productive work. Employees at the home office—*and their families*—go to professional baseball games in Chicago . . . paid for by the company.

Employees receive holiday gifts—at many holidays, not just Christmas. As purveyors of advertising specialties and incentive gifts, HA-LO encourages clients to recognize employees on a regular basis: they practice what they preach! The company believes it's important to recognize people on an ongoing basis.

As a company philosophy, HA-LO Marketing and Promotion will do practically anything to help its employees. It's an attitude thing. Whether the problems involve childcare issues, a death in the family, buying a home, or something else, the company—and its people—are there to help. It's a true example of caring and sharing. Since employees know they can count on the company and each other for whatever kind of support they need—time, money, physical help, or a shoulder to cry on, they have less stress and more confidence.

Leisure Craft/USA Display, Hendersonville, North Carolina, sponsors monthly lunches for its employees. These events build a greater family feeling among the employees. The company's extended family is included at the annual celebration dinner at the end of each year. Spouses and children of employees—even babes-in-arms, are invited. Employees receive bonus checks, then employees, their spouses, *and their children* receive gifts. And everyone gets a copy of a group photo of the entire workforce, suitable for framing.

Ask for Suggestions

Although it may seem dated, the suggestion box, when designed well, can be a great source of new ideas and an inexpensive way to get employees involved in the organization. Many companies that employ this concept have gone far beyond the familiar slotted box on the wall. Suggestions are actively solicited, rather than merely accepted passively.

Dana Corp., an auto-parts manufacturer with locations worldwide, received an average of 1.22 ideas from each of its 45,500 employees in one year. These ideas saved money and improved productivity. Ideas like making a tiny weld in sheets of steel to make it possible to load them automatically into a forming press, saving $250,000; or staggering schedules slightly so that a new $110,000 parking lot didn't need to be built make a difference. CEO Woody Morcott has made the suggestion box a core element of the organization.

At each Dana plant, workers know they are responsible for keeping the plant competitive; ideas that contribute to that goal are very valuable. Every plant handles the process differently. A plant in Mexico offers $1.89 for an idea and another $1.89 if it gets used. In Reading, Pennsylvania, all suggestions get logged into a computer. The Kentucky plant has 3 x 5 cards that can be carried easily, then posted on a bulletin board. In Missouri, the employees are organized into teams to implement ideas that cost less than $500. The program is very successful—about 70 percent of the ideas get implemented.[8] As a result, workers see the impact they have and know that they are respected.

Training for Continuous Improvement

Organizations must give workers training to prepare them for the responsibility of decision making. Enlightened companies know the value of self-directed teams and give employees ongoing training to develop the necessary skills.

Wainwright Industries manufactures stamped and machined parts for customers in a number of different industries, including aerospace, automotive, and information processing. Winner of the 1994 Baldrige Award, Wainwright has a thorough program of employee involvement, putting employees in charge of accomplishing goals, meeting customer requirements, implementing improvement actions, and making spending decisions.

At Wainwright the process starts with new hires, who are given a comprehensive orientation explaining the company's approach to continuous improvement. Follow-up sessions are held 24 and 72 days after the initial orientation and managers reinforce the quality measures during semiannual performance appraisals.

The company backs up its desire for continuous improvement by giving employees the education and tools necessary to accomplish their tasks. In fact, Wainwright invests seven percent of its payroll in training and education. This education includes not only skills training, but courses on communication, problem solving, and quality values as well. For employees who take classes elsewhere, Wainwright offers full reimbursement.

As a result of the commitment to education and the supporting corporate culture, employees implemented 54 improvement ideas *each* in 1993. Supervisors provide the support necessary to make the process a success by responding to suggestions within 24 hours. The workers benefit by larger profit-sharing payments and a safer workplace. Wainwright benefits with a decrease in recordable accidents, lower workers compensation costs, higher rates of attendance, and lower turnover.[9]

American Airlines pays out millions of dollars per year to its employees who offer suggestions that result in cost savings. Numerous other companies similarly share the benefits with workers who identify opportunities for improvement and help implement solutions.

Collaborate with Employees to Make Changes

Engaging employees in workplace improvements is extremely valuable. It is also valuable to demonstrate in other ways that the organization cares about what employees think. Unlike organizations where production workers never see the owners, Ben & Jerry's employees have the opportunity to interact with both Ben and Jerry directly at bimonthly staff meetings. Not only do the owners attend the meetings, but they also sport the same casual dress as the employees. They believe little communication can occur when the "suits" show up to talk "to" employees about the company.

At these staff meetings, Ben and Jerry interact casually

with employees and share vital information about the company. The company has also conducted a comprehensive survey asking employees what they think about a number of topics, ranging from the company benefit plan to farm aid. The results are not just buried in a file. The information gathered from employees at all levels is used to solve problems and make changes in the company.

The Human Resources Advisory Group, made up of employees from throughout the company, discusses changes with the line workers and gives feedback to the Human Resources Department. This collaborative approach to making changes may take longer, but it is more effective in the long run. Ben & Jerry's also wants to know how workers feel about management, so they conduct annual "rate-the-boss" surveys. The results are used to find problem areas that are then addressed by the Human Resources staff.[10]

Trust Is Essential

As you move decision making deeper into the organization, trust is a critical factor. The success of the transformation will depend in part on how the employees feel about the organization. The corporate culture, as well as the programs, must support the sharing of knowledge. Without both in place, workers may well feel that the company is just paying lip service to employee involvement. Even worse, if there is a lack of trust, employees may withhold negative information, such as waste emissions figures or manufacturing defects if they don't feel that the organization honestly respects their contributions.

A common thread here? To optimize their productivity, employees need to be respected as adults. Given the right training and knowledge, adults take on responsibility, accept accountability, and become more productive, active members of the organization. Some companies have adopted open book management principles and involved employees in every aspect of running the business; others use teams to create a continuous improvement culture; and still others reward suggestions and survey for employee opinions.

Regardless of the method, the concept is to acknowledge the value of employees and the investment they make with their intellectual capital. Unlike organizations in the past, where workers put in their perfunctory 9 to 5, enlightened corporations will maximize the contributions of all employees to remain competitive. The involvement comes from knowledge about the organization and how individual contributions enhance the whole.

Technology makes it possible to share more knowledge more easily than ever before. Enlightened companies take advantage of this opportunity and share as much knowledge about the organization as they can. The broader the employees' understanding of the organization, the greater the contributions they can make. Work will be meaningful and employees will stay.

Their stay will be even more meaningful—and enjoyable—for employees if they maintain a good balance between their work and personal lives. More about this topic will be found in the next chapter.

KEY CONCEPTS

- Employees in forward-thinking organizations make decisions on all aspects of the workplace.
- Employees understand all the financial information of the company.
- Education and training are good investments.
- Employees have intellectual capital that is crucial to the success of the organization.
- Trust between the company and the employees is a critical factor in employee participation.

ACTION PLAN

- Determine if your company has "hired hands" or contributing, involved employees. If you have "hired hands," figure out why. Is there an issue about trust?
- Identify ways employees can contribute their knowledge of the organization to solve problems and make work more productive.
- Identify any skills or education gaps that will stand in the way of increased employee participation.
- Develop training to bridge the gaps.
- Implement and reward ideas and suggestions from employees to reinforce the cultural change.
- Demonstrate trust in employees and respect for their contributions.

Endnotes

1. Case, John, *Open Book Management*, p. xx.
2. Semler, Ricardo, "Managing Without Managers," *Harvard Business Review*, 1989.
3. Markels, Alex, "Power to the People," *Fast Company*, February/March 1998.
4. Reder, Alan, *In Pursuit of Principle and Profit*, G.P. Putnam's Sons, New York, NY, 1994.
5. Flynn, Gillian, "Tapping Employee Insights to Expand Productivity," *Nations Business*, November 1996.
6. "HR Leaders Stay Close to the Line," *Workforce*, February 1997.
7. Sanders, Chris, "Back to the Farm," *Fast Company*, February/March 1997.
8. Teitelbaum, Richard, "How to Harness Gray Matter," *Fortune*, June 9, 1997.
9. http://www.nist.gov/director/quality_program/doc
10. Laabs, Jennifer, "Ben & Jerry's Caring Capitalism," *Personnel Journal*, November 1992.

7

Balancing Work & Personal Life

Today everyone seems to work harder, spend more hours on the job, and assume responsibility for more things—both at work and at home. Workers at all levels—and their families—experience greater stress than ever before in history. The stress is more intense, explosive, and even violence-prone. Flash points are lower as people feel more helpless in their desire for control and security. The stress of this balancing act is taking its toll.

For many families, the balancing act between work and home is done without a safety net. They lack adequate childcare; work in an inflexible environment; and have poor or nonexistent healthcare. The increased stress shows up in high rates of absenteeism, lower productivity, and more long-term health problems. People are searching for ways to make their lives work, to meet the needs of their employers *and* their families.

For organizations to recruit and retain good employees, they must create ways to help employees address these issues. To do so requires more than merely implementing new employee benefits. To successfully address these quality of life issues, there must be a dramatic change in the relationship between the organization and the employees. Evolving corporate cultures are developing new relationships that respect the interaction of employees' work and private lives. Enlightened companies are already well along in this evolution and are creating environments that enhance the quality of life for their employees.

Challenging the Myths in Corporate Culture

This evolution of corporate culture and societal trends will challenge many of the traditional myths held about the relationship of work and family. These myths are embedded in most corporate cultures as well as in the attitudes of managers and co-workers. Until these myths and corporate cultures themselves change, "family-friendly" programs cannot be successful. Employees will be unwilling to take advantage of programs that might be valuable to them, if they believe there will be a negative consequence for their careers. Consider some of the following myths about work and family. How deeply embedded are they in your organization?

Myth: *Family and personal problems should be left at the door when entering the workplace.*

As women move into the workforce in greater numbers, assuming more professional, management, and leadership positions, the awareness of family issues—primarily childcare—have increased. In the past, family issues were considered women's issues. After all, it was working women who needed childcare support.

Myth: *Men's careers are unaffected by family issues.*

Time has shown us that whatever is happening in the family has a significant effect on all workers—both men and women. The number of single fathers in the workforce is increasing.

Myth: *Childcare is the only family issue for employees.*

While "family" issues have centered on childcare in the past, eldercare will become increasingly important as the Baby Boomers age. In the short term, Boomers will be the "sandwich" generation, caught between children and dependent elderly family members. Looking farther into the future, the children of the Boomers will feel the pinch as this bulge in the population ages, many without the financial reserves for a comfortable retirement.

Myth: *People retire at age 65 and leave the workforce.*

For many workers retirement is not financially feasible. With a longer life expectancy, Boomers may choose not to retire or to return to the workforce in lower-paying positions.

Myth: *A family is a working father and a mother who stays at home with the children.*

Despite the realities of the workplace, many senior executives and managers still hold this antiquated view as the way a family *should be.* So while they may intellectually support quality of life programs, they send out corporate culture signals that discourage participation.

The reality of what constitutes a family is dramatically different from the past myth. A family can have two parents or only one; it can be same-sex or heterosexual; it can include children, elders, or other dependents. And as those definitions of family change, so do the needs of the employees who are part of those families.

Women in the Workforce

Let's look at some statistics about families. Today, about 60 million women work outside the home. The workforce is expected to increase by 26 million between 1990 and 2005. Of that increase, women will account for 15 million or about 62 percent of the net growth. In 1990, the civilian labor force was about 45 percent women, but by 2005 that number will be about 47 percent of the labor force.

The largest-growing segments of women are Hispanic and Asian women, whose participation in the workforce will increase 80 percent.[1] Of the women in the workforce, about 75 percent will become pregnant during their careers and half of those women will go back to work full-time.

Parents in the Workforce

Currently 37 percent of the workforce are parents and 4 percent of those are single parents. Of those parents, 17 percent have children under the age of 6. It's no wonder workers are experiencing stress trying to balance work and family responsibilities. Even with a two-parent family, the logistics are often overwhelming.

Stress points between work and family are manifested in the business environment as increasing turnover rates, absenteeism, and lower productivity. After keeping the pace of business and meeting the needs of family, workers have little reserve to keep themselves healthy, so health insurance programs may be negatively affected. Furthermore, workers must stay home to take care of sick children that cannot go to daycare. Co-workers taking up the slack cannot always produce the quality and quantity required.

Family Economics

In many families both adults are working and their combined income is just not keeping pace with their expenses.

They work long and hard, but still find too much month left over at the end of the money.

Statistics tell the story. Median income of the American worker between 1975 and 1994 rose only 6.7 percent. For the top 5 percent of men it rose 16.7 percent and the top 5 percent of families it rose 31.6 percent. During that same period, the cost of a car rose 65.8 percent and the cost of a college education rose as much as 66.5 percent! But the most difficult increase was in the cost of childcare, which rose an astonishing 202.2 percent![2] In two-parent families, both spouses are now working for necessities, not luxuries. For a single parent, the cost can be staggering.

Aging in the Workplace and in Families

By the year 2005 the age of people in the workforce will be concentrated in the 25 to 54 age range, but the number of workers over 55 will increase from 12.3 percent in 1990 to 14.7 percent in 2005. The average age of the American worker will be 38.9.

These "older" workers may also be responsible for caregiving for children, aging parents, or relatives. These responsibilities can be as simple as weekly visits to relatives that live independently to providing time-consuming daily care in the worker's home. Making arrangements for doctor appointments, balancing checkbooks, and negotiating and paying for nursing home care not only takes time during working hours, but also increases workers' stress levels.

As the parents of workers over 55 live longer, they will need even greater assistance. *Newsweek Magazine* reports that American women will spend 17 years raising children and 18 years caring for elderly parents. That's a whole career's worth of family responsibilities.

The costs to companies for employees who have eldercare responsibilities are increasing as well. MetLife indicated in a recent report that absenteeism for eldercare is costing companies nearly $4 million. Furthermore, the cost to replace workers who quit to care for elders is nearly $5 million.[3] These costs will only go up as the Boomers and their parents age.

As organizations evolve, the changing face of the workforce will be the catalyst for the new definitions of family that will replace the old paradigms. While this evolution will help companies create more effective benefit programs to help people balance work and family, there are still some powerful corporate myths that can make even the best programs unsuccessful.

Evaluating Performance

There is a lingering attitude that only people who work long hours and come in on weekends are serious about their careers. For employees who are serious about both their careers and their children, this belief poses an impossible problem. The result is that both work and family suffer, since neither gets the attention it really deserves. This myth is reinforced by managers and supervisors who still use the old methods to assess whether employees are working hard. That standard is "face time." How much time employees are at work—what hours and how many—often still forms the basis for evaluating employees' work.

Telecommuting can be a viable option for employees, but they will be reluctant to participate if their managers are still evaluating performance on "face time." This is particularly important since most companies report that telecommuters are actually more productive working at home.

The same problem occurs with employees on flextime. They may not be in the office late in the evenings or early in the mornings because their time schedule is different. If the corporate culture is designed around working late every night, these flextime workers may be considered less dedicated, even though they produce the same amount of work.

Family leave benefits can also be undermined for both women and men when "face time" is the criteria for career advancement. Many men feel especially pressured between the desire to take time off for family issues and the old beliefs about men being committed to their work first and family second. Younger men in the workforce frustrate and irritate their older bosses when they insist on a more personal or family-centered balance.

While salaried employees are expected to work long hours, the family pressures for hourly workers can be just as strong. Working in an environment that offers no flexibility can make it impossible to handle family matters, which seldom conform to a work schedule. Employees of companies with family programs in place report that the flexibility and understanding demonstrated by their managers or supervisors play a key role in their willingness to take advantage of the opportunities available.

In designing quality of life programs, it is essential that companies support these programs by changing the managers' and supervisors' perspectives on nontraditional workers. They will need new skills for evaluating performance that focus on results, rather than time at work. Supervisors of hourly workers will need to learn to manage with more flexibility, keeping an eye on the end product, not the clock. This shift to results management will be particularly challenging for managers supervising workers in virtual environments, such as telecommuters and distance workers.

Corporate Benefits from Work-Life Programs

Beyond helping employees manage their lives better, there are compelling financial reasons for organizations to develop successful work-life programs. Given the economic imperatives to have a stable, productive workforce and the increasing costs of absenteeism and turnover, enlightened companies are not only developing programs to help employees balance work and family, but are changing their corporate cultures to support these programs.

In 1995, DuPont documented the value of their work-life programs. A survey of 6,366 employees found that 52 percent of the people who had used three or more of the work-life programs responded that they would "go the extra mile" for DuPont. Only 36 percent of those who had not used the programs were willing to put in extra effort. The basics of the program included flexible scheduling, dependent care programs, and flexible spending accounts for dependent and medical care.

DuPont started its work-life program in 1986 and spent $1.8 million to expand it between 1990 and 1995. The positive results of the 1995 survey indicate that the money was well spent and according to Gary Pfeiffer, VP and General Manager of DuPont Nylon North America, "having the programs creates a business value that is several multiples of the cost of supporting those programs." The value is apparent in increased performance, employee retention, lower absenteeism, and reduced stress.[4]

Recruiting and Retaining Good Employees

Businesses operating in highly competitive markets know that to be successful, productivity must be up and costs must be kept down. The cost of replacing a worker, especially a knowledge worker, can be as high as 1.5 times the worker's annual salary. That doesn't take into account the cost of training, assimilation, team building, or experience building.

Hewlett Packard and other companies spend upwards of $10,000 in training new employees. Others cite costs of $20,000 and more, especially for salespeople. Add that cost to lower productivity during the training period and supervisor/trainer time spent training instead of doing regular work and replacing an employee becomes a very expensive process. We've calculated estimates, based on actual figures from clients, that suggest the total cost of replacing a valued employee could be as much as seven times annualized income!

It is in the best interests of every business to keep its best employees. But companies need to do more than just retain people. Employers must create an environment where worker productivity is at optimum levels. In an environment where employees have the opportunity and flexibility to care for both their families and their careers, workforce stability is enhanced.

Faced with these challenges of high recruiting costs and the need for a stable workforce, a number of large organizations developed employee surveys to determine just what is important to employees. Increasingly, in the past couple of years particularly, mid-sized and smaller organizations are utilizing surveys to measure turnover vulnerability. Practically every time we have used such surveys in our consulting work, we have discovered a wealth of information—knowledge that corporate management had ignored or been oblivious to. It's clear that management needs to pay more attention to workforce stability issues.

As an example of the kind of data being gathered, the Marriott Corporation targeted 1,600 of its 206,000 employees nationwide for an in-depth survey. The results brought family issues to the forefront. Marriott management discovered that 35 percent of their workforce had children under 12 and that the average worker in this group was absent four days per year and tardy five days because of childcare responsibilities. Marriott discovered that balancing work and family was a significant issue for both male and female employees and that this balance had a significant effect on their performance. In addition, eldercare was becoming a greater concern.[5]

Given the pressures of the workplace and the increasing

pressures of family responsibilities, businesses that will be successful in the future must find ways to help workers cope with the ever-increasing demands. Companies will need to be family-friendly, not just in words, but also in deeds. If people seeking family support don't find it at your company, they'll go somewhere else to get their needs met.

Although companies across the board are beginning to provide some programs to help employees balance their work and family responsibilities, in some cases the participation levels are not as high as might be expected. When this lack of participation occurs, it is often because the organization did not take into account the beliefs embedded deep in the corporate culture . . . beliefs like a high-performance work culture may be at odds with quality of life programs. Evolving companies are developing new cultures that balance performance and quality of life.

Examine your corporate culture to identify myths and beliefs that might stand in the way of a successful program. Address these myths and beliefs first and your chances of building viable work-life programs will increase dramatically.

A number of both small and large companies that have developed creative ways to help workers balance the demands of work and family. Included in the following chapters are some ideas that you can build on. Take what can work for your company. You may come up with a hybrid that's even better than the approaches shared in this book. Always keep in mind, that by assisting your workers with their difficult family issues you will bond them to the organization. That bonding will be instrumental in helping you recruit and keep good employees, lower your absenteeism rates, and increase productivity.

An editorial comment is appropriate here. Our research uncovered wonderful programs to balance work and life. We discovered that the reality of implementation does not always match the design, intent, and hype of the program.

Astute corporate leaders should invest the time to talk with (and listen to) their front-line employees to learn just how well the programs are actually being run.

If the culture or policy/procedure barriers block the support programs' success, all the grand intent in the world won't have an impact on workers and their families. The cognitive dissonance between design and reality will destroy, rather than support, the sense and spirit of meaningfulness.

A substantial part of life balance for workers is their relationship with their families. They'll be looking for companies that demonstrate what's called "family centeredness." We'll discuss this issue in the next chapter.

KEY CONCEPTS

▸ The success of any work-life/family-life program is dependent upon the existence of a supportive and consistent corporate culture. There must be congruence between culture and programs.

▸ Balancing work and family is a high priority among employees.

▸ To recruit and retain good employees, companies will need to help employees achieve the balance they seek.

ACTION PLAN

• Survey your employees to see what they need most.
• Identify how your corporate culture responds to work/family issues.
• Develop training to break down old beliefs and affirm a quality of life culture.

Endnotes

1. Williams, Paul, "A Look to the Future: Women in Business Through the Year 2005," *Los Angeles and Orange County Business Journals*, Fall 1997.
2. *Fortune*, March 17, 1997.
3. Micco, Linda, "Caring for Elderly Relatives Affects Productivity," *HR News*, November 1997, Vol.16: No. 11.
4. Clifford, Hal, "The Perfect Chemistry: DuPont's Work-Life Program," *Hemispheres*, May 1996.
5. Solomon, Charlene Marmer, "Marriott's Family Matters," *Personnel Journal*, October 1991.

8

Family Centeredness

Being a parent is the most challenging job most people ever face. People who are struggling with parenting issues find it difficult to be effective at work. Learning better ways to manage children helps workers decrease stress and increase productivity. Companies that help employees be more effective as parents also find that employee retention rates are higher. Educational programs can cover any number of topics: expectant parent training, childhood development, educational support, family relationships, and support groups.

With the changing demographics of the workforce, family issues have an increasing importance to organizations. Childcare is a serious concern for both employees and organizations. Elder care will be an issue in the near future. Time off for family events is cherished, as is time to attend to personal business.

Employees often struggle to find good daycare, getting children to and from daycare on time, and finding alternate care when children are sick. Employers, on the other hand, have discovered that childcare issues are the primary reasons for increased absences and tardiness among employees—both mothers *and* fathers. Because both of these problems are costly, companies have sought ways to assist parents with childcare responsibilities.

The solutions are as varied as the children and families themselves. Some companies have established comprehensive daycare centers on site, while others have experimented with school holiday care. Many companies have developed a referral service for child and family services to help workers find good facilities.

Elder care is looming on the horizon as an additional need for families, so some companies are also offering seminars and referrals to help care for aging parents and relatives. With the increasing pressures of work and family responsibilities, companies are also concerned about the good health of employees, both physically and psychologically. There are many ways to help employees balance all these responsibilities. The companies included here are only a few among many that have developed ways to enhance the quality of work and family life. Use their examples as a catalyst for creating your own quality of life programs.

Referral Programs

Providing parents with a referral source for childcare options is a component of programs offered by many companies. Through these referral services, parents can locate a number of valuable services—childcare and eldercare facilities, parenting classes, training in eldercare, financial planning for aging parents and relatives. For referral lists to be truly valuable to employees, they must be more comprehensive than a list from the phone book. While organizations may be hesitant to "recommend" a particular facility, gathering additional information about companies on the referral list would make them much more useful to employees.

Rather than digging for the information yourself, invite the facilities on your list to complete a questionnaire, including caregiver-to-child ratios and qualifications of the professionals involved. Ask for feedback from your employees about their experiences with the facilities. Put those pieces together and you have a fairly complete picture of the local facilities available—and how you and your employees rate them. For instance, childcare facilities could be sorted by the ages of children they take, the educational components, the costs and hours. Licenses and certifications of employees might also be included.

Larger organizations might want to consider establishing a list of criteria for facilities to meet in order to be placed on their referral list. The benefit to the care facility is an ongoing list of potential customers. The benefit to the employer is the assurance that the children of employees are being placed in quality daycare.

Parent Education

At the Los Angeles Department of Water and Power, 76 percent of their 11,000 employees are men. This public service department is an unlikely place to find a highly family-friendly environment. Yet the DWP has developed a significant program based on parent education for both men and women. Like many companies, the DWP offers child and dependent care referrals, as well as care for sick children, but the cornerstone of their program is parent education.

One of the many education programs offered is for expectant parents. This course is designed to include fathers in the process. As an extension of this class, DWP makes it possible for nursing mothers to return to work and continue breast feeding by providing breast pumps, ice packs to save the milk until they get home, and special rooms where they can express the milk. The breast pumps are also made available for the spouses of the men at the company. The lactation program has dual benefits. Since breast-fed babies tend to be healthier, the program lowers health care costs and absenteeism rates of parents staying home with sick children.

The fathering programs that have been particularly successful include parenting classes, support groups, and networking opportunities. As a result of this training for fathers, employees initiated a program for voluntary child support deductions from payroll. They have also established a mentoring program for first-time fathers. They are paired with other male employees who have been through the parenting and lactation program training. To help expectant fathers stay in touch, the DWP provides beepers. The beepers were so successful that now they are provided to employees for other family issues such as sick children, elderly parents, and loved ones with AIDS.

The benefit of all this to the DWP? Where once they had $1 million in lost productivity because of childcare issues, the company found that they received a $5 return for every 50¢ they invested.[1] That's quite a good return by any standard.

At Motorola, parenting classes count toward the 40 hours a year employees are required to spend in training. Since 44 percent of Motorola employees have children under 18, the classes can be very valuable, particularly because the subject matter ranges from early childhood development to raising teenagers.

Chase Manhattan is also concerned about the fathers as well as mothers in the workplace. They have developed lunch hour sessions to help fathers develop good relationships with their children and wives. In addition, there is an eight-week transitioning period for parents coming back to work after the birth or adoption of a child. Because parenting can be an overwhelming task, Chase also provides parenting and childcare tips for new parents.[2]

On-Site Childcare

Finding good, reliable childcare is difficult for most parents. The time spent screening facilities, the added commute time, and the concern about getting to the children in case of an emergency adds another layer of stress on both mothers and fathers in the workplace. One solution to this complex problem is to have a childcare facility at the workplace. Parents and children "come to work" together, eliminating the extra commute time. Their proximity during the day is a comfort to both parents and children.

The Marriott Corporation is another organization that places a high level of importance on family issues. In response to a broad-scope survey of employees, a comprehensive program was developed to help their employees create balance in their lives. The cornerstone of the project is their Child Development Center, located near their corporate headquarters in Washington, D.C. This center can accommodate up to 60 children, including infants. The programs are developmentally designed so that children are learning, not just being "watched." Along with the Child Development Center, Marriott offers referral and resource centers to help parents locate affordable, dependable childcare, including weekend care.

Because of the diversity among the Marriott employees, affordability was a major consideration. Marriott has also set up a Family Care Spending Account that allows employees to have a specific amount deducted, pre-tax, from their paychecks to pay for childcare, eldercare, or care for disabled dependents. Seminars on eldercare and other work and family issues are held at corporate headquarters during lunch time so employees can attend without taking time away from their families.[3]

Employees at Ben & Jerry's can take their preschool age children to a childcare center that is a renovated farmhouse adjacent to the company's headquarters. The center is also available for other families in the community who have children of the same ages. Fees are based on a sliding scale. Ben & Jerry's employees pay 10 percent of their income and non-Ben & Jerry's families pay 12 percent. Childcare is such an important issue for employees, that Ben & Jerry's is willing to spend $90,000 per year to maintain the center.

Long known for their environmental concerns, Patagonia, a manufacturer of outdoor wear in Ventura, California, is also concerned about the welfare of its employees and their families. Eight weeks of paid leave for new parents, including adopting parents, followed by eight weeks of unpaid leave, gives employees ample time to get their families off to a good start. When it's time to come back to work, Patagonia has an on-site childcare facility that is subsidized to make it affordable. For parents not choosing on-site childcare, the company offers a referral service for quality daycare in other locations. Based on low turnover rates, the benefits to Patagonia are savings of $661,657. The cost of replacing a worker at Patagonia averages $50,000, so retaining good employees is a significant factor in corporate profitability.

Outsourced Childcare Facility Management

Even though most companies do not have the experience to operate a childcare facility, they can still provide this valuable benefit to their employees by contracting with an outside service provider. The company may own or lease the building used for chilcare (and/or eldercare), but the facility is managed and maintained by an organization that specializes in childcare. There are numerous examples of this approach being used successfully in a wide variety of environments.

Campbell Soup Company, in Camden, New Jersey, St. Vincent Hospital and Health Care Center, in Indianapolis, and Opryland Hotel in Nashville, have all found this kind of outsourcing to be the best method to provide childcare to employees. By using a professional childcare firm, employees' children receive the highest quality in childcare and the employers are not involved in managing a business which is outside their expertise. In addition, the childcare management companies are responsible for insurance and quality control.

Opryland Hotel's Child Development Center, an on-site childcare facility, is unique in several ways. The facility is open 7 days a week and accommodates three full shifts of employees of the round-the-clock convention hotel. The facility accommodates 350 children.

The company subsidizes rates on a sliding scale so that the most any employee pays is 80 percent of the normal rate for services provided by LaPetite, the vendor responsible for managing the Center. The extremely low turnover among the staff enables more consistent quality care for the children. The facility is open on many holidays, typically busy work days for employees in the hospitality industry. Many Opryland employees travel from other cities to work in Nashville. They enjoy peace of mind knowing that their children are right next door rather than miles away in the event of an illness or emergency.

Outsourced Family Services Programs

Sometimes, just knowing where to look for family services is half the battle. Locating childcare and eldercare facilities can be a time-consuming process that takes time away from work and causes a high level of stress and anxiety. Services like seminars and information on parenting issues or healthcare for elders are available, but developing a list of referrals can be complicated.

For employers that do not have the staff available to research and design family services programs, there are companies that specialize in providing full programs. One such company, Corporate Family Services, in Charlotte, North Carolina, provides resources and referrals for childcare and eldercare, on-site seminars, and collateral materials on family issues. To assist companies in providing financial support for dependent care, Corporate Family Services offers subsidy administration. CFS also does a complete needs assessment to help companies determine where they are and how to get where they want to go with family services. This particular firm is one of a number of such companies that can also help design and manage an on-site childcare facility.

In some cases it makes good financial sense to rely on professionals in specific areas rather than develop the programs internally from scratch. Prior to hiring an outside firm, perform a cost analysis that includes cost projections for creating the programs internally, the current costs of absenteeism, turnover and recruitment, and the cost of using an outside firm. This should give you a good picture of the alternatives, as well as a clear understanding of the costs if no family services are put in place.

Holiday and Vacation Childcare

When children have school holidays and vacations that are different from business holidays, parents can find themselves scrambling to get everything covered. If childcare arrangements can't be made, chances are one parent will need to call in sick. To help employees with this dilemma, consider allowing children to come to work with their parents and setting up activities to keep them busy during the day.

Not all companies can support full-service daycare for children. John Hancock Financial Services in Boston came up with a program they call "Kids-to-Go."[4] This special program covers school holidays and vacations that don't coincide with business holidays. On those days, parents can bring their children to work and enroll them in "Kids-to-Go."

The program starts right from the workplace. Children come with their parents and then are divided into age groups for field trips that are age-appropriate. While older kids might be skating, younger kids might be at a puppet theater. The children take advantage of local cultural opportunities and travel by public transportation or walking when possible.

John Hancock partnered with a nonprofit, Ellis Memorial Hospital, to design "Kids-to-Go." Parents pay $20 per day for the program, which covers all activities during that day. For parents with a family income under $30,000, there are drawings for a limited number of $10 per day scholarships.

If you would like to give childcare a test ride, this kind of program might be a good start. Without a large investment, you can try it out for one holiday. Keep in mind the insurance needs for this activity; talk with your insurance agent. There may also be organizations in your area like Ellis Memorial who would be willing to co-venture a project and share part of the insurance expense.

In-Home Childcare Providers

Sometimes congregate childcare programs are not appropriate. Employers can support their employees by maintaining a listing of caregivers who will work in employees' homes. This resource can serve as a viable substitute for, or supplement to, company-provided childcare. Access to well-trained, in-home caregivers is extremely valuable to parents and can be a viable, attractive alternative to taking children to a daycare facility.

Because of the 24-hour schedule for employees at America West Airlines, their program had to be a bit different. Responding to the particular needs of the airline industry, America West developed a system for home childcare. Rather than refer out to childcare centers or develop their own facilities, the company instituted a procedure to qualify childcare providers who could care for children in their own homes. This concept works equally well at the corporate headquarters as at the field stations. America West contracts with an outside agency to recruit and train the caregivers. The training is ongoing, providing the caregivers additional knowledge, and an opportunity to meet and network with each other.

Families are encouraged to get to know more than one caregiver, so that in case of an emergency, they will feel comfortable using a different person. This kind of stability is a benefit to both parents and children. To keep top-quality caregivers, America West provides incentives of free air travel. Parents also get a break, with 25 to 50 percent of childcare costs subsidized by the company, depending on family income. For employees at the lowest levels of compensation, a sliding payment scale is used.[5]

On-Site Elementary Schools

Companies can provide a benefit to employees by partnering with a local school district to provide classroom facilities for schoolchildren at the workplace. Many school districts could use more classrooms and parents want something different for their children. Operating on-site schools has a dual benefit—the school district gets the facilities it needs and parents get to be closer to their children during the day. Such schools can be established for one company or for a number of companies located nearby.

In Florida, the needs of Honeywell, Inc. and the local school district combined to create an on-site school. Honeywell built a facility to accommodate grades K through 2. The staffing and teaching materials are handled through the local elementary school and Honeywell manages the facilities. Now the parents of younger children can have them close by during the day. Before and after school care is also provided at a reasonable hourly rate. Employees have the opportunity to participate more in their children's education, spending time reading to classes or joining their children for lunch without disrupting their work responsibilities.

An added benefit is being close when a child gets sick at school. Sometimes a reassuring hug is all it takes, and both parent and child can go back to work. If it's more serious, Honeywell has two ill childcare programs and pays 80 percent of the cost. If this sounds too expensive for you, Honeywell's start-up costs for the school were $75,000 and its ill childcare program cost less than $20,000 the first year. Honeywell estimates that for every dollar spent on the program, they have saved $2.50.[6] That return looks good on the bottom line.

Internet Viewing of Childcare Facilities

Here's a new idea that can help employees feel more comfortable about their children's daycare. A company called ParentNet Inc. has designed a way for parents to see what's happening at daycare through the Internet. By logging on and using a password, parents can view whatever the camera at the center is recording. Knowing that everything is all right with their children, workers can go back to work with their minds at ease. For companies that have daycare on-site, this service could be an added benefit enabling employees to visit the care center without leaving their desks.[7]

Warning: Some people and organizations are concerned about privacy issues with this kind of viewing. Tread carefully.

Elder Care

As many companies have discovered in their surveys, employees are beginning to take on additional family responsibilities because of aging parents and relatives. In a recent study by the U.S. Department of Labor, the estimates were that 25 to 30 percent of the workforce is already caring for aging relatives. By the year 2000, there will be 9 million people over the age of 65 who will need assistance from others. The Conference Board predicts that 40 percent of employees will have eldercare responsibilities by the year 2000.

Many of the same problems exist with eldercare as childcare. Time must be spent finding appropriate community services, medical treatment, handling financial obligations, and daily physical care. Employees who have eldercare responsibilities report that they spend up to 15 hours per week handling these issues. That's why many companies are now including eldercare referrals along with childcare information. One company has hit on a unique way of handling both issues.

Intergenerational Care
(Elder and Childcare Combined)

If a childcare facility is in place, consider adding eldercare to the program. The elders and children will enjoy each other's company and employees will have an additional, stress-relieving benefit. The cost to the organization will be minimal, since the site and staff are already in place. Minor changes can be made, if necessary, to accommodate the older folks.

A number of family-centered companies provide both childcare and eldercare—in the same or adjacent facilities. There are some interesting advantages to this combination of services. The type of care given to the old and the young is often similar. The young people enjoy having the grandparent age folks around, and the older folks like to watch the younger ones. For the employees caught in the "sandwich" generation, the convenience factor is sincerely appreciated.

Stride Rite, a well-known shoe manufacturer and retailer headquartered in Cambridge, Massachusetts, has created an "intergenerational" center. In this busy place, dependent elders share space with children, enriching the lives of both groups. The current facility, which serves both Stride Rite employees and the community, can accommodate up to 24 elders. They must be over the age of 60 and be able to take care of their personal needs with minimal assistance. There are programs like armchair aerobics, discussion groups, and art classes especially for elders. They may participate with the children, but it is never required.

Stride Rite applies the same kind of sliding scale to elder-care as it does for childcare: full pay for most community children, a discounted rate for employees, a state-subsidized rate for low-income elders, or Stride Rite-subsidized rate for low-income families that don't qualify for state aid. For more than 20 years, Stride Rite has been concerned with family and quality of life issues. Decades ago, they were the first U.S. corporation to offer on-site daycare for employees and the community.[8]

Expanding Bereavement Policies

As more employees are caring for older family members, the issues of bereavement will become more significant. Currently most companies only offer three days of bereavement leave. Three days is not nearly adequate for someone who has been the long-term caregiver for an aging parent. Companies need to consider more liberal leave time for those employees to grieve. It is also important to help employees prepare both financially and legally prior to the death of a parent or relative. Providing employees with education on these matters will make the bereavement process easier.

Not only is it important to give employees the knowledge of what to do, but it is also important to provide sensitivity training to help managers deal with the grief of an employee. How an organization responds to a family crisis is as important as the programs it has in place. All employees are aware of how a grieving employee is treated. They will make an assessment of whether the corporate culture supports the process or if the programs are merely window dressing.

Life-Threatening Illness
(Viatical Settlements)

In the relationship with employees and their families, companies need to be prepared to address the issues of a life-threatening illness. For employees and their families who are in this situation, companies may want to consider what is called a "viatical settlement." The viatical settlement allows employees to sell their life insurance policies for cash, usually without paying any federal income tax. This sale gives employees the access to cash at a time when they need it most to care for their families.

There is a difference between viatical settlements and the "accelerated death benefits" (ADB) that most policies carry as a rider. A viatical settlement can provide up to 90 percent of the policy's face value, while an ADB generally only provides up to 50 percent. Another significant benefit is that employees can apply for a viatical settlement while they still have a life expectancy of up to five years. ADBs are often limited to employees who have a life expectancy of less than a year.

Talk with your insurance agent regarding these issues. It may affect only a small number of your employees, but the way the organization responds will affect every employee.

When an employee is facing a life-threatening illness, the company must go further than just providing insurance benefits. Fox, Inc., a motion picture company in Los Angeles, is supportive of terminally ill employees both financially and emotionally. This enlightened organization helps these employees financially through the living death benefits of their insurance program.

This program allows workers with less than a year to live to withdraw 50 percent of their life insurance benefits without affecting the balance. If being placed on disability is the best solution, the employees may continue with medical insurance at the same rate as active employees and may carry twice their annual salaries as life insurance for five years.

What makes Fox an enlightened company is that it is active in making benefits known to employees who might have a serious problem. When anyone leaves on long-term disability, the Human Resources Department contacts the employee to ensure that he is aware of all the benefits available. And at Fox, Lynn Franzoi, the Vice President for Benefits, stays in contact with employees who are terminally ill. She also helps families be sure that Social Security benefits and Medicare are put in place at the right time.[9]

Offering Domestic Partner Benefits

Being a family-friendly organization means more than just flextime and child/eldercare. It means responding to the needs of the employees as multifaceted individuals. Families can no longer be defined as Ozzie and Harriet and the boys. Families may be either same-sex or heterosexual couples living together, with or without child and eldercare needs. For these families, the ability to provide insurance for the domestic partner can be a critical issue. In the past, most companies have excluded these "families" from the kinds of healthcare coverage many employees receive.

Now more companies are following the lead of IBM, Disney, Hewlett Packard, Digital, the San Francisco 49ers, and Bank of America by offering dependent healthcare coverage to domestic partners. Lotus Development in Cambridge, Massachusetts, provides domestic partner benefits company-wide. For Lotus, it was a matter of treating everyone fairly and valuing diversity. Lotus is part of IBM, where domestic partner benefits were essential for the company to remain competitive in the marketplace.

Adoption Benefits

Companies are also becoming aware of the increasing costs of adoption and the hardship this process places on employees. While health insurance covers the cost of child-birth, most companies do not offer any program to defray the expense of adoption. A few companies are now offering the same benefits to adoptive parents as biological parents, such as paid leaves of absence and financial reimbursements. A big step in this area is a new federal tax law that gives a one-time credit for adoption of up to $5,000 or $6,000 for a child with special needs.

When Steve Steinour, an executive at Citizens Bank in Rhode Island, and his wife adopted a child, he became aware of just how expensive the process could be. As a result, he helped start a program at the bank called the Citizens' Adoptions Assistance Program. This program allots $5,000 per adopted child or $7,500 for a special needs child, with a maximum benefit of $15,000. Employees who adopt enjoy the usual unpaid leave and an additional six-week paid leave of absence. Assistance in adoption costs is especially important, since insurance policies do not ordinarily cover adoption.

A survey by the National Council for Adoption identified some 228 companies across the nation that provide some adoption benefits. Of those, only 160 offer any financial reimbursements. Wise companies are redefining "family" to include the adoption process. They provide support, in both time and money, comparable to that provided to biological parents.

In moving beyond the traditional definition of what con-stitutes a family, companies are acknowledging the value of each individual and are choosing to support the wide range of responsibilities that employees have beyond the work-place. Such support goes a long way toward building employee loyalty and increasing worker productivity.

Help for Trailing Spouses (Relocation Services)

There are challenges for dual career couples even if they don't have family care needs. When one partner gets a great job in another city, the other must give up a career to follow. While traditionally this surrender has been the woman's role, men now also find themselves in the role of the "trailing spouse." No matter who is following whom, companies need to provide more in relocation services than a moving van and a real estate agent.

Companies like General Mills, 3M, Honeywell, and Pillsbury hire relocation experts to help trailing spouses network to find new jobs. The commitment to making the move work for the new employees and their partners can build a strong bond with the company. It is a good way to let employees know how much they are valued.

Including Family in Social Functions

Your company can demonstrate its commitment to the importance of family by changing the kinds of social functions they sponsor. Instead of an annual holiday dinner, try a brunch that includes the children. Plan a summer picnic where employees can get to know each other and their families in a different way. This kind of outing can go a long way to improving teamwork and communication. At Ben & Jerry's, childcare is provided on site whenever a social event is planned. This subsidized childcare makes it easier for employees to attend, both in terms of scheduling and paying for a baby-sitter.

Providing car seats for new mothers or beepers for expectant fathers is very low cost. If you're looking for a no-cost idea, how about designating a parking space near the entrance for pregnant workers? How about putting up a bulletin board for children's artwork or family pictures? These little touches let your employees know that you understand and value their life beyond the workplace.

Little Things Mean a Lot:
Ideas for Smaller Companies

Not every company can provide comprehensive quality of life programs. The key issue for any company is to do *something*. Let your employees know that you understand the pressures they are under to meet the responsibilities of both work and home. You can do some small things that will mean a lot to your employees and be relatively inexpensive for your company.

Enlightened organizations recognize the significance of family-related issues in the workplace. Workers need support to balance the demands of career and family. As we have seen, companies can provide that support in a variety of ways—from complete on-site care facilities to changing how social functions are scheduled. Whatever a company does to acknowledge the significance of family in employees' lives will help in the balancing act.

Workers want to know that their commitment to their families is valued by the organization. Valuing the family, in all its configurations, demonstrates respect for the whole individual, a concept that is at the core of the meaningful relationship between the organization and its employees.

Ask your people what would be of value and significance to them. Some workers will be most concerned about their families; many will also be concerned about personal issues. Employees without family dependents will be more concerned about their individual relationship with the company. We'll address those aspects in Chapter 9.

KEY CONCEPTS

- The quality of life includes both work and family.
- Helping employees create a balance between work and family is critical.
- The relationship an organization has with its employees includes:
  - Child and eldercare issues.
  - Life-threatening illness and bereavement.
  - Spouses and domestic partners.
- By helping employees with family issues, companies reap rewards of lower absenteeism, increased loyalty, and employee satisfaction.
- Family-centered programs need not be costly to be effective.
- The definition of family is changing and enlightened companies provide benefits to meet the diverse needs of their employees.

ACTION PLAN

- Survey your employees to determine the needs of your workforce.
- Based on the responses, determine which programs will have the greatest impact.
- Perform analysis of program costs compared to current employee costs, such as absenteeism, turnover, lost productivity.
- Implement programs that match the scope and budget of your organization.
- Evaluate the results of the programs and make changes where necessary.

Endnotes

1. Solomon, Charlene Marmer, "Work Family Ideas That Break Boundaries," *Personnel Journal*, October 1992.
2. Smith, Vernita, "Helping Father Know Best," *Human Resource Executive*, August 1997.
3. Solomon, Charlene Marmer, "Marriott's Family Matters," *Personnel Journal*, October 1991.
4. Santora, Joyce E., "Kids-To-Go," *Personnel Journal*, March 1991.
5. Woodford, Karen, "Child Care Soars at America West," *Personnel Journal*, December 1990. (p. 114)
6. Laabs, Jennifer, "Students at Work," *Personnel Journal*, November 1991. (p. 115)
7. Smith, Vernita, "Kids in Cyberspace," *Human Resource Executive*, August 1997.
8. Laabs, Jennifer, "Family Issues Are a Priority at Stride Rite," *Personnel Journal*, July 1993. (p. 117)
9. Flynn, Gillian, "Fox Shows Employees It Has Heart," *Workforce*, February 1997.

9

Care of the Individual

Statistics indicate that 37 percent of the workforce are parents of school-age children. That also means that 63 percent are not. While some of these employees may have eldercare responsibilities, many do not. As a matter of fact, the Census Bureau reports that never-married adults are the fastest growing segment of the population and account for 25 percent of Americans over 18. The number of childless couples is also expected to increase by 50 percent between now and 2010.[1]

Organizations have put significant energy into developing programs and policies to assist parents in the workplace. And rightfully so. But all employees are feeling the pressure of downsizing, long workdays, and the need to find a balance between their work and personal lives. Forward-thinking companies are finding ways to increase the quality of life for all individuals who work with them, as well as those employees with families.

Wellness Programs

During the 1980s, a lot of companies initiated wellness programs for their employees. The concept included counseling, physical fitness, medical check-ups, classes on stress reduction, nutrition, and smoking cessation. Much of that service has now been shifted to Employee Assistance Programs (EAPs) provided by the company or by outside firms under contract to the employers.

Opryland Hotel's Employee Wellness Program is staffed with trained professional counselors who address the "whole person" concept. They provide such services as family counseling, marital counseling, financial counseling, drug and alcohol counseling, and career counseling. They also provide lunch time seminars on family issues such as parenting, new baby care, nutrition and exercise, relationships, and anger management.

If an employee needs a referral to a medical specialist, the Wellness counselors make the referral. If an employee needs to find adult daycare or a nursing home for an elderly parent, counselors connect the employee with the resources they need.

All the services are available for the employee and for all immediate family members of employees. All of this is provided at no cost to the employee as a benefit of working at Nashville's Opryland Hotel. The program is one of a wide range of advantages of employment provided under the leadership of Kathy Roadarmel, Director of Human Resources at the major hotel and convention center.

The Gift of Time

If you ask most working people what they need, they will respond "more time." In a survey reported in *Workplace*

Vitality Magazine in 1995, mothers who could have one more hour a day would spend it with their children (44 percent), in personal time (28 percent), sleeping (15 percent), or with their mates (10 percent).[2]

In a recent survey of human resource managers regarding compensatory time versus overtime pay, 83 percent of respondents said the people in their organization would like the opportunity to choose between the two. The managers felt that 50 percent of employees would choose equally between overtime pay and compensatory time and 37 percent believe that offering comp time would improve morale.[3] The results of the survey point out that time is at least as valuable, if not more valuable, to workers today than money. So what about giving all employees that precious gift of more time?

A Mental Health Day

People need time away from work. Employees working a Monday-through-Friday schedule may have weekends off, but that doesn't help if they need weekday time for certain business chores. Unfortunately, because of rigid corporate rules, people who need time off during normal working hours are often forced to lie—say they don't feel well or pretend they have a sick child.

Eddie Bauer gives employees a "Balance Day" to be used however the employees deem necessary. It can be used for any number of things, from running errands to pursuing hobbies.[4] It's sort of an official mental health day that's above and beyond sick and vacation time. This benefit can be particularly valuable to single employees who have to run all their errands themselves without anyone to share the load.

Laundry and Dry Cleaning Services

Another way you can give time is by finding ways to make the "work" of family easier, even if it's just a "family" of one. Look for those chores that can be time-consuming, yet might be conveniently provided in the work environment. How about arranging with a local dry cleaners to do pick up and delivery at your location? It would save your employees the time it costs on the weekends.

Wilton Connor Packaging Corporation in Charlotte, North Carolina, washes clothes for employees. The on-site service is provided by two people employed by the company using washing machines and dryers in a room off the plant's production floor. For a modest price per load, employees can bring their dirty laundry in at the start of their shift and take home clean folded clothes with them when they leave for the day.

The Opryland Hotel in Nashville, Tennessee, also provides laundry and dry cleaning services on premises for its employees. To determine a fair cost to charge for the convenient service, the company surveyed dry cleaners throughout the metropolitan area. They determined the average pricing, then discounted the prices by 40 percent for employees.

If you don't have laundry facilities on-site, consider making arrangements with a local dry cleaner to provide laundry and dry cleaning services for your employees at a discount . . . with convenient pick-up and delivery service. This service may involve a little clerical time at your facility, but the gain will outweigh the expense.

Home Repair Services

Those small home repair projects are not only a bother, but they can take up work time as employees make arrangements for the work to be done and then may need to stay home waiting for the repair person. Talk with local contractors to see who can provide a bonded person to do the work. You can keep a few names on file to help out when necessary.

Wilton Conner Packaging Corporation, previously mentioned in this chapter, has a company handyman on staff to fix all those little things that break or just need a little adjusting. In addition to his work in the company's facilities, he also performs minor repairs in employees' homes as an employee benefit. His home service work is all on company time and is really appreciated by employees who would have to wait at home—losing valuable time away from work—for repair people to show up. With this unusual benefit, employees can just give the handyman, a fellow worker, the keys to the house and the work gets done. No stress. No hassle. You can imagine how much Conner's employees appreciate this service!

Concierge Services for Anything and Everything

An emerging industry is making life easier for people—in their work setting and in their home environment. Concierge services are now operating in neighborhoods, office buildings, industrial parks, and even within single companies. These specialists in getting things done are able to save a considerable amount of time for employees who already have more to do than they can possibly find time for.

A company called Elite Concierges, based in Marina del Rey, California, provides a multitude of services from meeting planning to travel, shopping to home maintenance, tickets and reservations to errands. Their client list includes Johnson & Johnson, Cadillac Division of General Motors, Metropolitan Life, and Merrill Lynch. You can find Elite Concierges at www.leconcierge.com. This company provides many of its services regardless of where you are located. There are other smaller firms like this all around the country handling local and regional requests.

You might want to contract with a concierge firm for a specific service for all employees or have them on call for any situation where an employee might need help. You could also make the use of the service as an incentive for achieving a corporate goal. For instance, if the goal is reached, the individual, team, or organization can use the concierge service for a week. Or the employee of the month could have concierge service for a day.

One caveat—remember that cost can be a factor for employees. So to be sure everyone can take advantage of this great benefit, either subsidize the cost or make it complimentary. You can place a limit on the dollar amount of services used to make it cost-effective for your company. A good way to calculate the benefit is to determine the cost in lost productivity when employees spend company time taking care of family demands or are completely exhausted from doing it all.

If you work with individual vendors, arrange a discount with the vendor for putting him on your list or subsidize the cost for employees. The same kind of arrangements might be made with a housecleaning service. What a wonderful weekend it could be if there weren't so many chores. By providing referrals for services and negotiating a better price, you will give your employees more time. The free time you give them will relieve the stress and give them time to regenerate over the weekend.

Videotape Loan

"It's the usual thing, done in the unusual way, that captures the attention of the world."

Look for unusual benefit ideas; they definitely grab attention!

Brayton International, a division of Steelcase, Inc., offers a variety of benefits to encourage quality workers to join the company's workforce in High Point, North Carolina. During the interview process, applicants hear about gain sharing awards that are tied to individual productivity (average $2,300 per employee in 1997), the employee-funded retirement program, and the fitness center. Those benefits are relatively common.

To do something different, the company instituted a video loan program for its employees. More than 500 titles are available for loan through the human resources department, saving employees time and money. Workers borrowing the tapes build stronger relationships with human resource professionals, increasing their comfort in asking questions about benefits and talking about their problems.

Mini-Massages

And talking about stress relief, how about having someone come to the office to give mini-massages? Not expensive, but a wonderful way to show your concern for employees. It is a delightful interruption, noninvasive, and refreshing. Having a mini-massage in the office relieves tension, from both the act itself and the idea that it's even happening. Make the experience voluntary, since some people are uncomfortable with being touched by strangers.

If you want to take this a step further, arrange for quantity discounts with a massage therapist at a nearby health club. Employees can take advantage of the benefit on their own time and at their own expense to enjoy full-body massages. There are multiple benefits here: the employee treats himself to something special, the experience is relaxing and stress-reducing, and it's a personal health break from routine.

1-800-FLOWERS brings in massage therapists to relax their heavily worked employees around busy times—like around Mother's Day and Valentine's Day. Other companies arrange for shoulder massages for workers on a regular basis.

Convenience Services

Organizations that have large employee populations can offer a wide range of services to their workers. Outside contractors can be invited to operate their outlets on company property, subject to certain rules like hours of availability, competitive pricing, and range of services. The philosophy is to make common products and services conveniently available to employees, saving them the time of running errands all over town to manage certain aspects of their lives.

Oracle is a fine example of how convenience services can be provided. Over 10,000 people work at the company's headquarters campus in Redwood Shores, California. Taking advantage of the relatively large employee population, the company offers a wide range of services that enhance the quality of workers' lives.

An on-site florist provides a wide selection . . . a great benefit for workers who, at the last minute, remember birthdays, anniversaries, or special occasions. Film can be dropped off for developing; there are drop locations in all the buildings. Employees can drop off clothes for dry cleaning or shoes for repair at central kiosks; delivery is made to employees' workstations. ATM banking machines are readily available throughout the complex.

Half a dozen high-quality restaurants cater to diverse tastes. There's always something open to serve people who work at all different hours. And delivery to work locations is available. Take your choice of restaurants: sushi/Asian, southwestern cuisine, California style, a New York deli, or the main restaurant that serves just about everything. Food prices are very competitive with local restaurants.

The restaurants provide a "dinner for two" service. Call by 2:00 p.m. and your dinner will be ready for pick-up between 5:00 and 6:00. Salad, rolls, entrée, vegetables, and dessert cost about $15 for two.

There's a health club on the Oracle campus for physical conditioning. Cultural growth opportunities include special events such as book sales, speakers, and special observances like Black History Month. Just before Christmas 1997, employees were treated to a performance by the San Francisco Opera.

Most people drive to work at Oracle. A contracted automotive service company provides repair and auto detailing, with free pick-up and delivery.

There is an active, well-coordinated volunteer movement at Oracle. Community service opportunities are promoted to employees by e-mail. Staff members organize volunteers and make arrangements. One major effort is Project Read, where employee volunteers help people learn how to read.

Each office suite has a kitchen equipped with free soft drinks, juices, waters, soups, and over a dozen kinds of tea—all company-provided. And the facilities maintenance workers clean the refrigerator!

All these conveniences enable workers to concentrate on their jobs without time-consuming distractions caused by the errands of life. In addition, Oracle supports an extensive flextime program giving people the freedom to work whenever they wish around the clock.

All of these services are offered at the corporate headquarters; the range of services available at the company's other facilities is based on the size of the employee population. Companies that have smaller populations can collaborate with nearby employers, perhaps in an industrial park, to achieve the same results.

Organizing the Daily Workflow

You can also give employees more time by rethinking how tasks get done in the workplace. By finding out how the work is getting done, you may find some ways to make things run smoother. Challenge things that have been done for years "because we've always done it that way." We've discovered situations in our client organizations where reports were prepared each week, then filed without anyone ever looking at them. The work was important in the past, but now the information was available instantaneously on computers at managers' desks. No one needed the report anymore, so the work could be eliminated.

At Xerox, the engineers struggled to meet deadlines, coming in very early or staying very late to find the quiet time they needed to do their work. When they began to track how they used time, they discovered that a significant amount of time was spent meeting with each other. The result was they felt unable to complete their tasks in a reasonable amount of time.

The solution was to change the way they worked together. When certain times were set aside as uninterrupted time, they were able to accomplish their goal and meet their deadlines because they changed the way work was done.[5] They had effectively given themselves more time. The positive feelings of productivity and success had an impact on family members as well. If work itself is well managed and productive, the quality of personal time is improved.

Personal Time Management

Chris Reiter, founder of Time Finders, is one of a number of professional organizers who works with companies and individuals to help them get organized. By addressing everything from controlling the mountains of paper that cross people's desks to changing how people think about time, organizers help people gain more control over their lives. On a personal level, trying to manage everything sometimes overwhelms people. As a result, they put off the filing, miss payments, and can't find the documents they need for taxes or any number of things. This problem becomes so overwhelming, that over time the project of getting back on track becomes impossible without help.

Reiter steps in to provide a helping hand and teaches people new behaviors for handling personal business. What she has found over the years is that people who have used her services will call up a year later and say that things are "really in a mess." When she arrives, there is very little mess compared to what it was in the beginning. People have learned new behaviors and are now ready to take another growth step in managing their time.

In an organization, the same is true. For all the time spent in meaningless meetings or searching for lost files, Reiter has solutions. The changes in organizational behavior will be a good foundation for other work/life issues. By bringing in an expert like Reiter to help employees learn how to deal with time, work, and family priorities, you will help employees reduce stress levels and increase productivity. Seminars and personal training on time issues can be extremely valuable for your employees in their quality of life both at work and at home.

Pets Come to Work

Depending on your corporate culture, you may want to consider bringing pets into the work environment. Some companies allow pets—dogs mostly, because cats tend to roam too much—to come to work. There is, however, a three-accidents-and-you're-out rule that applies to pets at most companies. Nursing homes and other eldercare facilities have known for years the advantage of having well-behaved pets around.

At Autodesk, a high-tech company in the Silicon Valley, pets are a part of the work environment. Some employees actually take or keep their jobs there because of the pet policy. Other companies pay up to $100 annually for vet bills and others pay for kennels when employees are called out of town unexpectedly.

Although these benefits may sound a little too far out for you, consider how important the family pet may be. There is a distinctly familial atmosphere when pets are present. In environments where there is no health threat or significant customer contact, pets may add a valuable dimension to work life. Note that single employees may be particularly interested in bringing pets to work, since there may be no one else at home with the animal(s) during the work time.

Good Health Is Good Business

And what about showing your employees that you care about their good health? By taking care of their own health, employees will improve their work performance and the overall quality of their lives.

A study done of employees in various industries in southern California indicated that there were a number of health behaviors that could impact attendance, vitality, anxiety, self-control, and a sense of well-being. Those practices are: getting adequate sleep, seven or eight hours daily; eating breakfast and rarely eating between meals; being near average weight, based on height; regular physical activity; refraining from smoking; and moderate to no use of alcohol. Encouraging these healthy habits and making it easy to exercise can not only make employees more energetic and productive, but lower healthcare and absenteeism costs for organizations.

The employer's cost to put together a fitness or wellness program is quite small by comparison to the costs of health insurance. While a company might spend between $2,500 and $3,500 per year per employee for health care, a fitness program would cost only about 3 to 5 percent of the insurance costs. Factoring in lower absenteeism and higher productivity, the organization will surely come out ahead. Not to mention the positive response employees will have to the extra benefit.

Incentives for Healthy Habits

You might want to consider a program similar to the one developed by Alamco, a gas and oil company in West Virginia. The company decided to self-insure, seeking to manage healthcare costs and better serve employees and their families. They knew that healthy employees would keep the policy costs down, so they designed a program to support good health habits. The company gave cash incentives for not smoking or chewing tobacco, wearing seat belts, a cholesterol count below 150, good blood pressure, waist/hip ratios, and exercising 30 minutes three times a week. Spouses could even earn incentives at a 50 percent rate for the same behaviors.

The company brought in speakers, sponsored a health fair, and gave an extra half-hour for lunch for employees who used it to exercise. Yes, they paid out $19,000 in rebates—but their insurance premiums remained stable, morale went up, and absenteeism went down.[6] By allowing time at lunch for exercise, the company was not only promoting good health, but also was giving employees additional time. Time to exercise is something many workers simply don't have.

In-House Fitness Programs

At Corning, Inc. in Ithaca, New York, employees workplace fitness costs are entirely paid for if the employees use the in-house facility 80 percent of the eight-week sessions, which meet three days a week. The cost to Corning—only $60 per employee.

Establishing a fitness center need not be expensive, as demonstrated by One Valley Bank in Clarksburg, West Virginia. The bank's fitness program was started with a budget of just $700 and fitness equipment purchased at yard sales. The bank knew that healthier employees would be more productive employees. And they also wanted to set themselves apart as a preferred employer. The results were good. A 1994 survey indicated a 93 percent decrease in turnover, a 24 percent increase in productivity, and a 148 percent increase in employee morale. The program for the 120 employees at One Valley Bank includes the mini gym, walking challenges, weight loss programs, and health fairs.[7]

Sara Lee Knit Products, the manufacturer for Hanes in Winston-Salem, North Carolina, offers a program called Health Fit which includes a 24-hour fitness center, health screenings, classes for smoking cessation, weight loss, and massage therapy. The program is available for the company's 12,000 employees and their spouses.

The Englewood, Colorado facilities of Oppenheimer Funds Services is an example of companies providing space, equipment, and time for employees to stay fit. On the lower level of the building is a well-equipped workout facility that workers may use whenever they wish. It's just down the hall from the postal vending machine and the credit union's ATM.

Coca-Cola also has a full-scale fitness center in its Atlanta headquarters, as do many other organizations throughout the country. Some companies even employ personal trainers and exercise specialists.

Exercising together is a preferred social outlet for many single employees. Your facilities may provide an opportunity for people to meet each other and establish relationships that will help build productivity.

Education on Health Issues

Coca-Cola supplements its wellness program with seminars on smoking cessation and weight loss. Employees earn points for healthy behaviors such as increased physical activity at home or visits to the fitness center. The points can be redeemed for everything from tee shirts to vacations and cruises.

A number of companies produce health fairs for their employees and their families. A wide variety of healthcare providers from the community set up tables or booths to explain their services, perform health screenings, and answer questions. These events usually last a day or so. Compaq Computers and Lillian Vernon are examples of companies that provide this service. Lillian Vernon employees also benefit from a nutritionist who visits the company monthly.

Health Assessments and Fitness Services

As part of their wellness programs—and sometimes as a requirement of their health insurance programs, many employers furnish annual physical examinations. Some cover all costs; others contribute a set amount, like $100, toward the expense.

Giving employees the option to choose what healthy activities they will participate in has been successful for Healthtrax. Their HealthAssist plan gives the employees the opportunity to have a full health risk assessment, followed by a one-on-one session with a health professional to chart the best course for improvement. All employees who are eligible for benefits can receive up to $240 per family to apply to health and fitness services. Approximately 85 percent of their employees take advantage of this benefit.

Partnering with Health Care Agencies to Provide Health Services

If you are wondering where to start when it comes to fitness, you may want to take advantage of turnkey programs. There are a number of fine programs available in communities around the country. The American Red Cross has a kit that focuses on lowering the risk of strokes and heart disease. The American Cancer Society will send trainers to conduct smoking cessation classes. Ask around and you'll discover other programs available that can give you ideas and even contain materials to use in seminar presentations.

You can take the ideas as far as you like, from simply providing information for self-help to forming groups to accomplish certain health goals. For companies that want to keep it simple, they can provide flu shots, cancer and blood-pressure screenings, classes on losing weight and quitting smoking, or annual physical exams to their employees at no cost. There are a number of nonprofit agencies like the American Red Cross that can help you provide these services. Check with your insurance company, local hospitals, or government agencies to find out what is available in your community.

Survey Employees to Determine Their Needs

Whatever you're planning to do, take the time in the beginning to survey your employees to learn what is important to them. One thing that all the companies we mentioned have in common is that they did a comprehensive assessment of their employees to determine what their needs were prior to implementing any program.

Every workplace is different and the needs of employees can differ dramatically from one year to the next. Thus, it is critical for organizations to be sure they continue to meet the needs of their employees. This monitoring is particularly important if you experience employee turnover: new employees may have different needs and preferences than those who departed.

Involve Employees in Developing the Services

Along with employee surveys, some organizations have created employee task forces to identify and design programs to meet employee needs. At Weyerhaeuser, a task force was constituted that included a wide cross-section of employees. In this way, Weyerhaeuser was able to enjoy the greatest input about what employees really needed and leverage the impact on senior management.

The action plan recommended by this task force was the implementation of a referral and resource program. Initially the group thought this program could be handled by employees, but soon discovered that it was too time-consuming and not as effective as they had hoped. In order to meet the needs of employees, they contracted with an outside firm that already had the resource database in place. The task force has remained in place to monitor the effectiveness of the program and to be sure that Weyerhaeuser is keeping up with the changing needs of the employees.[8]

Involvement of employees in program development is an important step in being sure that the participation levels are high. While surveys can provide much valuable information, the interaction of a broad range of employees who serve on task forces can bring new problems and solutions to light. And people like being involved.

People also appreciate flexibility in their lives. We'll talk about that in our next chapter.

KEY CONCEPTS

▶ All employees, regardless of marital or family status, whether they are married, single, with or without children, can benefit from opportunities and services to help them manage the chores of living.

▶ Making it easier for employees to handle the tasks of daily living is not costly and can reduce absenteeism and turnover, while increasing productivity and loyalty.

▶ Time management, both in the workplace and at home, helps employees accomplish tasks better and reduces stress due to lack of priorities.

▶ Good health is valuable to everyone. Providing opportunities and incentives to employees for healthy habits benefits the employees and the company.

▶ The needs of employees are different in every workplace, so it is important to involve everyone in determining the kinds of special benefits to offer.

ACTION PLAN

- Use surveys and task forces to identify the benefits and programs that are of greatest interest and value to your people.
- Do a cost analysis that includes the cost of implementing the benefits versus the time currently lost to absenteeism and lowered productivity.
- Review work processes to find ways to eliminate redundancy, to make interactions between employees more productive, and to maximize the technology that is available.
- Involve employees in the process of implementing and managing the special benefits that are put in place.
- Because employee needs are constantly changing, to be sure you are meeting current needs, evaluate what you offer on an ongoing basis.
- Think creatively about what special benefits you can offer and how they can be implemented, with an eye to cost-effectiveness and employee satisfaction.

Endnotes

1. *Workplace Visions*, November/December 1997.
2. "At A Glance," *Workplace Vitality*, November/December 1995.
3. H R Pulse, *HRMagazine*, December 1997.
4. Fraught, Leslie, "At Eddie Bauer You Can Work and Have a Life," *Workforce*, April 1997.
5. Shellenbarger, Sue, "Work and Family," *Wall Street Journal*, May 15, 1996.
6. Fenn, Donna, "Healthful Habits Payoff," *Inc.* Magazine, April 1996.
7. Cooper, Colleen, "Healthy, Wealthy & Wise," *Incentive* Magazine, December 1996. (p. 138—end first paragraph)
8. Haupt, Jennifer, "Employee Action Prompts Management to Respond to Work-and-Family Needs," *Personnel Journal*, February 1993.

10

The Flexible
Workplace

Flexibility in both hours and attitude is one of the most important factors in helping employees balance work and family. Until employees can take more control of their time, the imbalance will continue. As early as 1988, Dupont discovered that half of the women and one-quarter of the men had considered leaving their current jobs for positions with more flexibility.[1]

Unfortunately, for most workers the issue of work flexibility is still far from a reality. The current state of affairs for most shift and plant workers was made clear in a survey by Work/Family Directions. The results show that these workers have very little flexibility in their environment. While 51 percent of women and 45 percent of men felt that senior management was supportive, when it comes to supervisors the numbers drop to 30 percent for women and 26 percent for men. The lowest category of all was co-workers, where only 23 percent of women and 13 percent of men felt that their co-workers were supportive.[2]

These results reflect how much corporate culture must change in order to provide an environment where employees can meet both family and work responsibilities.

After so many years of using the clock as a measure of employees' reliability, commitment, and productivity, corporations must now take a more flexible approach. Doing so will challenge many assumptions organizations and people have about work, but the result will be a much more productive workplace.

Not only will hours need to be flexible, but managers and supervisors will need to take a much different view of how they evaluate employees' performance. As part of the evolution of corporate culture, employees will be evaluated based on their results, not the number of hours they spent on the task. Moving from a behavioral- to an achievement-based evaluation process gives employees responsibility for attaining measurable results. That focus, in turn, gives meaning to the work itself. Flexible scheduling allows employees to take more control of their time and how tasks are accomplished.

How *you* approach flexible scheduling will be unique to your organization, but here are some ideas that have worked in other organizations:

Flexible Arrival and Departure Times

Flexible schedules and work arrangements can mean a number of things. For some companies, it means that some workers arrive earlier than regular business hours while others leave later. Two working parents can cover responsibilities by being on slightly different schedules. While flextime might seem easy enough to institute for workers who ordinarily exercise judgment in how and when they will accomplish tasks, what about production workers?

In 1991, Levi Strauss conducted a pilot test of their sewing machine operators. These workers could come in up to 4 hours later than usual or leave 4 hours earlier, as long as the production was complete. They had core hours between 10 a.m. and 2 p.m., but were flexible on either side of that block of time.[3]

Lean and meaningfulness is not limited to the private sector. People who work in the office of the state attorney general in Bismarck, North Dakota, don't have to worry about juggling work and family. This most unusual state office understands the importance of parents to driving carpools and having lunch with their kids. There is no stigma attached to signing out for reasons like "carpool." Men, who are eligible for the same family time as women, actually take it. Attorneys are "on their own" to make up the time to get the work done. Employees in this environment are respected as whole persons.[4] This kind of flexibility gives employees the opportunity to handle *any* family issues that come up without the pressure of a rigid work schedule.

Working a Compressed Schedule

A flexible schedule can also be accomplished through a compressed workweek, such as, working ten hours a day for four days. There are several variations to this approach, including scheduling workdays and days off so employees can actually enjoy four-day weekends. Some companies that operate seven days a week offer rotating schedules of three days on and four days off followed by four days on and three days off. There is some room for creativity here.

The Financial Services Center for Hewlett-Packard went to a compressed workweek several years ago at the request of the employees. Workers presented the program to management stressing two advantages: (1) longer hours would allow them to service customers from other time zones more efficiently; and (2) a weekday off would reduce stress and improve morale. The result of implementing the program was a huge increase in productivity. Instead of processing 37 transactions, which was typical for an eight-hour day, the employees with compressed schedules processed an average of 63 transactions per day. An added benefit to Hewlett-Packard was that overtime hours were decreased from 7 percent to 2.7 percent, saving millions of dollars annually.[5] Now nearly 1,450 employees are on a compressed workweek. Hewlett-Packard has made flexible scheduling a key element in its culture, with 3,000 people working in virtual offices and 500 people job sharing.

Working 12-Hour Shifts

For companies that operate on a 24-hour schedule, a compressed work schedule may provide a number of benefits. Giving workers the opportunity to work 12-hour shifts for fewer days gives them more time at home and relieves stress. This value is particularly true for those workers on rotating shifts. Companies that are already on compressed weeks report better morale, decreased absenteeism, greater flexibility in meeting customer service needs, and better utilization of equipment. Some employers use wage incentives for less desirable shifts.

At Advanced Micro Devices in Sunnyvale, California, some married couples take different 12-hour shifts to reduce or eliminate childcare costs. Employees benefit in other ways, too. Having larger blocks of time away from work gives them an opportunity to spend more time with family members, handle personal business, and enjoy leisure time activities.

The James River Paper Company, a paper manufacturing and converting facility in Ashland, Wisconsin, developed a 12-hour, four days on, four days off rotating schedule for their manufacturing plant. To evaluate the benefits of the new scheduling, they had a second group work a rotating 8-

hour shift schedule. What they found was that employees on the 12-hour schedule were more satisfied with both work and leisure time, had less symptoms of stress, and felt that the alternative schedule was good for their personal lives. By continuing the study over 24 months, James River determined that the benefits of the compressed schedule continued over time, with workers reporting the same benefits even after 24 months on the program.

Condensed scheduling is not for every company or every job. The Duluth, Minnesota Police Department has patrol officers who respond to 911 calls on a compressed schedule. Investigators, who need long-term continuity and follow-up on their caseload, work more traditional shifts. The mental rest that patrol officers get during their four days off is one of the organization's most valuable benefits.[6]

Flexible Scheduling

Flexible scheduling is the cornerstone of the employee retention program at Crown Honda in Greensboro, North Carolina. When the Director of Parts & Service for the dealership instituted a flexible schedule, he enjoyed remarkable results.

The service department is on a 6-day/week schedule from 7:00 a.m. to 6:00 p.m.; however, not every technician works every day. With this sophisticated scheduling, the technicians work the same number of hours per week, but fewer days—and they receive an extra 24 paid days off per year. Every six weeks, Crown Honda's service technicians enjoy a mini vacation—four days off in a row! The 11-hour days allow them to complete more jobs.

But that's not the best part. The most exciting aspect to this nontraditional scheduling is what's in it for the dealership. The dealership benefits in many ways: First, they no longer have to give time off to schedule routine doctor or dentist visits. Those appointments are now scheduled on the employee's days off. Second, if an employee wants to attend a child's ball game or some other special event, he must arrange for an associate to cover for him. The employees handle the coverage themselves!

Turnover has virtually dropped to zero and technicians come in on their days off to work when they're needed. And they're needed often because the service department is so successful, so their incomes are up as well. Customers love the fact that the service department is open six days per week, from 7:00 a.m. to 6:00 p.m. Customer satisfaction has mirrored the rise in employee satisfaction, so Crown Honda's service business has continued to grow.

At first, the employees *and* management were skeptical, but now with so many days off and reduced turnover, respectively, everybody is happy—except jealous employees at the dealership on traditional schedules.[7]

If your business has shiftworkers and you are considering compressed scheduling, be sure to get buy-in from employees and unions before implementing a new design. As with any new program, involve as many people as possible in the decision-making process and provide open and honest communication. Creating a task force that includes employees and managers to develop the program will help overcome resistance to change.

With a flexible schedule, employees can integrate their family schedules with the work schedule, lowering tardiness and stress. While your employees are at work, they can concentrate on their tasks because they know that the family responsibilities are covered. Having the option of flextime also lets employees enjoy more control over their lives, a key factor in job satisfaction.

Flexible Leave Policies

Employers in all fields are becoming more flexible with leave time. Most companies stipulate a certain number of sick days, another number of vacation days, another number of funeral leave days, and have all sorts of complicated polices about time off. This complexity is confusing and often forces employees to lie about being sick to get a day off to care for an ill child or run some errands.

The Great American Cookie Company, Atlanta, Georgia, established a "personal hours" program that simplifies the whole issue of time off. Employees at the corporate offices earn 0.065 hours of personal time for every hour worked. At this rate, full-time workers (2,080 hours per year) earn 136 hours off—17 days a year. They accumulate time every paycheck, so they don't have to wait for a year to be eligible for paid vacation time. The personal time can be used in any amount, at any time, for any purpose.

Job Sharing—Two for the Price of One

Job sharing is another expression of flexible scheduling. In this approach, two people share the same responsibilities, with neither working a full schedule. This arrangement can be particularly attractive to parents with younger children.

Stride Rite Corporation has been an industry leader in employee benefits, but had not explored job sharing. When the assistant to the President of the Sperry Top-Sider™ division and the executive assistant to the Vice President of Human Resources both became pregnant, they knew that neither wanted to return to work full-time. Robert Lambert, the Vice President of Human Resources, decided he would give them the opportunity to job share. The three of them worked out the details of scheduling and terms, and he charged the women with responsibility for the success of the process.

The new partners were highly motivated to make the job sharing work, so they made sure to maintain good communication to prevent anything from falling through the cracks. One of the reasons they were successful is that they complemented each other's strengths and weaknesses. They both agree that a key element in job sharing is trust, which only develops over time.[8]

Part-Time Schedules

Part-time schedules are becoming more common, especially among managers and professionals. While the reasons for wanting part-time work are varied, the top three are: to care for children, to pursue professional interests, and to attend to personal interests. In a Conference Board study by the 1996 Work-Family Research and Advisory Panel, 94 percent of the companies reported that most of their part-time employees were women. Men, however, are starting to take advantage of part-time options. According to a part-time placement firm in Maryland, 60 percent of the part-time placements they make are now men, up from 25 percent in 1993.

Being flexible to these kinds of requests from valued workers can allow companies to keep them longer, even if only on a part-time basis. When their circumstances change, they may want to return to full-time work or continue part-time employment. As people seek variety and more control over their careers, they may choose to work several jobs simultaneously on a part-time basis.

Changing Employee Benefits to Support Alternative Work Schedules

When employees can choose a flexible schedule without losing benefits, the programs will be most effective. Companies that continue to extend benefits, even to those on reduced schedules, will be able to lower their employee turnover rates. A valuable consequence will be the customer loyalty that results from the relationships built through long-term workforce stability.

Flexible scheduling is at the core of the work/family programs at First Tennessee Bank in Memphis, Tennessee. In 1992, the bank started developing programs to help families balance their responsibilities as a business imperative. Customer complaints about employee turnover were the catalyst that got First Tennessee to reexamine its policies and procedures that were driving employees away.

The bank found that the rigid policies about vacations, sick days, and other personnel issues were making it difficult, if not impossible, for employees to take care of family needs. First Tennessee realized that flexibility needed to be built into the bank's culture. They started the process by asking employees what kind of schedule would work best for them and the programs grew from there. Over time, the flexible programs included condensed workweeks, job sharing, and telecommuting.

One of the most significant programs at First Tennessee is called "Prime Time." This program allows employees to decrease their working hours to as little as 20 hours per week and still maintain their benefits. Employees use this option to help manage childcare and elder care or to attend to other pressing personal needs. One employee changed her 8 a.m. to 5 p.m. schedule to 9 a.m. to 4 p.m., saving herself an hour of traffic and making it much easier to meet her childcare responsibilities.

Without the "Prime Time" program, First Tennessee would have lost about 85 percent of those employees who are now participating in this alternative scheduling option. As many as 70 percent of First Tennessee's employees use some kind of flextime. In a 1996 survey of the bank's employees, 94 percent said that the work/life programs met or exceeded their expectations.[9]

But the process wasn't just about programs; it was about a complete cultural change. CEO Ralph Horn said in an interview in 1996, "We flip-flopped our entire corporate philosophy. The philosophy now is that profit begins with satisfied employees."[10] After four long years of intensive training on empowerment, family values, and continuous improvement, this winner of the 1997 Optimas Award (awarded by *Workforce* Magazine) substantially increased its customer retention rate. The improvements translated into a 55 percent profit gain in two years, with a 50 percent increase in customer satisfaction.[11] Not only is flextime a good move to bond employees to the company; its benefits are also reflected on the bottom line.

Telecommuting

With all the advancements in technology, telecommuting has become a viable option for many employees. The estimates on the number of telecommuters range from 4.3 million to 9 million. The American Telecommuting Association believes that telecommuting could work for as many as one-half of American workers.[12] Telecommuting can provide employees with an opportunity to take more control in their lives, to balance work and family issues, and to be more efficient in their use of time.

In an industry where change occurs by the nanosecond, high tech companies can use family-friendly programs like telecommuting as a strong recruiting tool. Hewlett-Packard estimates that it costs between $7,000 and $10,000 to recruit an employee. In such a competitive, knowledge-intensive industry, the expense and loss of time caused by employee turnover can be critical. In response, Hewlett-Packard offers flexible hours and job sharing.

Kinetix, a division of Autodesk, is using telecommuting as a key recruitment tool. Their employees who have long commutes only come into the office one day a week.[13] Since Kinetix has offered that option, their recruiting costs have dropped significantly.

Companies are beginning to experiment with telecommuting for other kinds of workers. One such employee, an art director of *Incentive* magazine, wanted to spend more time with her young daughter. The magazine decided to try it out. They discovered that the employee was able to get more done at home and her time in the office was more productive. The bad news was that they missed having her around.[14]

Aetna Insurance Company based in Hartford, Connecticut, the nation's largest publicly owned insurance and financial services company, reports that 5 percent of their 30,000 employees telecommute. Among those 1,500 telecommuters are senior claims processors. When they worked at the office, these senior claims processors could process 250 claims per day. Now, working from home, they process 400 claims per day. That's productivity!

Keeping Telecommuters Connected

As more employees use alternative schedules and work at home, they have less opportunity to interact with co-workers. While there are many benefits to telecommuting, it is important to remember that most people still need personal interaction with their co-workers to feel connected to the organization and to each other.

Xerox now has 3,000 telecommuters. To help them maintain social contact, they arrange for people in each of their cities to get together three or four times a year for an informal event. Meetings have taken on a new meaning as well. With only a limited number of hours to meet with managers and other staff members, employees are well prepared for meetings and they actually look forward to them. For companies that need creative brainstorming, electronic media doesn't work as well as face-to-face interaction. And teams also need to interact in person to be most effective.

Setting Up a Telecommuting Program

Prior to implementing a telecommuting program, the company and the employee need to determine the specifics of how the arrangement will work. First, working at home does not mean that childcare is not necessary. Telecommuting makes those arrangements more flexible and allows parents to spend more time with their children. Second, companies must provide employees with all the equipment they need to work at home. One consultant recommends that every detail of the home office working environment be discussed in advance. This conversation can include how the office will be set up, childcare arrangements, and how the worker will submit work and receive assignments from the company.

There is even a new line of mid-priced furniture specifically designed for telecommuting employees. Named "Altra," this Italian import provides an important piece in the telecommuting puzzle for organizations that are serious about making telecommuting work. Other furniture manufacturers also produce office furniture that fits nicely in the home environment. Some pieces even close up when work is done and appear from the outside to be customary home furnishings.

With such a dramatic change in how and where work is done managers and supervisors will need training in new ways to relate with telecommuters and evaluate their performance. How well the relationship between telecommuting employees and their supervisors is managed will determine the success of the program. Communication is a key element with this arrangement. Employees need to have a clear understanding of their job responsibilities, goals, and deadlines. Managers must learn to evaluate the work based on the results, not "face time." Some managers hold the assumption that workers who are not in the facility must certainly not be working.

Companies already using telecommuting strategies know that employees who work at home are actually more productive. Chris Reiter, owner of TimeFinders, a time management firm, points out that in an eight-hour day, only 3.2 hours are really spent working. The rest of the time is spent in meetings, talking with co-workers, maybe playing computer solitaire. Just because an employee is visible, it does not mean he is working. Employees who telecommute are responsible for how they use their time. Telecommuters can make the decision to attend a soccer match with their children, then work from 8 to 11 p.m. to complete their work. Employees who are in an office have hours set for them and may or may not use them as effectively as telecommuters do.

Hoteling

A variation on the telecommuting concept—people not spending all their time in the congregate workspace—is a design called "hoteling." Under this arrangement, workers move from office to office, from home to office, or from customer site to office. When at the office, they're "visitors." They don't have specific assigned spaces—"their" offices. Instead, they learn where there are open workspaces, much like finding parking spaces in a multilevel parking deck.

The person in charge of space assignment connects the visitors with the facility's communication system, so when calls come for them, the calls will be routed to the right desks. Visitors can connect their computers and perform their work as if they were housed in a permanent office.

Arthur Andersen and IBM both have extensive hoteling programs, increasing the flexibility and efficiency of their employees. Employers are finding that hoteling enables them to make much better use of space, controlling real estate costs.

Virtual Officing

Some companies have moved beyond telecommuting to virtual officing. In this instance, work gets done wherever and whenever it is most efficient. People not only do not come into the office; they have no office to come into. This change can create significant savings for companies in the cost of space and maintenance.

Employees who work from virtual offices may be working at a client's office, at home, at a distant location, or in the local coffeeshop. This concept pushes the limits of most workplace assumptions. With this design, "my" office or "my" desk, becomes instead a shared workspace when necessary. The corner office isn't a sign of power and prestige anymore. What now sets workers and teams apart from the rest are the results produced and the customers satisfied. For employees to work in this environment they need to be open to evaluating themselves and others based on skills and results.

An industry that is moving ahead of the curve in virtual officing is information technology. In a study done by Advanced Technology Staffing, 93 percent of the workers said that they would like future contracts to include telecommuting.[15] Enlightened companies are responding to that desire by being more flexible with their information technology people. The short supply of these important employees demands that relationship.

TBWA Chiat/Day, an advertising agency in Santa Monica, California, went to a virtual office environment some time ago. Not only do the account executives and creative talent use virtual officing, but the Human Resources Department does as well. Only those people whose work must be tied to the physical plant are not virtual, such as receptionists and maintenance people. To facilitate their virtual officing, the company has developed a concierge service that takes care of forwarding mail and phone messages. Beyond that, employees can log into the company's computer to check e-mail and send faxes.

This idea seems to suit the employees and the organization, since TBWA Chiat/Day has 58 offices in 40 countries.[16]

For any business that deals with weather and geographic challenges (Chiat/Day is in Los Angeles' earthquake country and was immediately back in business after the 1994 quake), virtual officing can keep business going regardless of the elements. Employees who can work at home during a blizzard are relieved of the stress of having to try to get to work and deal with children home because the schools are closed.

As with telecommuting, a new corporate culture needs to be developed to support the evaluation of employees working in the virtual environment. There must be ongoing efforts to keep people connected, both electronically and in person. Technology will help.

Companies like Nortel provide powerful telephone technology to link people and data to facilitate high levels of productivity. Small video cameras mounted on top of computer monitors can now connect virtual workers to each other, their homes, and the office(s). Expect increased markets for torso clothing and bunny slippers!

Time is a key factor in the ability to balance work and family. Adjusting the hours spent in the workplace, sharing job responsibilities, telecommuting, or virtual officing can give employees the opportunity to meet their responsibilities both at work *and* at home. For organizations, the challenges come in changing the way they lead and evaluate employees and their work. Enlightened companies focus on *results*, not the *process* of working.

A study of relevant trends confirms that people will seek more and more flexibility in their lives. This orientation is particularly strong among younger workers who resist the relatively rigid rules and regulations that have characterized the workplace—and other aspects of their lives. The desire to self-manage is increasingly prevalent throughout our society. As more people strive to control their career destiny and their daily lives, we'll see more of a demand for flexibility. People want to grow and achieve in their own way. The next chapter explores how important growth is to meaningfulness.

KEY CONCEPTS

▶ Flexible scheduling is a way to help employees balance work and family.

▶ Flexible scheduling can include a compressed work-week, 12-hour shifts, job sharing, part-time, telecommuting, or virtual officing.

▶ Communication is a key element for success with employees working at different times and places.

▶ Telecommuting and virtual officing employees require opportunities to meet with co-workers in person—or at least visually—to keep them connected to the organization.

▶ Managers must learn to evaluate the results, not the process.

ACTION PLAN

• Review job requirements and responsibilities to find opportunities for flexible scheduling.

• Survey employees to determine their interest in alternative work opportunities.

• Include a full spectrum of employees in the design of any comprehensive schedule change.

• Give individuals the opportunity to develop schedules that are most effective for each of them.

• Establish strong lines of communication with employees who will be working off-site and clarify all the details of the new working arrangements.

- Develop a training program for managers who will need new skills to manage and evaluate employees working on alternative schedules or off-site.
- Evaluate the effectiveness of the program, taking into account productivity, overtime, absenteeism, and morale.

Endnotes

1. *Hemisphere Magazine*, May 1996.
2. "Inflexible Work Environments," *Personnel Journal*, May 1996.
3. Solomon, Charlene Marmer, "24 Hour Employees," *Personnel Journal*, August 1991.
4. Shapiro, Laura, et al., "The Myth of Quality Time," *Newsweek*, May 12, 1997.
5. Martinez, Michelle Neely, "Work-Life Programs Reap Business Benefits," *HRMagazine*, June 1997.
6. Conversation with David Blakewood, Director of Parts & Service for Crown Honda, Greensboro, North Carolina, April 22, 1997.
7. Maiwald, Connie R., et al., "Workin' 8 p.m. to 8 a.m. and Lovin' Every Minute of It!," *Workforce*, July 1997.
8. Laabs, Jennifer, "Family Issues Are a Priority at Stride Rite," *Personnel Journal*, July 1993.
9. Flynn, Gillian, "A Bank Profits From Its Worklife Program," *Workforce*, February 1997.
10. Hein, Kenneth, "Family Values," *Incentive*, December 1996.
11. Flynn, Gillian, "A Virtual Workplace Frees Creativity," *Workforce*, February 1997.
12. Rakoske, Alison, *Corporate Meetings & Incentives*, January 1996.
13. Schmit, Julie, *USA TODAY*, April 22, 1997.
14. Juergens, Jennifer, "Incentive Tests Telecommuting," *Incentive*, 1995
15. HRWire, "Virtual Office Virtually a Reality," RIA Group, September 8, 1997.
16. Flynn, Gillian, "A Virtual Workplace Frees Creativity," *Workforce*, February 1997.

11

Personal &
Professional
Growth

To stay competitive in the marketplace, companies must create an environment where learning is part of the corporate culture. Because the core business of today may be obsolete tomorrow, companies need people who have the knowledge and skills to adapt to the changing environment.

Workers want the opportunity to increase their capabilities and remain marketable in a constantly changing work environment. Education is the link. When people are learning, whether it's personally or professionally, they are growing. This growth equates to workers' job advancement, satisfaction, and self-esteem. Companies that invest in continuous learning by their employees are positioning themselves for success in the future.

A common axiom: "The only thing worse than training employees and losing them, is not training them and keeping them."

Companies that are already evolving for the future understand that they will benefit in significant ways if they support and encourage learning by their employees. A study by the National Center of Educational Quality of the Workforce indicated that a 10 percent increase in education resulted in an 8.6 percent increase in productivity and in nonmanufacturing companies the productivity increase was 11 percent. The same 10 percent increase in tools and machinery netted only a 3.4 percent increase in productivity.[1] This clearly underscores the value of investing in intellectual capital.

Providing Basic Skills

In the process of empowering employees, companies may not realize that their people lack the basic skills to handle the changes. Companies that fail to address this problem in the beginning of the process may not discover the skills gap until it has an impact on their relationships with customers.

Baldor Electric Company in Fort Smith, Arkansas, makes industrial electric motors and competes with companies like Reliance Electric, Emerson Electric, and General Electric. With $418 million in sales, Baldor is tiny by comparison. To stay competitive, CEO "Rollie" Boreham changed the company's manufacturing processes by shortening delivery times. Workers were given the parts and a computer printout with instructions, so they could build complete units from start to finish.

This change was a good process decision for quicker turn-around and a good personnel decision to make work more meaningful. In this case, however, the change exposed a problem area. After a shipment of motors was sent to a major customer, it was discovered that the motors did not match the written specifications. Investigation revealed that the cause of the problem was poor reading skills.

Company executives asked the workers what to do about it. Amid the choices were "fire us all and hire Harvard MBAs," "go back to the old methods," or "be sure everyone can read." The first option didn't have a chance, nor did the workers want to go back to the old methods. But they were ready to improve their reading skills. The company arranged for employees to take courses in reading at the local community college. Now all Baldor employees go through 48 hours of training on a variety of subjects, including value, quality, and cost analysis.

After putting the educational process in place, productivity rose 10 percent. Baldor now projects sales of $1 billion by 2000. Although the company is very small compared to its competitors, the net income per dollar of sales meets or exceeds that of the much larger companies. Boreham believes in his workers and knows that taking care of his customers starts with taking care of his employees. Now employee education and training are an integral part of his strategy to keep the company competitive.[2]

The high-tech industry has its own challenges with educating workers. While many employees in this industry are highly trained, there are many others who have remained at lower educational levels working in manufacturing plants. For these workers, additional education is critical. As the industry evolves, there will be less and less need for unskilled employees. And as companies push decision making lower in the organization, their workers will need more training to assume more responsibility and accountability.

Advanced Micro Devices (AMD), Sunnyvale, California, is already preparing workers for the future. For plant workers, it is increasingly important to be able to identify when a machine is running poorly and to be able to take steps to solve the problem. This identification and correction work requires some technical knowledge. So AMD provides the basic reading, English, and math skills workers need to move into the more technical classes the company has to offer. Education labs are open 24 hours a day to accommodate the various shift schedules. After the company started providing the basic skills and technical training, it saw benefits in increased manufacturing yields. Better-educated employees work more efficiently and make fewer errors.

There were other benefits, too. Workers participated more in meetings, earned more promotions, and had higher self-esteem and job satisfaction. AMD made an investment in their workers. Rather than replace their workers with more educated employees, AMD gave them the opportunity to gain the basic skills and then the technical knowledge to move forward with the organization.

The additional education brought these employees into the mainstream of the organization so that they could understand more about the company as a whole. With the greater perspective afforded by the education and the technical training, the employees were able to see career opportunities and take the steps necessary for advancement.[3]

The city of Phoenix earned the 1998 Optimas Quality of Life award for their work/life programs, many of which are centered in education. The city has established a comprehensive literacy program. The impetus for the program came from a study in 1988 that uncovered the fact that many city employees were not qualified for promotion because they lacked basic skills. Since its inception, the literacy program has touched the lives of 830 employees. Providing basic skills gives workers opportunities to be promoted within the city or to find better paying jobs in private industry.

Educate Workers Prior to Hiring

Being certain that prospective employees have basic knowledge benefits a company in the hiring process. At the Light, Gas & Water Division of the city of Memphis, people seeking employment must first attend classes at the State Technical Institute to be trained in utility jobs. By hiring only those who have completed the developmental training, LG&W gains employees who are ready to work on day one. This preemployment training saves money for the utility and ultimately keeps rates down for consumers.[4]

Making Learning a Part of the Corporate Culture

Enlightened companies know that education and training are not isolated events, but are instead, an ongoing process throughout the organization. These forward-thinking companies not only provide formal opportunities for learning, but also encourage and support the informal exchange of knowledge between workers as well.

This kind of continuous learning was the key factor in the turnaround of PIPSA, a paper manufacturing company in Mexico. Run as a monopoly for 60 years with newsprint as its only product, PIPSA faced an incredible challenge when its monopoly was abolished in 1989. Privatization by the government was imminent. CEO Rene Villarreal led an organization that would have to compete against much larger companies that owned much better equipment. He understood that to survive in this changing marketplace, PIPSA would need to have productive workers, not just cheap labor.

Villarreal met the challenge by creating "learning cells." Of the 2,000 employees, 65 percent belong to one or more learning cells that meet weekly to address current business issues. Some cells focus on functional issues such as marketing, finance, and quality, while others handle process issues between various plants. The results have been spectacular. In 1994 annual revenues were $78 million. A short two years later, revenues were up to $179 million. Plans were made to double capacity. The company recaptured 79 percent of the market in newsprint and expanded into the telephone book market. In addition, PIPSA now manufactures bond paper for office use.

Villarreal bases his "learning cell" concept on three basic principles. The first principle is that learning must be productive. By productive, he means that it must address at least one of the four goals of the company: to increase market share, to reduce costs, to increase quality, and to enhance service. The process of learning within the cells is clearly outlined to address specific areas: working more efficiently, identifying what new knowledge has been gained, sharing and teaching the new knowledge, and identifying how the new knowledge was applied.

The cells also address performance issues relating to quality, efficiency, and customer service. Because the learning process is directly tied to the performance of the company, employees can see the connections between what they do, what they are learning, and the success of the organization.

The second principle is that there must be respect for the different ways people collect and disseminate information. In PIPSA, the range of people runs from international executives with university educations to plant workers who have minimal schooling. For plant workers, knowledge is often passed along through an oral tradition of storytelling and song. Since it's the learning that counts, not the method of transmission, meetings may be short on overheads and long on stories and songs. In this case the corporate culture demonstrates a respect for the individual—a key tenet for future-oriented companies.

The third principle is that learning must continue beyond the company walls. PIPSA pays for the education of the employees *and* their families, providing tuition for private schools, because public education is so poor. The company's support of nontraditional education also gives value to workers who have years of experience. Villarreal and his team know that experienced technicians often have a sixth sense about the nature of a problem. This kind of knowledge is encouraged, too.

What the example of PIPSA illustrates so clearly is that continuous learning can be applied to *any* kind of company with any kind of workers. The PIPSA system can be as successful in an environment with few traditionally educated workers as it is in a high-tech environment with many.[5]

A Departmental Approach

There is great value in building department-level learning, especially when the effort is directed toward solving real problems. People enjoy becoming involved in solutions, if they know that their suggestions and problem-solving efforts will be listened to and acted upon. By working together to improve the way they do things, departmentally focused employees learn more about the department's mission, what kind of work is done—and why, and how to perform their jobs even better.

Opryland Hotel, Nashville, Tennessee, has earned a national reputation in the hospitality industry for its work in this area. The quality assurance program, under the leadership of Emily Ellis, has been widely recognized. Departmental, as well as cross-functional, teams meet frequently to study problems. The team members present their findings and recommendations to management committees, who either ask for more information, grant approval, or suggest modifications. The process remains employee-driven.

Sharing individual and group knowledge became a critical factor when Eastman Kodak went through a dramatic restructuring. Kodak created six groups within its manufacturing operations that would produce film and paper in continuous processes. Each group was made accountable for its own success. To be successful, diverse groups would need to communicate and share knowledge as never before.

After the restructuring, managers of the Black and White Film Manufacturing (BWFM) division realized that they had some serious problems. They also realized that they would have to find the solutions within the group. They started by making all 1,500 employees partners in turning the division around. An important part of the solution was to find ways for employees to share their knowledge with each other. It was essential that everyone understand how each part of the business operation fit with the others to impact the whole.

The leadership tcam asked for volunteers to help in this education process. Over 200 people came forward. The resulting video, in keeping with their identity as Team Zebra, was called "Dances with Zebras," a takeoff on the award-winning movie, "Dances with Wolves."

Each department created a segment that lasted three to four minutes to explain what function their unit performed. The only parameters were that the presentation had to reflect the mission, values, and principles of the organization. One group rented black-and-white prison suits; another had a worker in a zebra suit leading a chorus. There were takeoffs on musicals, rap songs, and skits. Although it did not receive Academy Award recognition, "Dances with Zebras" was a box office smash at BWFM.[6]

The special value came from employees' involvement in the process and the creativity it inspired. Like the continuous learning at PIPSA, BWFM/Kodak acknowledged that workers could learn in many different ways. What is most important is that all employees have the knowledge and skill to accomplish the tasks at hand and that they understand the importance of their work for the organization as a whole.

Partnering with Local Educational Institutions

There are many ways to educate employees. Educational institutions are often willing to partner with companies to provide a broad range of learning opportunities for workers. National Semiconductor is bringing the college campus to the workplace through the Economic Development Institute of the West Valley-Mission Community College District.

To help workers increase their skills and education, the company not only pays for tuition, but also provides on-site classrooms. Employees can actually earn their college degrees at work. The program is compressed—nine weeks instead of 18—and has the same academic standards as the classes at the local community colleges. In many cases, the same college instructors present the courses for National Semiconductor. The additional education helps employees perform better in their current jobs as well as prepares them for advancement opportunities.[7]

Education for Employees and Customers

Education doesn't need to stop with employees. Extending educational opportunities to customers can increase *their* loyalty. Whether companies provide product information or act as a business resource for customers, the result is increased profitability on both sides.

Say "Harley Davidson," and the first image you get probably doesn't have anything to do with education. But the Harley Company is dedicated to the education of its employees, dealers, and customers. Employees at Harley get 80 hours of training every year. Training at the Harley Leadership Institute is centered around three basic competencies that all employees are required to have: interaction, which encompasses communication and team skills; execution, which covers planning, evaluation, and decision-making skills; and technology, which teaches task skills and the continuous improvement process.

To help dealers, there is the Harley-Davidson University. At this facility, dealers attend three-day training sessions. Training here is diverse and covers everything from customer service issues to planning for retirement—all engineered to ensure that their dealers are successful.

The Harley Owners Group, HOG, is a factory-sponsored motorcycle club with 325,000 members and 940 chapters. Harley-Davidson's education program goes so far as to train leaders of the motorcycle club chapters to help them keep their chapters growing and viable.

Harley completes the continuous learning process by having employee volunteers from all levels of the organization attend a company-sponsored event to interact directly with customers. Employees bring back valuable information that allows Harley to improve product quality and meet customers' changing needs. This last component is especially valuable because employees have the opportunity to contribute to the organization by gathering and sharing knowledge that will have a direct effect on profitability.[8] They see how the pieces fit together to keep their company responsive and strong—and their work experience more meaningful.

Free Training as a Sign-on Bonus

Additional education opportunities are a powerful lure for employees in any industry, but even more valuable to people in high tech. Consulting firms in high-tech fields offer free training to recruit and retain good contractors. Manpower, Inc. will download $1,000 worth of courseware to any Information Systems professional who sends a resumé.

Another firm offers certification training in Microsoft and Novell networking technologies for any contractor who registers with them. For independent contractors, it is a great way to get the training they need to stay current in such a rapidly changing environment. By this method, Manpower recruits contractors who are highly trained and can be more valuable to clients.

When people apply to work as help-desk analysts for IHS HelpDesk Service, headquartered in New York City, they choose a two-year, personalized growth program. This growth program offers free Novell and Microsoft network certifications and opportunities to learn all kinds of software. This personalized training enables IHS to compete very successfully for the limited pool of help-desk analysts and call center personnel. Offering this training opportunity has helped IHS reduce their turnover from 300 percent to 25 percent, where it has remained stable.

Personal Development

When companies design and implement education for employees, they can go beyond work-related learning to help their people with their personal development as well. Helping employees increase their life management skills can help reduce stress and demonstrate the organization's concern for employees beyond the workplace.

Wimberly, Allison, Tong and Goo, an architectural firm based in Newport Beach, California operates internationally. In 1997, they had projects in 34 countries. As a benefit to its employees, the firm pays for language training for any employee who wants to learn different languages.

Cardinal Meat Specialists in Mississauga, Ontario employs 75 full-time employees, plus contract workers who are hired as-needed—an average of 120 people year-round. Sixty percent of the employees have been with the company five years or more. The company encourages personal development by paying the cost, books, and all associated expenses. The learning does not have to be related to the employee's work. Mark Cator, president of the company, "just knows that the company benefits—directly or indirectly—from employee growth of any kind."[9] Employees currently are engaged in courses ranging from woodworking to an executive MBA.

Since many of Cardinal's employees are recent immigrants to their new homeland, the company offers courses in English as a second language every couple of years. The enhanced language capability helps workers in their personal lives, as well as on the job.

Personal Financial Planning

For companies that offer 401(k) or similar plans that allow employees to make investment decisions, it is valuable to provide employees with the knowledge to make sound choices. Most employers explain the plan(s), the investment options, and the nature of risk and risk tolerance, but don't give employees much else to go on. Firms that give more information and training provide a very valuable service in helping employees maximize their retirement savings. Options for such education include providing sample investment portfolios, seminars on investment terminology, asset allocation, retirement needs analysis and inflation, and publishing an investment newsletter.

An enlightened attorney in the San Diego area, Donald English, Esq., was frustrated by the fact that he was paying a great deal of money to provide benefits to his employees, and the value of his generosity was not being perceived by his people. Now, each person, from the hourly file clerks to the highly paid partners, receives free financial planning.

As part of the financial planning services, the employee is given a thorough understanding of the financial planning process, together with the cost, of the company benefits being provided—including the financial planning services. Now, his employees really comprehend their employer's beneficence. While this benefit is only one of many this attorney provides, it is not surprising that his rate of turnover is very low.

Some of the large accounting firms, Ernst & Young, for example, now offer these services to their large corporate clients. The "new" perspective provided by the financial planner helps the employee understand that his employer really cares, which, of course, builds loyalty.

For corporations on a shoestring, there's a firm called Better Benefits, Inc. in New York City. Better Benefits sells "voluntary, employee-paid" insurance programs, offering group rates to the employees of mid-size to large companies for types of insurance that the employer doesn't want to cover. Some examples include car, homeowner's, and dental insurance. As a value-added service, in order to "earn" an audience with the employee, Better Benefits provides some financial planning advice. This information, of course, again includes a description of the fees paid by the employer. Everybody wins.

Retirement Planning

Every eight seconds another Baby Boomer turns 50. That means that retirement planning is more critical than ever. Unfortunately many people don't take the time or wait too long to get their retirement plans in order. Sensitive employers respond to the concerns of their older (and middle-aged) employees by supporting them in the retirement planning process.

The city of Phoenix is taking an active role in helping their employees with the financial and legal decisions that they will face as they near retirement. The city has established three different preretirement programs to address the retirement needs of employees in different age brackets. For the 36 to 54 age bracket the "Successful Retirement Planning" seminar teaches employees about life insurance, IRAs, setting goals, wills, and power of attorney.

Employees in the 55 and older group have a different set of needs, so their program is "Planning Your Tomorrows." This seminar focuses on the Social Security, city retirement benefits, tax and financial planning, and health services available to the employee. If retirement will occur within the year, employees can attend the "Choices and Decisions" classes to learn about insurance issues, deferred compensation distributions, and the retirement process as a city employee. Since 1992, this retirement planning education has been provided to about 1,200 employees.[10]

Managing the Family Budget

In some cases, financial education can be presented on a more practical level. With expenses increasing at a greater rate than income, managing the family budget can be a source of major stress and conflict. For some families basic budgeting, debt reduction, and buying techniques can make a real difference in the quality of their lives.

To help employees manage money better on a monthly basis, consider arranging with an accounting firm or a financial planner—who understands the significance of the basics—to provide seminars on family money matters. Once their finances are in order, employees' stress levels will be significantly reduced.

The professionals you hire for the seminars will appreciate an opportunity to meet with potential clients. Be careful, however, to be clear that those professionals understand that their role is education, not solicitation. A misstep here could undermine the whole program, if employees feel they are being "sold" instead of helped.

Preparing Children for College

Although it is sometimes seen as only a financial issue, some families can benefit greatly from assistance in preparing their children for college. Being able to afford college is certainly a major issue, but the testing and admission processes can also be intimidating.

GTE sponsored a teleconference for 1,400 of its employees and their children on preparing for college. The full-day conference, broadcast live to 18 locations, featured panels of experts to answer questions on admissions, financial aid, student life, and admissions testing. The GTE teleconference was so successful that the company plans to offer similar programs on topics such as career planning and saving for retirement.[11]

Not many companies can put together the kind of tele-conferencing that GTE can, but smaller companies could get several other businesses together to sponsor a "Getting Ready for College" fair at the local high school or community college. Connecting families with high school age children with college counselors, admissions staff, and student loan officers can help them put together the pieces that will work best for them. Not only will your employees appreciate the free information, but it will also underscore your commitment to education, both in the workplace and beyond.

Educational Opportunity Resources

There is a multitude of educational opportunities available for employees: in-house training, interactive computer-based training, courses at local community colleges and universities, commercial seminars, and free workshops delivered by local training professionals. Make your employees aware of all the opportunities through a general bulletin board posting or a referral list by topic. All learning opportunities are a benefit to both the employee and the organization.

Establish a policy regarding what kinds of education your company will pay for and the process required for application and financial support. For outside courses, you may choose to reimburse the employee/student based on grade point average or you may pay tuition directly to the school.

Career Development Opportunities

Along with job skills and educational opportunities, some companies provide a more formal career development process. To recruit and retain good employees, enlightened companies furnish employees with the tools and opportunities to make themselves more marketable—both internally and externally. Employees know that they are responsible for their own career development and will choose companies that give them the options they seek. Having control over career potential is a key element in making work meaningful.

In a survey done by Drake Beam Morin, Inc., of 700 companies in New York, researchers found that 80 percent of the companies studied were already doing something to help employees manage their careers. Here are the kinds of things these companies are doing: offering higher education tuition reimbursements, sponsoring training programs, maintaining libraries or resource centers, presenting career development workshops, and offering job coaching or mentoring. About 10 percent of the respondents indicated that they had complete career centers available to their people.[12]

Continuous learning is essential. Rosenbluth International has a strong learning and development program. Because the travel industry is based on technical skill, employees must continue to develop their skill base . . . for the present and the future. The company facilitates employees developing their own careers through career counseling provided by the Human Resources Department. Rosenbluth has a "shadowing" program where employees can visit any other department.

Each Rosenbluth employee has a personalized learning plan, which includes short- and long-term goals. By helping employees chart their own career path, the company effectively gives its workers job security. Employees who are skilled and prepared for the jobs of the future are assured opportunities for which they have invested their time. The company also has learning leaders who spend the majority of their time working with the individual units to determine their development issues.[13]

Companies that offer career development resources to employees give people the opportunity to become more employable. That growth can mean that these employees are more prepared to move into more responsible positions within the enterprise and/or that they will be more marketable if the firm must downsize. Giving support to the whole individual changes the relationship companies have with their employees. The partnership makes the employment more meaningful.

Job Rotation

Rotating employees into different jobs within the organization is a good career development strategy. Working in different areas, employees not only increase their knowledge and skills, but also learn more about the company as a whole. This breadth can be very valuable in positioning workers for any changes the company may be making in the future. Particularly in a large organization, employees can become isolated in their divisions and be unaware of the kinds of changes taking place that may, in fact, put them out of a job.

Job rotation gives employees a chance to explore and broaden their own career objectives. They may find a better fit for themselves in another division. And certainly the skills they obtain will be valuable should the organization change its core business. Building a broad set of competencies and experiences greatly benefits the employee—and the business.

Co-author Roger Herman gained significant experience working for The B. F. Goodrich Company after earning his bachelor's degree from Hiram College in the late 1960s. He was one of about a dozen recent graduates hired into a rotating management training program at the rubber company. The trainees worked about two months in each of a number of different departments, moving on a regular basis to gain new experiences in departments of their choice. Each week a different senior executive spent a couple of hours briefing trainees on his area of responsibility to give these fast-track employees greater learning and insight.

Participants in this rotation program were better equipped to serve the company with a wider range of experience and cross-functional understanding. The company benefited, and so did the employees.

Career Development Programs

Because the changes in business are occurring at an ever-increasing rate, employees need to prepare themselves for the jobs that will be most valuable to the organization in the next two to five years. Enlightened companies give workers the resources to identify future job opportunities and develop the new skills required to fill those positions.

Preparing employees for jobs in the future was an important consideration at Amoco. As part of a dramatic reorganization in the late 1980s, Amoco realized that to meet changing business needs, their employees needed to prepare themselves to function in a rapidly changing environment. To make this transition possible, Amoco needed to design a comprehensive career development program to help its people grow.

Because the organization was comprised of 18 individual business groups, career development plans were customized to each unit. The Exploration and Production group, with employees worldwide, took on the task of developing the framework for the project. This particular sector was affected greatly by rapidly changing technology, so career development was essential to this business unit's success.

They started out with a task force to create a model that would include strategic staffing, employee satisfaction, and skill enhancement. The model also had to be compatible with management practices of compensation, promotion, and performance management. The objective was to create a system in which employees could gather information about the company, then determine the skills they needed to continue to be viable and valuable in the organization.

To gather as much information as possible, each task force member developed an advisory board comprised of a range of fellow employees. The involvement of many people in the process was one of the reasons the career development program was ultimately so successful.

It took two and a half years to develop the program, but the result was worth the time invested. The Career Management program (ACM) was built on four basic principles: education, assessment, development planning, and outcomes. Employees using the process have the opportunity to do personal assessments that make the education and planning portions of the program much more effective. Personal assessments, such as Check Start and Prevue have been proven to be highly effective. Similar instruments are also available, such as the Empowerment Mirror from Development Dimensions International.

The ACM program was launched at employee meetings held at each site and offered a half-day session for employees to explore the center. Since the beginning, response to the process has been positive. ACM professionals attribute their success to the following factors:

- The program was put in place, as a direct response to business needs.

- ACM was not a one-time event, but part of a complete change process. Management development specialists took time in designing the program, so that when it was presented there was a high participation rate by employees. Employees were encouraged to take a more active role in their own career development and were supported by the company through career advisors. Supervisors also had their variable pay tied to their employee development skills.

- The implementation of the program came through business units so that it was kept close to the employees. Prior to canvassing for a new job in the Amoco organization, employees use the development aids of assessment and planning. Feedback from employees using the program was evaluated for continuous improvement.[14]

ACM's process provides a good framework for any company considering a career development program.

Employees Create Their Own Career Development Centers

TRW, a space and technology company, is competing— not only with other companies in its industry, but with the telecommunications business for top technical talent. To give the company an edge, TRW developed two comprehensive career development centers, one at a manufacturing facility and one at the Space and Electronics Group. What makes the TRW centers unique is that they have been developed and are serviced almost entirely by volunteers. Rather than present the center as a benefit created by Human Resources and "given" to employees, the company chose to provide the opportunity for employees to develop the centers themselves. Employees, managers, and the company worked together as partners to develop relevant learning facilities.

Since the plant runs three shifts, the manufacturing location created a center that could function 24 hours a day. At start-up, TRW provided $21.76 per person to support accumulation of the basics. After that, groups contributed manuals, learning materials, subscriptions, everything they had that could be valuable to the learning process of other employees. The facility is staffed by front-line supervisors, human resources staff, and training personnel. Employees use the facility whenever it is convenient for them, checking out materials to use for self-paced learning.

Employees are asked to complete a form after using the center to identify what was learned, how it was applied, and the result of that application. This input enables TRW to quantify the effect of the center at the manufacturing plant. When they reviewed the forms, executives discovered that learning had increased tenfold. The center now averages 250 checkouts a month! Because it was a collaborative effort, the center itself is a point of pride for the employees and is part of every facility tour.

Intranet Access to Internal Job Opportunities

The career development center at the TRW Space and Electronics Group is also supported by volunteers, who invest many hours collecting information to be placed on the company's intranet. At this facility, the high-tech employees use their computers to access educational materials through PDC (Personal Development Center) On-Line.

TRW's PDC On-Line service connects employees to internal and external web sites that can be helpful in their career development. The facility enables employees to check out materials, meet with counselors, and attend workshops. The center also functions as a vehicle to convey information to employees about business strategy, so they can actively direct their learning to meet the current and future needs of the organization.

The TRW programs have two key elements: first, the career development centers were supported by senior management; and second, in both instances employees were involved and responsible for the development and maintenance of the centers. Employees use the facilities more often because they have been involved from the beginning. As we emphasize in our speeches and consulting, "people support what they help to create." It is an example of the new relationship organizations must have with their employees. It is not about giving programs *to,* but partnering *with* employees, to meet the needs of both the employees and the organization.

Helping Employees Transition Out of the Organization

Sometimes, despite the best of career development programs, employees find themselves downsized out of a company. What, if any, responsibility does a Lean and Meaningful employer have to downsized workers? NOVA Corp., a

Canadian-based natural gas and petrochemical company, thinks that the corporation has a significant responsibility to departing employees. NOVA developed its Employment Transition and Continuity (ET&C) program to support employees in finding employment both internally and externally. The program serves the 6,000 employees in North America.

Since 1993, when the program began, over 1,000 employees have used ET&C to help with a variety of career issues. ET&C covers the areas of education and training, business and volunteer opportunities, reassignments internally, and retirement. One of the most unique aspects of the program is the entrepreneurial venture support.

Through this unusual support program, employees whose positions are eliminated have the opportunity to receive awards up to $25,000 to start their own businesses. To qualify, employees must submit a business plan, and the company provides both resources and support in the development process. Even after setting up their new businesses, former employees can continue to get valuable feedback to help them run their businesses.

For other employees, whose jobs are gone, opportunities might lie in community service. NOVA provides 50 percent of the employee's salary and full medical and profit sharing for employees who volunteer a minimum of 20 hours per week to a qualified nonprofit organization. When the assignment is complete, the employee can expect a full severance package. The nonprofit experience can sometimes provide people with skills they can use in finding new jobs elsewhere. These opportunities enable a meaningful transition to the next career phase.

Education is also a component of employees shifting to a new position. Tuition and book reimbursements, plus a 50 percent salary, can make it possible for people to get a college education that they might never have achieved otherwise. This additional education can then be used to pursue new career opportunities after graduation. The Education Option of ET&C also financially supports part-time enrollment for both employees and their spouses to a maximum of $5,000.

In addition, NOVA maintains full-service career development centers that provide assessments, career and financial planning information, training workshops, job postings, and counseling. For employees who move at least 25 miles from their current address in order to find employment, NOVA's relocation services provide grants of up to $5,000.[15] The flexibility of this program to meet the diverse needs of the affected employees makes it successful.

In the rapidly changing work environment, employees need to know that there are many options for their career development. Because of the way NOVA Corp. treats employees when a change in the business environment eliminates their jobs, the morale and productivity of remaining employees does not drop nearly as low as it does in companies without this kind of program. Supporting employees in transition is a reflection of a corporate culture that values individuals, and as a result, builds loyalty on the part of all the remaining employees.

Enlightened companies provide continuous learning opportunities for employees, both professionally and personally, so that both the company and the individuals are prepared for the future. The demands of the marketplace require that employees be educated problem solvers. Companies that build on the intellectual capital of their employees by offering a wide range of educational opportunities will come out on top. Good employees are always looking for ways to increase their knowledge and skills, and will seek the employers that offer them the most educational opportunities.

The commitment of the organization to employees' growth not only produces better-educated people, but also creates a loyalty to the organization. What company in the world doesn't want its people to be well-educated?

Encouraging employees to be well-educated is part of

being socially responsible. Social responsibility is a key component of meaningfulness. Let's begin our journey through this concern with Chapter 12.

KEY CONCEPTS

> ▶ Continuous learning will be part of the organization culture of Lean and Meaningful companies.
> ▶ Employees at every level need and want ongoing professional and personal education.
> ▶ Employers need to provide resources to help employees define, develop, and control their own careers.
> ▶ Getting employees involved in helping other workers creates a supportive, growth-oriented environment.

ACTION PLAN

- Assess the educational needs of your employees.
- Find resources, such as community colleges, training consultants, or government programs, to address those needs and consider bringing them on-site.
- Provide career-planning resources either by developing a career center on-site or preparing a referral list for outside sources. Consider having the company pay any fees associated with the use of outside resources.
- Keep employees up to date on the kinds of jobs that will be important in your company or industry in the future.
- Make the career and personal development of staff part of managers' evaluations.
- Involve the employees in the design and development of the learning programs.

Endnotes

1. Applebome, Peter, "Study Ties Education Gains to More Productivity Growth," *New York Times*, May 14, 1995.
2. Groves, Martha, "Knowledge at Work," *Los Angeles Times*, December 17, 1995.
3. Ladendorf, Kirk, *Knight-Ridder/Tribune Business News*.
4. Waters, David, *Commercial Appeal*, Memphis, Tennessee.
5. Matson, Eric, "You Can Teach This Old Company New Tricks," *Fast Company*, October/November 1997.
6. Anfuso, Dawn, "Kodak Employees Bring a Department into the Black," *Personnel Journal*, September 1994. (p. 168)
7. *CMP Publications*, July 29, 1997.
8. Imperato, Gina, "Harley Shifts Gears," *Fast Company*, June/July 1997.
9. Telephone conversation with Mark Cator, February 25, 1998.
10. Piña, Phillip, "Early Lessons for the College-bound," *USA Today*, November 15, 1995.
11. "Companies Believe in Helping Workers With Their Careers," *Personnel Journal*, January 1996.
12. Sanders, Chris, "Back to the Farm," *Fast Company,* February/March 1997.
13. Ibid.
14. "Amoco's 7 Design Factors for a Better Career System," *Personnel Journal*, February 1996.
15. Wensky, Arnold, & Galer, Susan, "Helping Employees Help Themselves," *HRMagazine*, August 1997.

12

Social
Responsibility

To be successful in the changing marketplace, it is imperative for businesses to identify how they will demonstrate social responsibility. Customers and investors make decisions more often based on the quality of the relationship an organization has with employees, the environment, and the community. They use these criteria in their buying and investment decisions.

In the clothing industry, people are concerned about the kind of labor being used to produce the garments. In the medical industry, the public is aware of the testing methods for new drugs, the safety of packaging, and the disposal of hazardous waste. For manufacturers, communities are knowledgeable about their environmental protection record or their use of materials that deplete natural resources.

Not only are consumers, stakeholders, and investors concerned about what happens outside the company; they're also alert to internal issues and philosophies. These stakeholders are understandably curious about how a company handles diversity in its workforce, what level of tolerance it has for harassment, and how its leaders manage their employees.

Socially Responsible Investing

In a tight labor market, employees will choose to work for a company that not only takes good care of its employees, but also one that is considered a responsible corporate citizen. Being able to maintain a stable, productive workforce and recruit the best people in the industry is the basis for ongoing profitability and investor confidence. A company that does not have a clear idea of its values and social responsibilities will have a difficult time navigating the troubled waters of tomorrow's society and attracting the investment dollars essential to success.

The idea of responsible investing, that is, choosing companies for both their financial performance and their values, actually began in 1928, when companies were "sin screened" prior to being included in funds. Over the years, funds have been developed based on individual social stands, such as doing business with South Africa or providing materials that supported the Vietnam War. Initially investors chose not to invest with companies that had a bad record, but—over time—they also began to consider what companies were "doing right."

The Ernst & Young Center of Business Innovation, in a study with 275 portfolio managers, found that 35 percent of them make decisions based on nonfinancial factors. The ability of companies to recruit and retain employees was ranked fifth in the list of 39 criteria used in picking stocks.[1] Essential for the long-term success of any company is the ability to hire and retain good employees and the provision of a harassment-free, diverse, and safe work environment. Meaningful companies will emphasize these issues.

As early as 1972, the Dreyfus Third Century Fund's annual report included company records for equal opportunity, safety, health, and environmental issues. The Calvert Group began in 1982 developing funds that included only socially responsible companies. Some institutional investors acknowledge that employee-related issues have an impact on corporate profitability. This kind of responsible investing has had significant effect on how companies do business. When mutual funds, retirement funds, annuities, and other investment vehicles are taken into account, responsible investing dollars amount to over $300 billion.

The California Public Employees Retirement System (CALPERS) is using its investment clout to push firms to be more loyal to employees and provide more job security, because these are both factors in productivity. CALPERS also encourages these companies to keep layoffs to a minimum and develop better relationships with their employees.

Stockholders' interest in social issues is forcing a change in the legal climate. Significant resolutions have been placed successfully on ballots of major companies by concerned shareholders. They're asking for votes on measures that ordinarily would not require corporate reporting—issues like minority hiring policies and working conditions of suppliers. How do these socially responsible companies perform against other companies? Quite well, actually.

One organization that tracks socially responsible corporate performance is the Domini Social Index. Amy Domini began screening companies for social responsibility when she was asked to invest the money from her church. Her current portfolio consists of 400 stocks that make up the Domini Social Index. In the past five years the returns on the Domini Index have been 19.59 percent, while the Standard & Poor returns were 18.38 percent; in the past three years the Domini Index returns were 26.92 percent to Standard & Poor's

25.93 percent. For investors those returns are attractive.

Being socially responsible requires a company to look beyond the immediate and identify issues that have a long-term impact on both the local and global communities. A socially responsible company identifies its basic social values and makes them the foundation for all corporate decision making. Rather than measure decisions only by stock price, increased profitability, and market share, a values-based company demonstrates its responsibility to the society, both locally and globally, and the people that make its very existence possible. As the market indicates, this kind of decision making ultimately results in better workforce stability, increased customer loyalty, and enhanced bottom-line profitability.

Observers of trends in the design of annual reports have noticed an increasing use of photographs of employees. This focus demonstrates a heightened awareness among corporate communications professionals for the importance of humanizing the corporate image. Enlightened corporations are showcasing their employees—their greatest asset.

Building Social Responsibility

Although there has been a good deal of conversation about social responsibility, it has been difficult sometimes to get programs up and running. One group, however, the Colorado Network of Businesses for Social Responsibility, has more than 1,000 corporate members who are trying to make a difference in the world. While the membership includes such well-known companies as Ben & Jerry's Ice Cream, Levi Strauss & Co., and Tom's of Maine, most of the members are smaller companies looking for ways to do business differently.

The organization is focused on helping businesses find the ways they can respond to larger social issues. The Network accomplishes its goal in a number of ways, including offering publications, employee handbooks that address new pay methods, family-friendly policies, and research on environmentally sound practices. Because corporate cultures and environments are very different, the solutions for one company might never work in another. But in general, even very small companies can contribute through volunteerism, environmental awareness, and making socially responsible investment choices.

The Social Venture Network (SVN) is an organization dedicated to helping companies use their influence to find solutions to social issues. SVN has a number of resources that may help you in the process. The group is comprised of over 450 business owners and others with an interest and commitment in changing the way business is done. SVN is designed around seven objectives:

1. **Sustainability** within the environment through mindful use of resources;
2. **Social Justice** through equitable business practices;
3. **Community Contribution** by businesses and their employees;
4. **Innovation** in ways to do business and contribute to a just society;
5. **Cooperation** to expand social responsibility in the business community;
6. **Diversity** in the workplace by creating an environment that allows everyone to flourish;
7. **Education** about new business practices and ways for the business community to have an impact for the social good.

Information about this network group can be found at www.svn.org.

Making a Positive Difference

An emphasis in socially responsible companies is to make a positive difference in the world around them. Many are active in their local communities, while others are (also) active in national or international efforts to make this a better world.

Organizations like Make a Wish Foundation and Starlight Foundation work diligently to make dreams come true for children with chronic or fatal diseases. Whether it's a trip to Disney World, a visit with an astronaut, or a chance to meet Michael Jordan, these special kids benefit from the support of organizations and their volunteering employees. The money's important, but so is the personal touch.

A number of employees of HA-LO Marketing and Promotion are being trained, as of this writing, to serve as "wish grantors" for the Starlight Foundation. Companies in a wide variety of industries support these kinds of organizations.

Using its love of professional sports, HA-LO donates tickets to professional games, as well as sports team memorabilia, to charities around the country for use in fund-raising auctions or raffles.

Broad-based national movements like Habitat for Humanity enjoy wonderful corporate and volunteer support. Home Depot has made this project practically a special mission of the company and its employees. The company benefits as its employees have a chance to use the products they sell. Their personal familiarity with the products enables them to better answer questions and help their customers in the store.

Responding to Crisis

Companies in crisis, like McNeil Laboratories, Fort Washington, Pennsylvania, during the Tylenol tampering incident, were able to show the world that they were socially responsible, regardless of any financial losses to themselves. It may have been costly to remove all Tylenol from the counters and design safer packaging in the short term, but the long-term benefit was employee, customer, and investor loyalty.

When there are disasters, natural or man-made, companies have an opportunity to help their communities and the environment. Tom's of Maine stepped up to help out when a barge carrying diesel heating oil ran aground off the coast of Rhode Island. The barge spilled 800,000 gallons of the toxic substance in an area that was a sanctuary for waterfowl.

After hearing of the spill, Tom's of Maine contacted Save the Bay, a nonprofit group dedicated to preserving Narragansett Bay, and began asking other businesses for donations that would help. Next, they put together a work party to go by van to the site of the spill to help out with the cleanup. The actual cleaning of the animals and shoreline required special expertise, but the people from Tom's had plenty to do at the Save the Bay headquarters stuffing envelopes and sharing skills in communications and database design.

The time and energy they spent was valuable to the cleanup efforts and the Save the Bay organization. But there were also benefits for Tom's of Maine. The group that worked on this project included a broad range of employees from hourly workers to the CEO. These dedicated people worked together as a team doing something meaningful outside the workplace. They demonstrated elements of the company's mission statement that include being socially and environmentally responsible and being concerned about the well-being of customers, co-workers, and the community. This kind of commitment reinforces why Tom's of Maine is a special place to work.[2]

When you look at your company, there are a number of things you'll want to consider. Use the following list as a guideline to begin the process of determining how and where your company will take its place as a socially responsible corporate citizen.

1. The relationship with employees: Does the company hire and promote minorities in all levels? Is the work environment healthy and safe? Are there family-friendly programs in place to help employees balance work and family life? Are employees fairly compensated and do they have the opportunity to share in the wealth they help create in the company?

2. **The relationship to the community, both locally and globally**: Does the company support or deplete the local community? Does the company invest in the economic future of the community and its residents? In what countries does the company do business and what products does it sell? What effect does the company have on host countries around the world in terms of society and the environment?

3. **The relationship to the environment**: What does the company do to reduce the detrimental impact it may have on the environment? In what ways does the company conserve resources or energy both in usage and purchasing?

4. **The relationship with customers**: Are the products high in quality, safe, and durable? Do the products benefit society? Are products marketed in a socially responsible way, that is, free of stereotypes and not exploiting children or Third World populations?

These are not easy questions. The answers require some serious thought and the solutions will demand creative thinking.

Enlightened companies take all these issues into consideration when developing corporate strategies. The added benefit for them is that their social responsibility can be a factor in recruiting and retaining good employees. How a company responds to the larger social issues makes a difference to employees. People want to be associated with companies that have a strong set of values that are demonstrated both in the marketplace and internally.

The following chapters will show you how successful companies have been socially responsible. We'll begin with the importance of demonstrating responsibility to employees.

KEY CONCEPTS

▶ Employees, customers, stockholders, and other stake-holders are taking into account what companies stand for when making decisions.

▶ Being socially responsible does not mean a lower shareholder return.

▶ Social responsibility includes:

  ▶ Environmental responsibility.

  ▶ Relationships with the community, both locally and globally.

  ▶ Relationships with employees.

  ▶ Relationships with customers.

  ▶ Taking the long view of corporate actions.

ACTION PLAN

• Determine what your company stands for, that is, what are the things you would do or not do regardless of the financial implications.

• Communicate these values to your employees, your customers, and your shareholders in both words and deeds.

• Make your values the framework for all decision making.

• Identify opportunities within and outside your company to demonstrate your company values.

Endnotes

1. Shellenbarger, Sue, Work and Family, *The Wall Street Journal*, March 19, 1997.
2. toms-of-maine.com, "Tom's Helps Out in Wake of Oil Spill" 1995–1996.

13

Responsibility to Employees

S ocial responsibility begins at home. The relationship the organization has with its employees is a defining factor for lean and meaningful companies. Customers, investors, and potential employees will be asking:

- How does a company handle employees during a down-sizing or a crisis?
- What are the company's wage and benefit standards?
- Do part-time, temps, and perma-temp workers replace full-time workers?
- Does the company have a diverse workforce that is treated equitably?
- Does the company take a strong stand against harassment of any kind?
- Does the company ensure the health and safety of its employees?

How would *your* company respond to these questions?

The news is filled with stories about companies that have neglected social responsibility to their employees. Over the long term, these organizations will have difficulty finding and keeping quality employees. As the labor market tightens, job searchers will seek out those companies that maintain a high standard of responsibility to their employees. These are the companies that will attract the caliber of workers they want and need.

One of the most compelling examples of a company taking social responsibility is the story of Malden Mills, Methuen, Massachusetts, and its CEO, Aaron Feuerstein. Newspapers carried the story of how this textile company that employed 2,400 workers was destroyed by fire. Feuerstein could have closed the mill and walked away, but he didn't. Instead he kept all the employees on the payroll at a cost of $1.5 million per week. The mill reopened and workers increased production from 130,000 yards of Polartec fabric to 200,000 yards per week. For Feuerstein it was a matter of doing what was right. Closing the mill would have effectively destroyed the local community.

Feuerstein acknowledges that he has been paid back tenfold by the loyalty and productivity of his workers. His advice to fellow CEOs is to brag, not about the stock options, but about the social responsibility and charity they show to their workers and their community.

Equal Pay and a Living Wage

People work to earn a living, at a standard that is reasonable for them. Workers are concerned about equity—fair pay regardless of gender, race, national origin—and a sensible relationship between compensation of hourly workers and seemingly grossly overpaid senior executives.

Taking a unique position in regard to compensation, Ben & Jerry's has put limits on executive compensation. It is part of their belief that if the company does well, everybody does well. Executive compensation is based on a ratio, currently 7:1, with one equaling the lowest wage plus benefits for a full-time employee, who has been with the company for a year. Minimum wage at Ben & Jerry's is $8.00 per hour and other salary increases are capped until the lowest salary reaches $8.25. In a state where the per capita income is about $17,500, the lowest-paid employee at Ben & Jerry's makes $22,000 including benefits.

Furthermore, 40 percent of the highest-paid employees are women and overall, women's compensation is very close to parity. In addition, 5 percent of pretax profits are shared with employees based on the number of months they've worked. Profit sharing is the same for everyone, regardless of whether the employee is in management or works on the floor packing ice cream.[1]

Full-Time, Part-Time, and Perma-Temps

In some industries there has been an increasing reliance on part-time rather than full-time workers or perma-temp workers, who work for extended periods of time. In either case, these workers are not given the same benefits as their full-time counterparts, even though they may have similarly responsible positions. Clearly there are some employees who prefer to work on this basis; however, there are many others who continue in these categories but would prefer full-time employment.

The positions that organizations take regarding how they use and compensate these workers will be important. Meaningful companies, because of the relationships they have with their employees, will take an equitable position between market expediencies and social responsibility.

One company already taking a stand is Hewlett-Packard. In an industry that is rapidly expanding its use of temporary and perma-temp workers, Hewlett-Packard is maintaining its usage of temp workers at only 10 percent of their total work-force. Because the knowledge and experience of these work-ers is valuable, lean and meaningful companies will restruc-ture their compensation and benefit programs to make them more equitable to all employees, regardless of classification.

Valuing Diversity

Establishing a corporate culture that values diversity is a key element for a socially responsible company. In an era of increasing globalization, the workforce is becoming less and less homogeneous. Because different cultures communicate in different ways, it is essential that companies help employ-ees understand and appreciate each other's differences. In addition, it is important to provide opportunities for people to get to know each other on a more informal basis.

Learning to Communicate in an Informal Setting

Work can often become too formal, too structured for people to really communicate openly. Many employees will be more comfortable opening up with each other in a more informal environment.

Ziegler's Ace Hardware, a Chicago-area chain of 10 retail stores, holds a birthday lunch each month. All employ-ees with a birthday that month are invited by letter to have lunch together in a nice restaurant that is convenient to all participants. The letter asks them to bring along at least one wish to share regarding what management could do to make their stores better places to work.

After the orders are placed, co-owner Brian Ziegler asks each employee, in turn, to introduce himself giving his name, position, store, and how long he's been with the company. After the introductions, all the birthday guests share their wishes. If the wishes are easy to grant, like a new electric stapler or calculator, the owners respond on the spot. More complicated wishes are reviewed by management and written responses are sent to employees within 30 days.

An increasing number of employers, where employees typically wear suits and heels, proclaim "casual dress" days on Fridays—or even every day (like MasterCard International in Purchase, New York). Within reasonable guidelines, workers are encouraged to wear more relaxing clothes . . . the "corporate casual" look. Clothing manufacturers, like Van Heusen and Levi Strauss, have developed entire lines of clothing to respond to the trend. Human resource professionals report that both productivity and morale are higher on dress-down days.

Some companies declare special dress days, usually around holidays. A dress theme such as Halloween, Christmas, or Independence Day, brings out creativity in workers. Costume days often include contests and some fun activities.

An IBM storage division in San Jose sponsors a diversity day. Employees dress in ethnic costumes, prepare ethnic food for each other, and perform traditional dances. The event helps people get to know more about each other and build a base of commonality while celebrating the differences. The IBM event was so successful that the company prepared a monthly bulletin to announce other diversity events in the community. To continue to support diversity in the workplace, videos on different cultures are shown around the plant where people gather.

Learning to acknowledge the differences and finding common ground are powerful tools in creating a strong workforce. Creating a corporate culture that is open and accepting of fun, personal styles, and other forms of diversity is essential to making employees feel valued by the organization and fellow workers.

Setting Goals to Increase Diversity

Setting goals is the key to accomplishing any task. Unless companies set diversity goals that can be measured, there is little chance that any significant changes will be made. It is easy to quantify the level of diversity in any organization. Once the company knows the demographics of its workplace, setting goals for change will give the process urgency and meaning.

It wasn't until CEO Ernie Drew made a commitment to diversity at Hoechst Celanese, a textile plant in North Carolina, that changes really occurred. He established a very specific program for increasing diversity, which included setting specific goals: by 2001, females and minorities will fill at least 34 percent of the positions at all levels of the company. Managers' performance evaluations are tied to the success of their diversity initiatives.

Because life experience is a very good teacher, senior executives at Hoechst Celanese are required to join two organizations where they are a minority. What employees learn in these environments cannot be taught in the classroom. The additional benefit is providing something to the community through employee involvement. Drew also actively pursues diversity in hiring new employees by working with universities that are known for their diverse student populations. The company provides guest lecturers, donations, scholarships, and summer jobs.[2]

In 1991, executives at Bank of Montreal realized that they were not utilizing or developing the women in their organization. This oversight was particularly significant because 75 percent of the workforce was women. The bank was still operating under old assumptions about women. For example: women would have babies and leave or women weren't suited for upper-level bank management positions. As a result of this corporate culture, only 9 percent of the 28,000 women employees held executive positions and only 13 percent were senior managers.

Faced with these discouraging numbers, the bank put together a task force to make changes. Not only were changes to be made, but they were to occur in a timely manner. The culture change was jump-started. By 1996, women accounted for 20 percent of senior executives and 22 percent of senior managers. By retaining these knowledgeable and experienced women, the leadership of the Bank of Montreal gained a business advantage. They had a more stable workforce and could benefit from the skill these women already had.

The task force that tackled the advancement of women has also taken on the issue of diversity for other employees. The bank now provides diversity training and promotes the benefits of a multicultural workforce that includes a Task Force for Employment of People with Disabilities, a Task Force on the Advancement of Visible Minorities, and a Task Force on the Advancement of Aboriginal Employment.

Recruiting and Hiring
Differently Abled Workers

An area where companies may not think about diversity is in hiring disabled or "differently abled" workers. While the federal law mandates certain standards about discrimination, enlightened companies actively recruit people from this group because they can be exceptional employees.

In 1996 Dupont Merck hired eight developmentally disabled workers through a nonprofit organization called Rights of Citizens with Mental Retardation in Delaware. In addition to hiring these workers, DuPont Merck helped pay for two facilities to house residents in the program.

To be successful in the hiring of mentally disabled workers, begin with clear job descriptions and expectations. Carefully match jobs with prospective employees. DuPont Merck assigned a mentor to help the workers get off to a good start. This investment is similar to what you should do with any other new hire. These employees have been an asset to the organization, handling essential support tasks such as answering phones, copying, and making deliveries.

The American Association for the Advancement of Science helped identify disabled students at the college and graduate level to work with IBM. Looking for people interested in computer programming and engineering, IBM hired ten interns the first year and to date has sixteen working throughout the United States. IBM has always been proactive in this area and began preparing for the Americans with Disabilities Act (ADA) a year before it was enacted.

The Marriott Foundation works with disabled high school seniors through a program they call "Bridges." Their goal is to link these students with local employers. Since its beginnings in 1989, they have placed more than 2,700 students in paid internships around the country. Even better, 87 percent of the students they place end up with permanent jobs at the company where they intern.

Sears, Roebuck and Company also uses interns, including disabled workers. Physically challenged workers do not usually consider retail careers. Through internships, Sears shows the many opportunities that are available for disabled workers to make satisfying contributions in the retail environment.

Resources for Hiring Disabled Workers

If you are considering hiring disabled workers, you may want to contact the President's Committee on the Employment of People with Disabilities. They maintain a database of 1,100 job candidates that have been prescreened in personal interviews. The database includes information about the workers' skill levels and qualifications.

You can access this information by calling the President's Committee at 202-376-6200 or by e-mail at info@ pcepd.gov. The Committee's web site address is www.pcepd. gov. One added benefit to organizations that hire disabled workers is that they change jobs much less frequently and are genuinely glad to be working.[3]

Developing a Diversity Program

There are many resources available to assist you in establishing your diversity programs. What follows is a list of things to consider when you are developing or evaluating the programs in your company.

- Provide awareness through education on an ongoing basis. One seminar will not be effective in establishing a corporate culture that is open to diversity.
- Get employees involved. If your company is large enough, get employees from different groups and backgrounds involved in presenting workshops on diversity. The best way to open people's minds about disabled workers is to see for themselves how well these workers can perform their jobs.
- Make work groups and decision-making groups models of diversity.
- Evaluate and reward employees for behaviors that support diversity. Respect and cooperation among diverse employee groups is essential for a company to be profitable and socially responsible.

Welfare to Work

In a tight labor market, the Welfare to Work program creates a new source of entry-level employees. As a result of federal welfare reform, there will be nearly 4 million people looking for work. This labor pool is diverse, with 36 percent white, 37 percent African American, and 21 percent Hispanic. Of the women in this group, over two-thirds have had recent work experience, prior to going on assistance. Not surprisingly, welfare mothers are most often the sole breadwinners for the family. These individuals can be valuable employees with minimal job readiness training and retention services.

Businesses that already hire former welfare recipients find that they have motivated, trainable employees, and—best of all—low turnover rates. United Airlines has hired over 360 former welfare recipients. Their track record is very good, with the turnover rate among these employees only half that of employees not drawn from public assistance rolls. As employers bring these people into the workforce, they strengthen the community both economically and socially.

A nonprofit organization called The Partnership can help employers recruit welfare-to-work employees. The Partnership offers publications, a toll-free number for information, and a web page (www.welfaretowork.org). There are no dues or requirements to belong, but participants are asked to "have hired or pledge to hire at least one person off public assistance without displacing existing workers."

Maintaining a
Harassment-Free Workplace

In addition to supporting diversity, companies have a responsibility to maintain a work environment that is free of every kind of harassment. While the law requires certain policies and procedures regarding harassment, the prevailing culture may not support them. It is essential that employees know what constitutes harassment and procedures for reporting incidents.

While the financial impact of a failure to comply with the law is well known, there are other costs that usually go unnoticed in an environment where harassment is tolerated. Lost productivity through absenteeism and employee turnover due to a hostile work environment can have a significant negative impact on any business. The cost of these intangible factors is substantial.

Sometimes it is best to look outside your company for

assistance in these areas. There are a number of highly qualified consultants who can help you through employee training and coaching to resolve issues surrounding harassment. The investment in time and money will reap rewards by creating a work environment where everyone feels safe, comfortable and able to give their best performance.

Employee Discounts

When the company's products or services are of value to consumers, offering discounts on merchandise provides a measurable value to employees. There's also a feeling of pride when people purchase and use what they helped produce. Employees of Vanity Fair Corporation, Greensboro, North Carolina, are eligible to shop in a company store that offers Wrangler® clothing manufactured by a subsidiary. You can be sure they appreciate the discounted prices . . . and wear the products with pride.

Most companies offer the advantage of employee discounts on a year-round basis, but some make it a special event as well. Ziegler's Ace Hardware hosts a family night in November each year. The two-hour open house features a sundae bar (with one of the owners serving) and discounts of 35 percent or pricing at 5 to 10 percent over cost, depending on the item.

Employees are invited to bring their immediate families, and Ziegler's definition is very liberal—parents, brothers and sisters, cousins, grandparents. The popular experience, scheduled late on a Sunday when the store is normally closed, gives people an opportunity to buy everything from nuts and bolts to snowblowers.

Physical Safety

Employees' physical safety and health are also a part of being socially responsible. Companies must maintain an environment that is free from pollutants that are hazardous to employees, including second-hand cigarette smoke. Equipment and machinery should have regular maintenance, so that workers feel secure operating them. Floors need to be clean and free from debris that could cause a fall. Ventilation needs to be good and temperatures moderate, taking into consideration the exposure to natural weather elements.

Office workers need some of the same protections. Most recently the awareness of the ergonomic issues surrounding carpal tunnel syndrome and repetitive stress disorder has increased. The effects of poor workstations on employees' physical health will increase as more and more people spend long hours in sedentary tasks.

For the health of your workforce, be sure that you have a complete and current safety program in place. Obviously, the urgency in a manufacturing environment is greater than in a service organization, but it is good business to protect employees in the workplace from hazards to their health.

To make your safety program most effective, involve staff members from various parts of the organization. By involving people from a broad range of disciplines and viewpoints, the program will be more thorough and more effective. Different perspectives of how to address issues and correct problems will be helpful to increasing the value of the program. The side benefit of using employees from various parts of the organization is that it will develop teamwork, allow employees to get to know each other, and create pride of authorship in the process.

Safety programs are prevalent in many organizations, though not thought of as part of "meaningfulness." An effective safety program prevents lost-time accidents . . . and *that* is certainly meaningful!

Bill Lutsch, President of Farm Fresh Bakery in Lawton, Oklahoma, credits his managers and employees with the innovation that has kept his bakery on the leading edge. Farm Fresh's safety program is second to none in his industry. The folks in charge at this bakery make great efforts to reinforce responsibilities and clarify expectations.

The results of their safety program are dramatic. The entire company has not had an accident or any other workers' compensation loss in over three years. As of this writing, the shipping department has enjoyed over 4,600 days without an accident—that's over 12 years!

Of course, Lutsch rewards his employees for their vigilance. With frequent raffles and drawings—monthly and yearly—employees have won pick-up trucks, washers, dryers, cash, and other items the committee decided were appropriate. One year Lutsch and his Director of Safety rewarded the production and sanitation crews by wearing hula skirts while roasting a pig for lunch. This kind of fun bonds employees to the company and encourages employees to be careful.

Cardinal Meat Specialists emphasizes safety with periodic reminders (like mugs or sweatshirts), an aggressive communications system, and an annual dinner dance and awards night. The program is working: the meat processing company has enjoyed six years without a lost-time accident.

The relationship of an organization and its employees must evolve into one of mutual respect. Those companies that demonstrate their commitment by creating such a workplace will attract and keep the very best employees. In doing so, they will be able to compete more effectively in the marketplace and continue to be viable into the next century. Those who fail to make the transition not only risk loss of market share, but face the possibilities of extensive and costly legal struggles.

Responsibility to Employees During Downsizing

To get "lean" and stay "lean" some organizations will need to continue their reengineering efforts. Employees need not merely be dismissed with a pink slip and a wave. Socially responsible organizations are finding more effective ways to cut costs and minimize involuntary separations. One of the most unlikely places to find such an attitude is the federal government. But that's exactly where *Workforce* Magazine found its 1998 Optimas Award winner in the category of Managing Change.

The U.S. Office of Personnel Management (OPM), in response to President Clinton's initiative to create a more efficient and cost-effective government, has reduced its workforce by 48 percent and decreased its expenses by 33 percent. Even more remarkable is that 96 percent of the employees whose jobs were eliminated have been placed in other positions.

To accomplish this kind of significant downsizing without massive layoffs, OPM came up with nearly 30 options. They recommended things like job sharing, furloughs, voluntary reassignment, and retraining. The key to the success of any downsizing process is to keep a clear focus on the objectives. The desired results—for the employers and the workers—will be determine what kinds of options work best.

OPM also established a comprehensive career assessment center for federal employees. The center provides counseling, training, career resources, and job-search assistance. In addition, access is also available through the center's web site.

OPM applied one unique strategy to salvage a floundering division—privatization. Using an approach unheard of in American government, OPM developed an Employee Stock Ownership Plan for the employees in its investigation unit. This division had lost money for 10 years; but rather than close it down, the division was recreated as a private, employee-owned entity.

The objectives of the new company were to serve the tax payers and make a smooth transition without diminishing quality for the federal agencies that were its customers. They were also charged with ensuring that the new partnership was in the best interest of the employees and their unions. It wasn't an easy road, but the new company, called United States Investigations Services, Inc. (USIS, Inc.), was able to reduce the price of services by 18 percent, saving federal agencies nearly $1 million each year. Tax payers came out on top, too, with a value of $14.7 million, which will continue over the next five years of the contract USIS has with OPM.[4]

If the federal government can downsize and place nearly all of the employees, surely a large company can do the same. The key element is keeping the goals in focus and being open to multiple options beyond letting workers go. Enlightened companies keep employees, their most valuable asset, and capitalize on their knowledge by creatively reworking the system to meet new challenges.

Be sure that your company takes a stand now and builds a strong, socially responsible relationship with all your employees. Corporate responsibility reaches beyond the walls of the company. Astute employers also demonstrate their responsibility as citizens of their communities. On to Chapter 14 . . .

KEY CONCEPTS

Social responsibility to employees includes:
- Providing equal pay and a living wage.
- Valuing diversity in the workplace.
- Supporting welfare-to-work programs.
- Maintaining a workplace free from harassment.
- Creating a safe physical environment for workers.

ACTION PLAN

Compensation
- Review the current salary/wage structure to ensure that it is equitable.
- If you find inequities, develop a financial strategy to equalize compensation.
- Examine the use of temps or part-time workers.
- Set limits on the number of workers in these classifications.
- Restructure the benefit qualifications to include these workers in some way.

Diversity
- Assess and evaluate your workplace diversity.
- If there is little diversity, set goals and develop a strategy to recruit employees from more diverse backgrounds.
- Provide training within the organization about valuing diversity.
- Consider ways to hire disabled workers.
- Include diversity management as part of performance evaluations for upper-level managers.

Harassment

- Review harassment policies and procedures to ensure they are effective.
- Respond immediately and thoroughly to all complaints.
- Provide ongoing training on harassment issues.

Physical safety

- Review all current safety programs.
- Involve employees in developing and implementing safety programs.
- Provide ongoing training on safety compliance.
- Consider an incentive program for outstanding safety records.
- Review the ergonomics of clerical and service staff work space.

Endnotes

1. Laabs, Jennifer, "Ben and Jerry's Caring Capitalism," *Personnel Journal*, November 1992.
2. Rice, Fay, "How to Make Diversity Pay," *Fortune*, August 8, 1994, pp. 79–86.
3. Sugarman, Jolene, "Willing and Able," *Human Resource Executive*, August 1997.
4. Sunoo, Brenda Park, "Reinventing Government," *Workforce*, February 1998. (p. 211)

14

Responsibility to the Local Community

Community involvement is a way for companies to demonstrate that they are good corporate citizens. While some kinds of involvement can have far-reaching impacts on society at large, other activities are about neighbors helping neighbors. That helping can come in many forms. Sometimes donations of money can be very effective; other times direct employee involvement has the greatest effect on the community.

Regardless of how you contribute, it makes good business sense to be involved, since people like to do business with people they know. Your company's involvement in the community lets your customers know that you are willing to give something back to the people that make your business possible.

There is another benefit to community involvement. How a company interacts with the community makes a difference in how employees feel about their organization. When employees know not only what significance their job has in the company, but what significance the company has the community, it makes their work more meaningful. Employees value, and feel proud to be associated with, a company that is active in supporting the community. When employees are encouraged to make their own commitments to the community, it increases their personal sense of meaning and value, as well as loyalty to the company.

The Increasing Need for Volunteers

In the current work environment, people barely have enough time to take care of their job and family responsibilities. Many people feel that there is virtually no time left over to volunteer for nonprofit organizations. This deficiency of volunteers was brought to the fore when a group of Chicago ministers developed a program to mentor troubled teenagers. They were able to get foundation money to start the program and recruit an initial group of volunteers. Unfortunately, they couldn't schedule adequate training for the prospective mentors. With only Saturdays available to train, the program has not gotten off the ground . . . even after two years. Unfortunately, this program is only one example of many across the country with similar challenges.

With increasing demands on our time and money, people have less time to volunteer and less to give financially. In 1995, 68.5 percent of American households gave to charity, which included contributions to churches, a 6.6 percent drop from the 75.1 percent contributing in 1989. The same kind of decline is seen in volunteerism. In 1989 there were 98.4 million volunteers, about 54.4 percent of adults, but in 1995 the number dropped to 93 million, or less than 50 percent. The statistics indicate that, although the numbers are decreasing, Americans are motivated to support community organizations. A possible cause for dropping numbers is the increase in the number of hours spent at work, as well as increasing child- and eldercare responsibilities.

Given this decline in individual giving and the decrease in government funding, General Colin Powell called upon businesses and individuals to fill the gap and get involved in their communities. His movement, America's Promise, asks that all Americans make a commitment to be sure that 2 million children have the five basic resources they need by the year 2000. The basics are a caring adult, a safe place, a healthy start, a marketable skill, and a chance to give back to the community. He has enrolled businesses, individuals, local governments, and Chambers of Commerce to help America's Promise meet these goals for the nation's children. The individuals and companies that have made commitments are too numerous to name, but here are just a few.

- A Chamber of Commerce in Lancaster County, Pennsylvania, has a book filled with pledges of its members to provide at least one of the five basic resources.

- The owners of a local dinner theater in Pennsylvania ask their employees for ideas to implement the five basic goals. The proprietors also ask for their employees' personal commitments to accomplish those goals.

- In St. Louis, a volunteer fair was held at a shopping center where representatives from community service organizations were available to talk with people to let them know how they could contribute. In these one-on-one meetings, people were able to learn how they could contribute to a community service organization in their community.

- Allstate insurance CEO, Jerry Choate, sits on the board of America's Promise and his company has pledged over

$25 million in support of the organization. In addition, when Colin Powell spoke to the Allstate employees in Northbrook, Illinois, the event was broadcast to the 50,000 other employees at Allstate.

- At a summit meeting in West Virginia, it was announced that the state would be able to exceed its original goal of providing resources to 20,000 youngsters. General Powell is encouraging every state and every community to commit to being States and Communities of Promise and as such, hold summits of their own to enlist support for America's Promise.

- The Boys and Girls Clubs are already responding to the call to give something back to the community. At the annual Congressional Breakfast of the Boys and Girls Clubs of America, they presented General Powell with a book of pledges of their commitments for community service. The America's Promise campaign provides a focal point for any organization to develop its own community service program.[1]

Your company can take advantage of this national movement to boost volunteerism. Jump on the bandwagon by encouraging your employees to volunteer on their own, establishing company community service program(s) that people can join, and/or make corporate pledges to support local (or national) service organizations with funds, time, equipment, product, space, or other resources. Emphasizing how your company and your people can make a positive difference is a message that will be well received by your stakeholders.

Volunteerism Benefits
Employees at Work

Companies that actively participate in community service have found that their employees are actually more productive on the job. Spending time in a completely different environment can refresh employees and give them a better sense of purpose. Employees who volunteer are 10 times more likely to report that they are in good health than those who do not volunteer. And these employees also report that they feel happier and more confident at work.[2]

When employees are more involved in the community, companies experience lower turnover and a stronger reputation that aids in recruiting new employees. In a tight labor market, recruits seek employers that share their values. Those values often include commitments to the community.

Many companies focus their community involvement energies on supporting their local United Way organizations. In addition to the fund drives, some employers encourage their people to participate in charity walks or special project days. Armstrong World Industries, headquartered in Lancaster, Pennsylvania, participates in the United Way's annual Day of Caring. In 1997, over 300 of the company's employees invested half of a day on a Saturday helping United Way agencies in the community.

In addition, employees who volunteer for community activities seem to be more adaptable in the face of organizational change. At a time when flexibility is highly desired by companies and demanded by the marketplace, an activity that increases employee adaptability is highly beneficial.

When employees from the same company work together on a project, they are able to bond much more effectively as a team. In some cases, employees demonstrate leadership abilities that might not have been discovered without the experience.

One of the largest catalog companies in the country, Arizona Mail Order, located in Tucson, Arizona, knows how this teamwork can benefit the company and the local community. Every December holiday season, each department adopts a needy family from the local community. The department holds in-company bake sales and looks for other ways to raise money. Team members shop together for the food and gifts; then on Christmas Eve, the department, as a group, delivers the goodies to the needy family.

Can you imagine how the team members feel as they look into the smiling faces of their recipients? Can you imagine how that bonds them as a team? The Adopt-A-Family program is a heart-warming example of how—*at no cost to the company*—an organization can provide service to the community and to its employees at the same time.

Volunteerism Based on Business Expertise

The volunteer experience can be expressed in many different ways. Some companies choose to have employees volunteer time in their own area of expertise. For example, Lens Crafters has its employees donate time giving eye exams, while Home Depot is active in its support of Habitat for Humanity.

PetSmart, a chain of pet product stores, supports its business by sponsoring "adopt-a-pet" community service events. CEO Mark Hansen bases his company on taking good care of animals, so by encouraging customers to find their pet from the many animals at the pound, he demonstrates company values and provides a community service at the same time. Customers and employees feel good about the events and PetSmart's values.[3]

Community Service Based on Business Expertise

Home Depot Corporation focuses its community involvement in three areas that affect its business: affordable housing, the environment, and preparing at-risk youth for the job market. Capitalizing on their business of building supplies, they donate products to Habitat for Humanity and give seminars to customers on how to make their homes more energy-efficient.

Their commitment to at-risk youth works well for them on a business level because they hire up to 500 entry-level employees per week. The time spent with these young people teaching them about getting jobs has a value beyond Home Depot's hiring needs. When at-risk youth find they really have the option of being employed, it changes their whole outlook. Adding them to the workforce can increase the socioeconomic level of the whole community. Those who are successful at the entry level can provide powerful role models for other at-risk kids. In this situation the community at large receives a benefit and so does the Home Depot Corporation.

Giving Employees Time Off to Volunteer

In a *USA TODAY*/CNN/Gallup Poll, researchers found that 51 percent of the employees surveyed would take time off to volunteer in the community if the company paid for it. A number of companies are doing just that.

- KPMG Peat Marwick and Brink's Home Security give one day off per year to every employee to volunteer in community service.
- Kimberly Clark Corporation donates $2 million as well as the time of thousands of employees to build playgrounds.
- Time Warner is contributing 1 million employee volunteer hours by the year 2000 to provide literacy tutoring.
- Timberland employees may use up to 40 hours paid time per year for volunteer work.
- Federated Department Stores donates 50,000 employee hours for tutoring and mentoring.
- The Walt Disney Company is committed to contribute 1 million volunteer hours through the year 2000.
- The American Booksellers Association will enroll 50,000 employees and customers to tutor children in reading.

- The National Football League Players Association will bring together both active and retired players to mentor Native American teenagers.

Some of these efforts are in response to the America's Promise campaign, but many companies have been involved in this kind of activity for years. Your contribution does not have to be on a grand scale; do what is appropriate for your company and your people.

Some employees at Citibank spend vacations working with Operation Smile, a nonprofit organization that supports volunteer plastic surgeons to help children with facial deformities in impoverished countries. The Citibank employees, who may have never met each other, find power in teams as they work for the common goal of restoring children's hope in the future.

Financial Contributions

Corporations have also committed big dollars to community service. While the amounts shown here may be far beyond your budget, remember that a few hundred dollars to a local group may have a substantial impact.

- Coca-Cola committed a total of $100 million to recruit at-risk teens that will serve as tutors and mentors for elementary school children.

- Ronald McDonald House will donate $100 million to help in the prevention of child abuse and teen suicide. McDonald's already has a well-deserved reputation for reaching out through a number of national and local efforts to strengthen communities.

- General Mills supports education through a $2.1 million grant for scholarships for troubled children.

- Pfizer is contributing $5 million to community health centers through grants and medicines.[4]

- The Ronald McDonald charities receive support from AT&T Wireless Services and their customers. The original marketing promotion was that AT&T would give a free cellular phone to any customer that donated $25 to the Ronald McDonald charities. After three years of donations, AT&T Wireless makes the donation themselves and still gives the customer the free phone. Contributions to date exceed $457,000.

- HA-LO Industries is known for its charitable work. Each year, the company sends hundreds of underprivileged children to professional sporting events. The HA-LO Kids Heaven program has provided free tickets to Chicago Bulls and Chicago White Sox games for years. In 1998, 2,400 of these deserving kids will attend Chicago Cubs games as HA-LO supports its hometown of Chicago.

Community Services
a Corporate Value

At Warner Lambert's Consumer Healthcare division, they consider not only the competencies and skills of prospective new hires, but also their commitment to society through community involvement. The company culture is so strongly influenced by their commitment to community involvement, that how an employee values community service plays a key role in determining how compatible the worker is with the company.

Warner Lambert also supports Operation Smile with donations and a unique approach to sales incentives. Rather than the standard vacation or list of prize options, the top sales people have a child sponsored in their names in Operation Smile. So far this program has shown itself to be a powerful motivator for the sales staff.

Matching Employee Contributions

For employees who make financial donations, Warner Lambert makes a matching contribution. When employees have the backing of a large corporation, they can have a much greater impact on their chosen programs. Gateway 2000 also supports employee involvement in community activities. When requests come in to Gateway to participate on a board, they find employees who have an interest in the particular area and refer them. Gateway provides matching funds for employee contributions, because they know that board positions require a certain amount of fund raising.[5]

To increase contributions to charitable organizations by employees, Computer Associates of Islandia, New York, decided to match donations at the rate of 200 percent. The new matching program had its effect and employee contributions increased. Not only does the company match employee funds, but it also makes corporate contributions to organizations such as Make A Wish Foundation and Operation Smile.[6]

Employees Decide How to Serve the Community

It is important to keep the volunteer programs meaningful to the employees. To that end, some companies let employees choose how and when to spend their volunteer time. While one employee might volunteer for an AIDS project, another might spend time with a community arts foundation.

Encouraging employees to find their own ways to contribute is an important component of Warner Lambert's commitment to the community. The company is so large that it relies on employees to know what's most important in their local communities. Employees choose within the broad parameters of health care, education, civic, and social activities. Letting employees run with an idea can produce a tremendous result. When a new employee was looking to fill her holiday time, Evelyn Self, the Director of Community Affairs at Warner Lambert, gave her some ideas. Soon, the employee had connected with the Salvation Army on Project Angel Tree and more than 2,000 gifts were distributed to children through the generosity of Warner Lambert employees.

At Ben & Jerry's social responsibility is a core value. It even appears as part of their mission statement. The corporation holds social responsibility, inside and outside the organization, at the same value level as being profitable for shareholders. Each year, Ben & Jerry's contributes 7.5 percent of pretax profits to a cause that both the owners and the workers choose together.

Ben & Jerry's also encourages employees to develop their own programs for community service. Employees are paid their regular wages and may spend up to 50 hours a year in community service. During slow summer and fall months of 1991, when Ben & Jerry's needed to close down the second shift in Springfield Vermont, 35 of the workers stayed on the payroll at their regular rate. These employees spent their time doing work in the community—doing everything from painting fire hydrants to winterizing homes for the elderly and families with a disabled member. They were also able to put on a benefit at Halloween to support local children's causes.[7]

One of the reasons Ben & Jerry's has such a successful community service program is that they rely on employees to come up with the ideas for the corporate involvement. In this way the organization not only meets the diverse needs of the community, but also demonstrates its commitment to the corporate mission statement.

One of the latest projects is to provide the resources for all children to have access to the Internet through the "Lids for Kids" project. For every product lid sent to Ben & Jerry's by consumers of their products, 10 cents will be donated to grassroots organizations to connect schools to the Internet.

Ben & Jerry's has co-ventured this project with Yahoo, an Internet search engine provider. To promote consumer participation in this program, every lid enters the consumer in a sweepstakes to win a lifetime supply of ice cream and a trip to Vermont.

The employees of T.G.I.Friday's raised money for the Texas Special Olympics by pulling an airplane. While they didn't win the competition, working together raising money and attending the event was a great teambuilder.[8]

When the huge flood hit Fargo, North Dakota, the 3M company sent $1 million in cash and products to help out. The company agreed to match gifts of employees and retirees up to $700,000. As if that weren't enough, the employees at 3M in Minneapolis went to help their North Dakota neighbors, too, volunteering their time to help with cleanup. They even collected hoses and rakes to take along. This generosity is an example of the company and the employees working together to make an impact on the community.

Businesses, both large and small, have found that employees want to be associated with companies that are "doing the right thing." Such involvement enhances how the employees feel—not only about the company, but also about themselves by being associated with such an upstanding organization. Increasingly, customers are also making decisions based on what companies stand for—particularly when it comes to smaller businesses. People want to do business with people they know and people who are involved the issues that concern them.

The president of the North American subsidiary of Aladdin Knowledge Systems, Ami Dar, developed a non-profit organization called Action Without Borders that links volunteers from around the world. Dar says, "Even the smallest companies and the busiest people can make a big difference. Start by changing your perspective. Recognize that your company has a lot to offer—whatever its size."[9]

Here are some more ideas, illustrated with examples of

some things smaller companies are doing in their communities.

Make a Donation and Challenge Others to Do the Same

Corporations can provide a valuable service by pledging seed money to charitable organizations. One strategy is to donate a specified amount of money to a cause, say National Public Radio, if other supporters will match the funds within some certain period of time. This approach gives the community group valuable leverage in encouraging other companies or individuals to contribute.

Powell's Lumber & Ace Home Center in Rolla, Missouri, has supported the community for years by sponsoring sports teams. For the company's 85th anniversary, management wanted to do something special. In keeping with the 85th anniversary theme, they donated $100 for each year in business to help get new sports fields built. They also enlisted community support, challenging other businesses in the area to make the same kind of contribution. These caring community leaders got customers involved, sponsored a car wash, and sold hot dogs. This overall campaign generated $10,391 to begin the ball park expansion. Along the way, they involved the whole community.[10]

Donate Equipment, Supplies, or Products to a Nonprofit Organization

Consider what products or services you manufacture or sell that might have value to community organizations. Either make direct donations, sell the merchandise at cost, or provide merchandise or services that can be raffled, auctioned, or used as door prizes. Remember that community organizations—and schools—need computers and other technology. What may be obsolete for you could be of tremendous value to a deserving group.

One young entrepreneur, Kevin Bristol, wanted to be sure he gave something back to his community. This young man started his own personal pager company in Baltimore, competing with plenty of larger companies. Now his company has 8,000 subscribers and nine locations. Kevin gave back to the community by donating 25 pagers to a local hospital to be used by expectant fathers, patients waiting for transplants, and families with members in shock trauma.[11]

Klosterman's Bakery in Cincinnati is deeply committed to its community. The bakery regularly donates first quality product straight off of the bakery line to two local nonprofit organizations. One local nonprofit, called The Free Store, coordinates food distribution to needy families in the area. The Food Pantry of the Bond Hill Presbyterian Church, located near Klosterman's corporate office and one of its bakeries, regularly feeds 8 to 10 underprivileged families. The bakery supplies all of the bread products for this worthy cause as well. Klosterman's employees take pride in serving the local community.

Community involvement doesn't have to be big to be valuable. If you are a small business, consider donations other than cash. Nonprofit organizations are always in need of office supplies and machines, food, clothing, and volunteer hours. Sometimes a very small gift is all it takes to get a project off the ground. A quick call to your favorite local charity—a neighborhood school, a church, or a nearby homeless shelter—will elicit their wish list.

You may discover many items gathering dust in your storage closets, consuming very little space. Consider equipment and supplies you're no longer using, as well as what your employees may want to bring in and donate. Your company receives a tax deduction, and you also gain points with your people.

McGunn Safe Company launched an early childhood literacy program with only $1,500. The company added to the contribution by having employees ask for used book donations to build the children's library. Consider offering seed money and volunteers to help organizations get started.

Partner with a Nonprofit

Find a nonprofit organization that is similar in size to your company. Then you can grow together. Be sure to find ways for employees to help where they can. Local Chambers of Commerce or trade associations most likely have fundraisers like golf tournaments or children's fairs that could benefit significantly from your participation.

If you would like to be involved with a large charitable organization, look for activities that partner smaller companies with larger ones. An example is the American Express "Dine Across America" program. American Express subsidized the big expenses like administration and advertising, but local restaurants participate by donating the proceeds from a particular entree to the fund or asking customers to add a donation to their credit card bills.[12]

Every community has opportunities for companies—and their employees—to make a valuable contribution. San Antonio, Texas, like many cities, has people who need greater knowledge of life skills to become more self-sufficient. The local Tourism Council developed a relationship with St. Phillips College to provide volunteers from member companies to work with the Adult Literacy for Life program.

Advantage Rent-A-Car and its sister company, Star Shuttle and Charter, agreed to become the pilot group to serve as tutors and mentors. Their work established the benchmark for how corporate volunteers would help these adults who are deficient in some basic life skills, helping them become more productive members of society. The community service was accomplished on Saturdays for a month.

Use Your Business Space
for the Community

Judy Wicks, founder and president of the White Dog Cafe in Philadelphia, Pennsylvania, knows that a restaurant is more than just a place to get something to eat. She sees her restaurant as a place to help build a sense of community. In developing her business, she built in social goals as well as business goals.

The nationally known restaurant is now a major center for community involvement. The White Dog Cafe won the Business Enterprise Trust Award for combining business management and social vision. Wicks believes that "social change isn't about heroic gestures. It happens gradually and with the help of many people."[13]

Support School Fund-Raisers

Most communities have a high school band that could use additional financial resources. A typical fund-raising strategy is for the band students to stage car washes. Call the band director to learn how much the band usually earns for a day's car wash, then offer that amount or more for the students to come to your business and wash cars for all your employees. Your donation will be appreciated and your employees will love having their cars washed. For a real bonus, provide the same service for customers who visit you that day. You'll be supporting your employees, their families, and the community.

Partner with Other Businesses
for a Special Project

Elliot and Gail Hoffman, the owners of Just Desserts, a bakery in San Francisco, put together a coalition of businesses to renovate a local school. Mobilizing 800 business volunteers, including some of the biggest corporations in the area, Hoffman and their crew took $280,000 in donated supplies to a neighborhood school and completely renovated the property.

Their purpose in the school project extended beyond the renovation itself. For the Hoffmans, the project was a way to give people the opportunity for community involvement, to volunteer, to make a difference. Elliot Hoffman believes that there are many people who, given the opportunity to participate, will gladly get involved to serve the community.[14]

There are more opportunities for community involvement than we could ever list here.

Ideas to Get You Started

We've begun a list that may spark ideas that meet needs in your particular community. How about . . .

- Support holiday activities such as Toys for Tots through the Marine Corps.
- Work with local missions and homeless shelters to serve food on holidays or at other special times.
- Collect and distribute clothing, toys, or furniture for those in your community that need them.
- Provide financial support to help pay utility bills when cash-hungry people need help.
- Furnish blankets and care packages for the elderly during harsh winter months.
- Donate a van to a nonprofit for childcare, eldercare, or medical care transportation.
- Engage in year-round support of a local food bank.
- Provide tutors and equipment for schools that need them.
- Design and implement ongoing support programs for inner-city or poverty-level children who need everything.
- Offer support to elders living alone, who may need home

maintenance or just someone to come by to visit.

• Sponsor or start an athletic program for kids—baseball, soccer, volleyball—even chess!

• Support a local Boy Scout or Girl Scout troop through volunteering or funding.

The list can go on and on. Survey your employees to find out if and how *they* are involved already as a volunteer or know about an organization that could use your support. Brainstorm together to develop ways to have the most impact on the community with whatever resources you have available. Since people support what they help to create, getting people involved from the design phase makes a lot of sense.

Beyond Volunteerism:
Responsibility to the Local Economy

When a company is involved in its community, employees, applicants, and other stakeholders see—and support—that local emphasis. Everyone is concerned about local economic health, so when corporations champion the local economy, they make a positive difference inside and outside their company.

You don't have to be a large business to have a significant local impact. Small business is the backbone of the economy. What happens in the local economy will affect every business, regardless of its size. Evolving companies understand this connection and seek ways to support local economies. This commitment to help small businesses stand on their own will ultimately result in a stronger economy and increased profitability for businesses across the board. Like other examples of social responsibility, organizations that include supporting the local economy as part of being good corporate citizens will have a more loyal, productive workforce . . . people feel good about working for organizations that are good corporate citizens.

Using Buying Power to Make a Difference

Your customers are critical to the success of your organization. Being a customer for area companies enables you to support the local economy while improving your own profitability. A stronger economy means more customers—for everyone. While it's easy to buy from the big name suppliers, choosing to do business with a small or minority-owned business can have an effect on the community and economy at large. For many of these small business owners, even a small sale of product to your company can make the difference between staying in business and closing their doors.

Look for Certified Businesses

Companies sometimes hesitate to buy from a lesser-known supplier because of concern about the quality of the goods and services. Whenever you purchase from any company, large or small, it is important to do your homework. One of the ways to find out about a small or minority-owned company is to inquire if they are "certified." Many minority- and women-owned businesses are certified by various government agencies and large corporations to be placed on their lists of suppliers.

To be on these lists, the companies must submit a comprehensive package of information about their ownership and operations. Asking a vendor if it is certified to do business with the government or large corporations may offer some indication of the stability of the business. There are also a number of organizations that can help you find the right minority vendors.

A Resource for Finding Minority-Owned Vendors

The National Minority Supplier Development Council (NMSDC) certifies minority-owned vendors and links them with other companies. The NMSDC has a database of more than 15,000 certified minority businesses. In addition to pairing companies and vendors, the organization helps minority businesses with the capital they need to fulfill purchase orders. You do not have to sever your relationships with current suppliers to support minority businesses. Just add the names of small and minority-owned businesses to a list for consideration when making new purchases.

Buying at a Fair Market Price

Ben & Jerry's and Stoneyfield Farms support local economies by purchasing milk products from the local dairies. Not only do both companies buy local products, but they also pay a premium. Given their size, they are both in a position to demand lower prices from local dairies based on volume. However, neither company does so, believing that their vendors deserve a fair price for their products.

Support Vendors by Sharing Business Knowledge

When Ben & Jerry's needed brownies for one of their ice cream flavors, they went to Greystone Bakery, a company affiliated with a Zen monastery that provides jobs and training for homeless and unemployable people in Yonkers, New York. After using the brownies for a while, Ben & Jerry's discovered some quality problems. Rather than change vendors, they worked with the company to address issues and improve the quality. Now Greystone Bakery sells about $3 million of brownies per year to Ben & Jerry's and the quality is superb.

Ben & Jerry's also purchases ingredients from La Soul Bakery, Newark, New Jersey, a company that employs former convicts and recovering drug addicts. Again, Ben & Jerry's made a commitment to help the business grow, not only by purchasing product, but also by sharing their expertise. Employees from finance, manufacturing, and quality control invested time sharing their knowledge with both Greystone Bakery and La Soul Bakery. The Ben & Jerry's employees who helped develop these suppliers received the added benefit of seeing the value they could have in the community.[15]

Partnering to Integrate
Business and Social Issues

The local economy also creates opportunities to address social issues. With little time and effort, minor modifications in the way you do business can make a big difference in your community. Your business has tremendous power to help others at little or no cost—and earn an even more positive reputation.

Catherine Sneed, a counselor at the San Francisco County Jail, developed a gardening project on prison grounds as a way to support counseling with inmates at the prison. Elliot and Gail Hoffman, owners of Just Desserts, learned about what Sneed was doing and offered a piece of land near their bakery to be used as a garden plot. They agreed to buy the produce at market price to use in their products. Now the produce is purchased by a number of businesses, including Ben & Jerry's and Chez Panisse, the famous Berkeley restaurant owned by Alice Waters.

The Hoffmans didn't stop at just buying produce from the Garden Project. Participants in the program learn life skills like opening a bank account and being at work on time. The Hoffmans hire graduates of the program. In keeping with the goal of teaching life skills, graduates must go through a complete interview process to be hired.[16] By supporting the garden project, this company took action to help with a social issue—the retraining of prison inmates to function as contributing members of society.

Gardening made a difference in another community, too. After the riots in Los Angeles in 1992, Tammy Bird, a biology teacher at Crenshaw High School, wanted to do something to help heal this battered neighborhood and give students some science experience. She enlisted volunteers from the business community and, along with 40 students, took over a lot behind the football field. Their goal was to sell produce at the local farmers market to provide college scholarship money and give food to needy families. The project, called "Food from the 'Hood," raised $600. With vegetables and herbs in the garden, the next step could only have been salad dressing. Their salad dressing, "Straight Out' the Garden," is now sold to 2,000 grocery stores in 23 states. Current revenues are around $50,000.

The mission statement of this unique organization is to create jobs for youth; to show that young people can and do make a difference; to prove that business can be socially responsible, environmentally friendly, and profitable; to give back to the community; and to use experience to prepare for the future. This mission statement is proudly printed on every salad dressing bottle.

Students must apply to the program to become an "owner" in Food from the 'Hood. They do everything in the business—weeding the garden, harvesting, marketing, maintaining the computer logs—their activities run the gamut. Students learn about working together and operating a business . . . and they are matched up with mentors to help them get into college. The mentors help these students identify their options, search for schools, and go through the application process.

Through this program, these inner-city kids have made a positive impact on their community and learned that they can be successful in ways they never dreamed possible. As Melinda McMullen, an adult volunteer for the project, said so well in a 1995 *Newsweek* article, "What comes from that garden is inspiration. From anything—even the riots—amazing things can grow."[17]

None of these business enterprises could have been successful if someone hadn't been willing to be a customer and if others hadn't been willing to share their knowledge. In doing so, they helped create new and viable businesses that put resources back into the local community. In each instance, employees of successful companies got involved in mentoring the smaller, local businesses. This involvement not only gave the employees a feeling of personal accomplishment, but also gave them a sense of pride in their own organization for supporting the community.

Building Your Business in Underserved Communities

The benefit to the community is the prime focus for basketball superhero Magic Johnson. Speaking at an event sponsored by the Minority Business Opportunity Committee, honoring minority businesspeople in Los Angeles, Magic talked about the theaters he is building in several underserved communities.

The first complex opened in Los Angeles; there are plans for similar theaters in Chicago and Atlanta. When Johnson first had the idea, everyone told him it could never work and that the kids would tear up the theaters. He persisted and, in partnership with Sony Pictures, he built the theater complex in Los Angeles. The project used 75 percent minority-owned contractors, who hired gang members and people from the community.

Johnson's theater is now the fifteenth highest grossing theater in the country. He has hired 100 young people to work in the complex, which is used not only for movies, but also for school graduations, educational projects for kids, and voting. "Young people come to work and take pride in what they are doing," Johnson said. For him, the goal is not to make money, but "to make the community better for our being there." Acknowledging the impact of minority business people on his life, he challenged other business leaders saying, "If you don't employ the kids and the people in the community, who will?"

Even Magic Johnson, with a college education and a successful basketball career, needed the support and knowledge of other business leaders. To make his theaters a success, he relied on resources of the mayor's office and Sony Pictures. This scenario underscores the need for businesses to get involved in helping community businesses be successful by sharing both time and resources the way Ben & Jerry's did with La Soul and Greystone Bakery.

Providing Capital for Entrepreneurs

Few entrepreneurs have the financial backing that Magic Johnson brought to his project. For many community businesses, access to capital is a key stumbling block. In Minnesota, the Corporate Report Minnesota Business Plan has a competition designed to support entrepreneurs. The organization awards two prizes, one academic and one professional, totaling $60,000. The money is to provide "seed" money for entrepreneurs in the community. For some businesses, it doesn't take much to get a start. This kind of start-up money, based on a good business plan, can be just what the doctor ordered for an energetic entrepreneur.

Not only does Ben & Jerry's support the local economy with purchasing and employee support, but also the company established the Entrepreneurial Fund. The purpose of the fund is to provide low-interest loans to people in the community who are starting new businesses. In keeping with the company's own commitment to being socially responsible, businesses that apply must also demonstrate social responsibility. The money for these loans is generated through the proceeds of tours through their manufacturing plant in Waterbury, Vermont. Ben & Jerry's puts half of the proceeds into the Entrepreneurial Fund and the other half goes into the Employee Community Fund Committee. Rank-and-file employees make decisions on how this money will be spent in the community.

Sharing Business Knowledge

Many communities have Small Business Development Centers. At no cost, these centers provide start-up and small business owners the kind of knowledge and advice they need to build their companies. The centers offer everything from developing a business plan to applying for an SBA loan. Every successful business has employees with skills that could be valuable for someone trying to get a start. Encouraging employees to share their knowledge in this arena can have a very positive effect on the local economy. Every new business provides jobs and generates cash flow for the community. This kind of social responsibility has long-term benefits for society as a whole.

Your organization can have an impact on the local economy in many ways. Whether you buy from minority-owned and small businesses, partner with others to create new businesses, provide funds for entrepreneurs, share your business knowledge, or find another way to contribute, both your business and the local economy will benefit. The perception of your organization in the community will influence employees, customers, and investors. As part of a strategy to create long-term stability and profitability, future-oriented companies are already actively building local economies.

KEY CONCEPTS

▶ There is an urgent need for volunteers and contributions from many community organizations.

▶ Local economies play a significant role in the health of the overall economy.

▶ Support the local economy by using local vendors or creating business opportunities.

▶ An advisory role with small business can influence a local economy, as well as give your employees an opportunity to make a difference.

▶ Supporting volunteerism by your employees can enhance their performance, increase their commitment to your company, and positively impact your customer base.

▶ Employees and employers alike benefit from involvement in community businesses.

▶ Involvement can occur in many ways and need not be too expensive.

ACTION PLAN

- Locate suppliers in the local community.
- Research these businesses regarding certification or through the local Better Business Bureau.
- Begin purchasing some items from local businesses.

- If there are problems, consider providing intellectual resources through your organization to help develop these small businesses.
- Partner with another organization or nonprofit to develop a mutually beneficial business.
- Give employees opportunities to share their business knowledge with local businesses through Business Development Centers, Chambers of Commerce, or other organization.
- Involve employees in finding a way to provide funds for entrepreneurs in the community.
- Identify a service you can supply to the community that is part of your business.
- Poll employees to find their areas of interest.
- Develop a plan that is most compatible with your workforce, for instance, a company-supported single activity or opportunities for individuals to contribute based on their personal interests.
- Involve both corporate resources and human resources to reach out into the community.

Endnotes

1. America's Promise—The Alliance for Youth web site, The Dispatch by General Colin Powell, May 1997 and October 1997.
2. Finney, Martha, "Operations that Build Smiles, Confidence, Skills and Community Goodwill," *HR Magazine*, April 1997.
3. Server, Andrew, "Lessons from America's Fastest Growing Companies," *Fortune*, August 8, 1994.
4. Hall, Mimi, *USA TODAY*, April 22, 1997.
5. Finney, Martha, "Operations that Build Smiles, Confidence, Skills and Community Goodwill," *HR Magazine*, April 1997.
6. Shadovitz, David, "Seeing Double," *Human Resource Executive*, August 1997.
7. Laabs, Jennifer, "Ben and Jerry's Caring Capitalism," *Personnel Journal*, November 1992.
8. *Nations Restaurant News*, June 2, 1997.
9. Muoio, Anna, "Ways to Give Back" *Fast Company*, December/January 1998.

10. *Ace Hardware Daily News.*
11. Warner, Elizabeth, "A Real Page Turner," *Nations Business*, January 1996.
12. Framer, Jill Andresky, "How to Give Wisely," *Inc.* Magazine, February 1997.
13. Muoio, Anna, "Ways to Give Back," *Fast Company*, December/January 1998.
14. Reder, Alan, ***In Pursuit of Principle and Profit***, G.P. Putnam & Sons, New York, N.Y., 1994.
15. Ibid., pp.175–179.
16. Ibid.
17. From *Newsweek*, May 29, 1995, web site www.ncl.org.

15

Educating Tomorrow's Workers

A major concern today is where we're going to find qualified workers in the future. It's difficult to find suitable employees now, and trends indicate that the labor shortage will intensify.

What can—or should—your company do to prepare today's young people to be productive employees tomorrow? There is a clear and vital social responsibility here, but your activity in this area may also be self-serving. Consider the value of building your corporation's reputation as a good place to work, your industry as a good career field, and hard-to-fill positions as worthwhile occupations.

Enlightened companies are taking steps now to help prepare young people to enter the workforce and be productive.
By doing so, employers reduce the cost of turnover in entry-
level workers who are unprepared for the work environment.
They also develop young workers, who will be able to learn
the skills to be successful and productive in a demanding
marketplace.

The number of young people who need job training is
mind-boggling. With government spending cuts, there will
be fewer opportunities for young people to get that training.
The Job Training Partnership Act, through the Labor
Department's Employment and Training Administration
(ETA), uses government funds to support 640 regional service areas in providing jobs for economically disadvantaged
youth. ETA anticipates providing as many as 550,000 jobs
during the peak summer months. This figure may sound like
a significant number of job opportunities, but to understand
the magnitude of the issue, look at the statistics in one region
in Minnesota.

There are 6,900 young people between 14 and 21 who
qualify as disadvantaged youth in this Minnesota region. Of
that total, only 850, or just 12 percent, were placed. With
more funding, ETA could have placed as many as 1,500 or
about 22 percent. This 22 percent is still a far cry from the
6,900 young people who need job opportunities.[1]

The gap between what is needed and what is available is
huge. In terms of society as a whole, the impact of young
people who cannot find or qualify for work is tremendous.
By investing in the education of these young citizens, companies can build the strong workforce needed to support a
healthy economy. Failure to do so will be costly to all concerned. For companies that are willing to provide jobs for
these young people, there are government tax credit programs to offset some of the expense.

With the prospect of more serious labor shortages looming on the horizon, it makes good sense to invest wisely in

raising the capability of young people. Recognizing that government programs can't possibly meet the needs, corporations and educational institutions have significant roles to play. Here are some ideas of what is already being done.

Managing Young Workers

The New York Eye and Ear Infirmary in Manhattan has summer workers doing everything from answering the phone to working in nursing units. Taking on these young people can be a challenge for supervisors, who become teacher, mentor, and parent. It requires clear communication of expectations and requirements, and a tolerance for youth, but the rewards are great. When students from the summer work programs stay in school, go to college, or start a successful career path, the supervisors, the company, and society all benefit.[2]

Providing summer jobs or internships during the school year can be done by businesses of any size. There are always a number of tasks that need doing, but always seem to stay on the bottom of the pile. One purpose of these jobs is to provide an environment where students can learn how to work. Job skills will develop over time as these young workers increase their confidence in their ability to fit into the working world. When taking these workers into your company, give some thought to what you'll have them do. Be sure to communicate your instructions and expectations clearly. Focus on having them grow, while you're getting work done.

A primary purpose of working with young people is to create opportunities for them to experience success. With every well-done task, the self-confidence of these developing workers will increase. In addition, they will become accustomed to the responsibilities and discipline of the work environment. Without this kind of experience, they might otherwise have no knowledge of the business world. When they are ready to apply for full-time work, they will have the advantage of knowing what to wear, how to act, and what working means. The chances that they will succeed will be greatly increased. And they could be your future workers . . . or customers. Working with young people can strengthen your company's future.

Teaching about the World of Work

Because a key problem for many businesses today is hiring qualified workers, programs like "Take Your Community to Work" are rapidly gaining support. This idea, developed by Dale Caldwell, President and Founder of Operation Education Incorporated, is to have businesses invite students from disadvantaged schools to visit the workplace for a day. As these students are introduced to environments and careers they may not have known existed, they are motivated to stay in school and more actively pursue career objectives. This program is now active in nine countries and 90 U.S. cities. Students who experience the real workplace are better prepared when they begin their first jobs.

When United Airlines brought Dallas students in for the day, they worked alongside United employees taking tickets, sorting baggage, and helping the concierges with frequent flyers; learning what airport security does; working with flight attendants onboard the aircraft before departure.[3] This kind of experience gives students a real taste of the working world.

Formal Classroom Training

To help young people succeed, Shell Oil Company developed the Shell Youth Training Academy. In the Chicago program, high school students work up to 20 hours a week at companies selected by Shell. Jobs may be in construction, at a law firm, retail shops, or Shell service stations. Because outstanding students have other opportunities at scholarships and financial aid, Shell targets young people who get average grades. Prior to going to the participating firms, the students receive two weeks of classroom instruction. They learn about communication in a business setting, how to write a resumé, how to dress for work, and basic computer skills. The program originated in Los Angeles, where Shell has helped 465 students. Of that group, 96 percent have either gone on to college or are working full-time.[4]

Agencies for Youth Employment

A & M Records in Los Angeles has established a non-profit organization called "Y.E.S. to Jobs." Through this program, corporations donate $500. Y.E.S. to Jobs screens the applicants and places them in summer jobs. The students need only have a C+ grade average. Good attendance records are more important. What participating companies have found is that these teenagers are anxious to learn and fit into the organizations quickly.[5]

Apprenticeship Programs

The Greensboro, North Carolina Chamber of Commerce and more than 120 local businesses work together to provide apprenticeship programs for high school students.

It is an important outreach program: the effect on these young people is already becoming apparent. Many of them had no idea how they were going to earn a living or if they could go to college. Through the program, they've been given the opportunity to achieve more than they ever thought possible.

One of the businesses is Dow Corning, where students are hired to work 20 hours a week during school and full-time during vacations. The students need a C average and must take algebra and chemistry. Edward Kelly III, the human resources and safety manager at the plant, expects that these apprentices will be making suggestions to the chemical engineers about new products once they get familiar with the manufacturing process.[6]

Aligning Job Skills and Education

In Virginia Big-Ed (Business, Industry, Government—Education) operates as a cooperative effort of business and educators, designed to give students the training and education they need to fill the available jobs. Because the requirements of industry are changing, students often leave high school without the skills they need.

Now, with business and schools working together, they can prepare students for the future. For example, if students want an entry-level drafting job, the employers want them to have Computer-Aided Drafting (CAD) experience. If these students can get the experience before leaving high school, they will be ready to step into entry-level positions immediately. Students can see the direct relationship between the classes and their application in the real world.[7] That's a motivator for students of any age.

Total Quality Goes to School

When employers clarify what skills they need in employees, educators can design programs to ensure those skills are taught.

Businesses in Winston-Salem, Forsyth County, North Carolina, are taking a more active role in helping educators prepare students for employment. Working as the North Carolina Business Committee For Education, 100 businesspeople have developed a list of competencies that high school graduates should have in order to be ready for work. The competencies are: communication (reading, writing, and public speaking), skill with numbers and data (math and science logical deductions), problem-solving techniques, critical thinking to organize information, teamwork, and technology skills.

These same 100 companies are also involved in helping schools apply business processes in running the school system. This program is called Total Quality in Education. In Forsyth County, 26 school systems are using the quality approach and students are learning to use these skills to increase their learning and problem-solving skills.

Even the bus mechanics in Forsyth County have applied TQE and decreased the backlog of busses waiting for service from 68 to 10. The Forsyth County Chamber of Commerce has worked with a number of businesses to show the school district ways to run more effectively, including saving $9.2 million over the next five years. If business techniques can help schools run more efficiently, more money is available for classrooms, supplies, and teacher salaries—an incentive for keeping good educators in the classroom.[8]

Helping Teachers Teach

Partnering of businesses and schools can be done in many different ways. Businesses are increasingly involved in providing resources to schools, resources like equipment, time for employees to volunteer, summer jobs, and student visits to the workplace. Some businesses adopt schools and give employees time to tutor children or give additional support to teachers during busy times before and after school. Other businesses encourage teachers to spend time observing their operations so that the teachers have a better understanding of how businesses work. This exposure to "the real world" gives teachers the knowledge and insight to help students acquire the education and experience they need to get good jobs.

The BellSouth Foundation has a $60,000 grant for teachers in Winston-Salem to visit local businesses, government agencies, and nonprofit organizations to gather information to make school curriculum more relevant.

Carolina Biological Supply encourages teachers and students to visit their workplace to see the kinds of specialized skills the company needs from its employees. This visitation generates summer employees for Carolina Biological Supply, when workers are busy preparing products to be sold to school biology departments. The students who are employed often become interested in science during their summer jobs and return as full-time workers after college.[9]

Developing Training Centers

Some employers develop and operate training centers for their own employees and invited nonemployee participants. Technical topics, process technology, and a variety of other subjects can be addressed in classes, seminars, and special conferences. Such programs reinforce a company's position as an industry leader, while providing opportunities for exchange of current knowledge and forward thinking in the field.

Dow Corning, along with nine other chemical companies, contributed $125,000 for the development of a training center for chemical processing. High school and community college students and trainees from private industry use this center.[10]

Teachers Learn in the Workplace

3M, known for innovation, understands that hands-on experience is the best way to learn about science. Every summer the company invites 25 math and science teachers to spend six weeks working on challenging research projects at 3M. These teachers have the opportunity to work with the best scientists at the company, then take back the knowledge to the classroom. The time spent in a corporate environment makes it easier to make the theoretical information of the classroom relevant to life in the world of work.[11]

Adopt a Class or a School

There are many ways you can partner with your local school system to your mutual benefit: Provide funds to a high school for equipment or supplies, mentoring, or tutoring. Consider providing workers to do repairs or renovations, sponsoring a job fair, or letting the school use your property or business for a fund-raising event. Offer matching funds for donations raised by parents or children. Create a summer job program to give high school students some job experience. Present a job search skills workshop to show students what is necessary to land a job after high school.

Consider offering a whole sixth-grade class a college education. There are many schools that can barely get students to graduate from high school. By starting early with students, your company could work with the school system to help motivate these young students to get the education they need to compete in the workplace. Give the students some guidelines, such as maintaining a certain grade point average, taking certain kinds of challenging classes, scoring in the top 25th percentile on the Scholastic Aptitude Test. Then get the employees of your company involved in mentoring and tutoring these students. Often, these young people can't do it alone; but with the support of caring adults, they will have a chance to go to college and be productive citizens.

You might want to get another company to sponsor a different class and create a friendly competition. Both businesses will benefit by having a better-educated labor pool, the community will benefit by having more people working, and the students will most certainly benefit by having opportunities to succeed.

A civil engineering company, Anderson & Associates, headquartered in Greensboro, North Carolina, adopted an elementary magnet school for science and technology. The purpose was to make science fun for students. Anderson & Associates had only eight employees, so they called on other engineering firms and the local university's engineering department to work with the students. With the help of all these people, students took apart toasters and put them back together, built a rocket, learned how much weight it takes to collapse a bridge (a sand bridge model), learned about what happens in an earthquake (with a Jell-O city), and surveyed the school yard. These students now make the connection between science and things used in daily life. The employees of the participating companies felt good about their contributions and the commitments of their firms to the well being of the community.[12]

Educating Parents

In Minneapolis/St. Paul, Twin Cities Public Television (TCPT) helps parents get children involved in other activities besides television. TCPT offers hands-on training, then provides collateral materials that encourage dialogue and interesting activities for parents and childcare providers to use with the children. The program, called "Ready to Learn," has become part of the curriculum for area nonprofit organizations. The course has been taken by more than 5,800 parents and childcare providers.[13]

Ideas to Get Started

Share the expertise of employees in the classroom: science, public speaking, communication, art and graphics, math, music, dance, computer technology, and . . . invite students to visit your place of business. Remember, children have boundless curiosity. What you may think is mundane, they may find fascinating. Consider these ideas. . . .

- Develop a mentor program with a school. Mentoring can be on many levels. Employees can become mentors for students, but business can also be a mentor for education.

Can your company mentor a local school in being more
efficient, creating more effective fund-raising activities, or
providing more effective parent-teacher communications?

- Create a way to provide incentives or scholarship funds,
  either to students for high school or college or to parents
  for daycare costs.
- Look for an opening or two to hire high school students
  during the summer or part-time during the school year.
- Partner with other businesses or the local Chamber of
  Commerce to put on a job fair or college fair to help
  young people learn about their options.
- Donate funds or volunteer time for a health fair in your
  community that focuses on children.
- Raise funds for free children's inoculations.
- Provide supplies and equipment for a preschool in your
  neighborhood.
- Support theater, music, or athletic programs at local ele-
  mentary schools.
- Partner with an agency or nonprofit that offers parenting
  classes and provides financial or volunteer support.

What these kinds of programs have in common is that
they are all an investment in the future. They go beyond the
short term to address the larger social issues of caring for and
educating the children of today so that they can be productive members of society tomorrow. The commitment of the
corporation and the involvement of employees create a common cause that builds loyalty and reinforces respect in the
workplace.

Educating tomorrow's workers is essential for the future
of the United States, but will have a significant impact on the
global community as well. Chapter 16 focuses on our
responsibility to the global community.

KEY CONCEPTS

- There is a gap in the education of young people and the needs of the business community.
- Organizations have a vested self-interest in helping young people prepare for the world of work.
- The partnership of education and business will create a solid foundation for young people to build a future.
- Companies can invest in their communities in a variety of ways, all of which return multiple benefits.

ACTION PLAN

- Identify gaps between the education of new recruits and job requirements.
- Survey your employees to see what kinds of skills they would be willing to share.
- Survey local schools to discover how your organization might meet some of their most pressing needs.
- Involve employees in finding a way to match the needs of the school, the needs of the business, and the skills of employees.
- Start small, by hiring just one high school student in the summer or part-time. Do what fits for *your* company.

Endnotes

1. Grossman, Robert J., "Summer Jobs Mold Tomorrow's Workforce," *HR Magazine*, April 1997.
2. Ibid.
3. BusinessWire, Dallas/Ft. Worth, March 1996.
4. "Shell Oil's Youth Training Program Aims to Assist Minority Communities," *Chicago Tribune*, February 24, 1997.
5. Grossman, Robert J., "Summer Jobs Mold Tomorrow's Workforce," *HR Magazine*, April 1997.
6. Johnson, Clint, "Schoolmates," *Triad Business News*, July 25, 1997.
7. *Daily Press/The Times-Herald*, March 25, 1991.
8. Johnson, Clint, "Schoolmates," *Triad Business News*, July 25, 1997.
9. Ibid.
10. Ibid.
11. "Greater Minneapolis Chamber of Commerce Announces Quality of Life Awards," PR Newswire, January 9, 1997.
12. Johnson, Clint, "Company Helps Students Have Fun with Science," *Triad Business News*, July 25, 1997.
13. "Greater Minneapolis Chamber of Commerce Announces Quality of Life Award Winners," PR Newswire, January 9, 1997.

16

Responsibility to the Global Community

In the future there will be growing global connections among communities. American companies will do business in and with countries around the world. As these connections become stronger, companies will be as aware of their impact on the world at-large as they are of their impact on the local community. Increasingly, even companies operating on a relatively local basis are involved in the global community.

Now, not only are the citizens of one country watching, but the whole world is watching and taking note of how these multinational organizations meet their responsibilities to the global community. For smaller businesses there are also opportunities to demonstrate their sense of social responsibility and have an impact around the world. Employees and customers have an increased loyalty to companies that respond to pressing worldwide issues.

Responsibilities to Host Countries

Companies that do business globally have a great challenge in protecting the local environments and populations. Simply deciding to do business in a country, particularly an underdeveloped country, can change everything, from the levels of pollution to the diet of the local people.

Enlightened companies will not put local communities in jeopardy in order to boost their shareholder values. Instead, these companies will pursue policies that protect the environment *and* enhance the community both economically and socially.

Global social responsibility requires that companies carefully analyze the potential results of their actions. Before a company decides to import technology, build a plant, or tap a natural resource in another country, executives must undertake a thorough examination of the impact on the host country.

This examination process should include a cost analysis of an environmental monitoring program and an exploration of *all* the consequences of opening a facility in the country. A study should be conducted to determine the raw material requirements for the facility and the processes. An audit of health and safety records at home and abroad is worthwhile. An analysis of the environmental demands of the facility on water, electricity, air, and waste disposal is essential.

As our understanding of how world ecology functions increases, companies must be ever mindful of the effects their actions may have around the world. Companies that have ignored these issues in the short term have felt the negative impact in the long term. Planning in the initial stages of global expansion can create a mutually beneficial relationship between the organization and the host country.

Building Global Economies

Many economies in Third World and emerging countries are unable to bring their products to the world marketplace. Large organizations can profit by seeking products made in small communities and establishing an ethical business relationship. Encouraging the development of these communities and countries strengthens the global economy and can change the lives of people for the better.

Anita Roddick, founder and CEO of The Body Shop, is an activist in pursuing ethical, sustainable trade relationships with developing countries around the world. The Body Shop's Community Trade program sets forth a list of criteria for global trade that focuses on bringing products from needy communities into the marketplace and providing long-term trading opportunities for those underprivileged areas. In doing so, The Body Shop positively influences local communities—increasing employment, skill levels, and income for the residents.

The criteria for Community Trade can stand as a framework for any company that does business globally. The five tenets are:

1. Work with established organizations within the community, such as a farming co-operative, tribal council, or an association of women, so the purchasing strengthens their collective interest.
2. Seek out groups that are disadvantaged in terms of education, resources, health care, or markets for their goods.
3. The trade must benefit the workers who provide the product by providing training, skills, and participation, as well as increased income.

4. The business relationship must be viable; price, quality, availability, and capacity must be taken into account.
5. The development of trade must be environmentally sound, protecting both the ecosystem and animals.[1]

The Body Shop purchases goods from developing countries around the world, with 23 Community Trade suppliers in 13 countries, including Nicaragua, Bangladesh, Zambia, Russia, and Mexico. The Community Trade program accounts for 7 percent of all Body Shop buying. One Community Trade supplier is Kuapa Kokoo, Ltd. which sells cocoa beans in Ghana. Thanks to The Body Shop, 9,000 farmers are now paid a fair price, on time, for their products.

Another Community Trade supplier is General Paper Industries in Nepal. This company supports The Body Shop tenets by teaching AIDs awareness, providing scholarships for girls, and planting sustainable shrubs on hillsides.

Purchasing Decisions to Save the Global Environment

Ben & Jerry's is a company that has always been associated with social responsibility. As their business grew, leaders of the company began to examine opportunities to have a positive global impact.

In developing a new ice cream flavor, Rain Forest Crunch, they made an environmentally conscious decision to use nuts from the rain forest. Their purchase of the nuts supported the economic value of a living rain forest, helping to save this precious resource. By designing the package to raise awareness of rain forest issues, they had a double impact. Every sale of Rain Forest Crunch meant buying more nuts and informing more customers about the crisis of the rain forest.

Through increased awareness, consumers might well make other purchasing decisions based on rain forest protection. The product had an impact on a worldwide environmental issue and increased Ben & Jerry's profitability. Customers not only liked the taste of the ice cream, but what the company stood for. Other like-minded people chose Rain Forest Crunch ice cream over another in support of their commitment to saving the rain forest.[2]

Define Values for International Business Relationships

Doing business in other parts of the world, particularly Third World countries, demands setting some standard values. High poverty levels force workers, often children, into abusive work environments for meager wages. Companies that are values-based will insist that vendors meet certain standards of humanity in order to receive contracts.

Levi Strauss has committed to doing business only with companies that share its values structure. Because of its increasing involvement in the world economy, the company has developed a list of criteria that defines the values they expect in their international manufacturers and suppliers. Potential suppliers and manufacturers are assessed based on their environmental records; ethical standards; health and safety in work and residential facilities; legal compliance with laws, both as individuals and a company; and employment practices—work must be voluntary. Levi Strauss also insists that there be no physical risks in the workplace, and that the workers not be exploited in any way.

In many situations these primary criteria would be almost impossible to meet, but the company goes on to include a secondary list. It evaluates vendors on their wages and benefits—working hours are not to exceed sixty hours per week and compensation must be paid for overtime. The company will not tolerate child labor, prison or forced labor, or discrimination based on personal characteristics or beliefs. The vendors may not use any corporal or other mental or physical discipline. And, the company must benefit the community.[3]

Getting a contract with Levi Strauss is so lucrative that vendors are willing to make sweeping changes in their companies to meet the criteria. As Levi Strauss takes a stand—on fair and humane conditions for workers, for protecting the environment, and for ethical business practices worldwide other companies will follow suit. The result will improve the quality of life for all of us.

Responsibilities to Host Country Employees

Establishing criteria for vendors is one thing. Making the criteria work in the face of economic reality can be another. Companies need to take an active role in helping Third World companies make the necessary changes.

In the competitive garment industry, it is not uncommon to have sweatshops in Third World countries where children work long hours for low pay. Levi Strauss insists on maintaining the International Labor Organization standards with all its contractors.

According to these standards children under 14 are not allowed to work. When applying the standards to two Bangladeshi contractors, company officials discovered that the children working in these factories were the sole support of their families.

Refusing to let them work would create unbearable hardship for the children and their families. Rather than back down, Levi Strauss negotiated a compromise. The contractors would continue to pay the underage children a wage and hire them back at age 14. The company would send the children to school, paying all costs for tuition, books, and uniforms. While this cost some money on both sides, it was the right thing to do.[4]

In the eyes of consumers and employees in the United States, the Levi Strauss value structure has meaning. The company policies are not just words. The company is willing to take action and find creative solutions to problems based on their established values.

Commitments to Worldwide Health

As we understand more about the interdependence of economies and ecologies, we also become more aware of our connections to people everywhere in the world. As individuals and organizations, there is a need to reach out, to share, and to improve the lives of other human beings. For millions of people, basic health issues must be addressed before there can be any consideration for commerce or ecology.

Many corporations, nonprofit organizations, and individuals are finding ways to have an impact on health issues for people around the world. We highlight a few companies here and acknowledge that there are many others committed to making a global difference. We hope that the ideas in these pages, plus what we'll share on our web site,
www.leanandmeaningful.com,
will stimulate your thinking about how you can have a positive influence on your organization's global community. The primary and secondary benefits of international involvement can be far-reaching.

Guide Dogs for the Blind in South Africa

The 3M Company supports health in the global community through their Move to Mobility program in South Africa. The concept is to help people become more mobile, whether it is by providing a guide dog or another device that will help them get around. 3M makes a particular kind of bandage called a Tegaderm dressing. Hospitals save the wrappers from these dressings and return them for credits toward the purchase of a guide dog or some other mobility aid. To date 16 guide dogs have been provided to people who otherwise would never have been able to afford these costly, highly trained animals.

Children's Health

Numerous programs concern themselves with the safety, health, and nutrition of children around the world. Opportunities to support these efforts range from "adopting" children financially, to bringing them to the United States for medical treatment, to arranging for their formal adoption by eligible families. You can provide various kinds of support through established organizations such as the Red Cross, the Red Crescent, church groups, or the United Nations Children's Emergency Fund (UNICEF). Alternatively, you can create your own program.

Johnson & Johnson created the Worldwide Child Survival Program. Partnering with UNICEF and the World Health Organization, Johnson & Johnson provides a range of programs to improve children's health around the world. With the needs so great, the company uses the mortality rate of children under five to identify the most pressing problems. Currently Johnson & Johnson is working with UNICEF in China to eliminate neonatal tetanus. Training on childbirth delivery for health care workers in 25 Chinese provinces is funded through the Worldwide Child Survival Program. In addition, the program also encourages public acceptance of the practice of immunizing children against disease.

Another interesting approach that might give you some ideas is something we encountered on a flight to Mauritius, an island country in the Indian Ocean. As we neared our destination, Air Mauritius flight attendants took up a collection of foreign change—for UNICEF-sponsored healthcare for the children of Mauritius. When we talked with them about this unusual practice, airline employees told us that the collection is very well received. Passengers have leftover change from their departure country (Air Mauritius flies from most of the major gateway airports in Europe) and are happy to empty their pockets of old currency to make room for Mauritian money.

Operation Smile

Founded in 1982 by Dr. William Magee and his wife Kathleen, Operation Smile travels the world with surgeons to treat children with facial deformities. The first trip in 1982 to the Philippines had 18 volunteers and provided care for 200 children. Now the organization has helped more than 20,000 children around the world and 21,000 children in the United States. The organization relies on volunteers and corporate sponsors, including Citibank, Johnson & Johnson, Warner Lambert, and Northwest Airlines. These large companies contribute in many different ways.

Some Citibank employees spend vacations as volunteers working with Operation Smile. Although these employees may have never met each other, they discover the power in teams as they work for the common goal of restoring children's hope for the future. The experience of working with Operation Smile changes employees. The team experience and the broader view of the world adds meaning to their lives, both personally and in the workplace.

Warner Lambert, an ongoing corporate partner of Operation Smile, sponsored a Youth Conference in the summer of 1997 to bring together high school and college Youth Clubs in the United States and abroad. To raise funds for Operation Smile, Warner Lambert agreed to match funds, dollar for dollar, raised by the youth groups. Employees in the company also got involved in fund raising by donating their pennies. The pennies filled a 75-gallon fish tank!

To get the pennies counted and wrapped, Warner Lambert enlisted the help of the Mercer County Special Services School for disabled children. These kids counted and wrapped all the pennies (it took three days) for a grand total of $3,488. Warner Lambert also supports Operation Smile with a unique approach to sales incentives. Rather than the standard vacation or list of prize options, the top salespeople have a child sponsored in their names in Operation Smile. So far this program has shown itself to be a powerful motivator for the sales staff.

Northwest Airlines got customers involved in Operation Smile by asking for cash or "World Perks" travel miles donations in their inflight magazine. Passengers also view a video presentation about the work of Operation Smile. As an added incentive to passengers, Northwest gave 500 bonus frequent flyer miles to passengers who contributed travel miles or $50 cash.

Operation Smile is a large, well-known organization. There are many more companies, both large and small, not named here, that have contributed to the success of the organization. What the Operation Smile story illustrates is how companies can get involved on a global level by supporting an existing nonprofit organization. Whether involvement in the community is local or global, the same principles apply: encourage and support employees' personal commitment of time; match funds; involve employees and customers in the activity.

Women's Health Fund

Through the Avon Worldwide Fund for Women's Health, Avon Products, Inc. takes a stand for women's health around the world. When local operations of this worldwide company identify women's health-related issues in their own communities, the Fund is available to work on a solution. Since its beginning in 1992, the fund has grown to over $45 million.

One particular issue for Avon worldwide is breast cancer. The company has launched a crusade to combat the disease by providing information on the benefits of early detection.

The Avon sales force, 450,000 strong, is encouraging women on a one-on-one basis to take the necessary steps to protect themselves from this health risk. By selling the "Breast Awareness" Pin and Pens, Avon has raised over $17 million, which is used in local communities for education and detection services.

To reach underserved women, Avon has contributed more than $9 million to the YWCA and the ENCOREplus program.

Media is an effective method to reach large numbers of people. Avon has effectively used both print and television to spread the word about breast cancer. To reach the women of the Spanish-speaking community, Avon developed a Hispanic version of their PBS special and broadcast it on Telemundo in 1994. Since then the special program has been condensed to a 30-minute video and is distributed worldwide.[5]

The Gift of Sight

LensCrafters, a large eyecare and glasses retailer, recycles old glasses for distribution worldwide. In conjunction with the Lions Club, LensCrafters collects, sorts by prescription, cleans, and repairs old glasses. LensCrafters' associates, who are optometrists, opticians, and technicians, go on missions to other countries to provide eye testing and to deliver the used glasses. Lions Club International determines the locations for the missions and makes all the arrangements for the associates. In a two-week mission, working 12 hours a day for seven to nine days, associates can help as many as 13,000 people. LensCrafters' goal is to provide glasses to one million needy people by the year 2003.[6]

It is a small world. The environment, the economy, and humanity all work together as a single system. The future will bring us closer together through more sophisticated communications and expanded international business. The level of worldwide social responsibility that companies demonstrate will influence the loyalty and commitment of their employees, customers, and investors. Enlightened companies are already part of the global community, through their businesses or the actions they take to improve the lives of people thousands of miles away.

There are many opportunities to provide support for nonprofit organizations that are doing good work around the world. This kind of outreach will benefit the direct recipients, while validating your corporation's sense of corporate responsibility. This dedication to building a better world will have far-reaching positive effects on employees, applicants, customers, and other stakeholders.

KEY CONCEPTS

- Establishing a business base in a host country can have a significant impact on every aspect of its society. A detailed analysis must be done prior to entering the market in a host country to determine the effect on its economy, ecology, and society.
- Purchasing decisions can help communities on the edge of poverty. Multidimensional support can help countries get their products to market. Criteria must be established for this relationship so that it remains beneficial to both the business and the community.
- Developing global business relationships around a defined set of values can promote more humane business practices and create new opportunities for host country workers.
- Partnering with nonprofit organizations is a way to have a positive effect on serious worldwide health issues.
- Enlightened companies acknowledge the whole world as their own community.

ACTION PLAN

- Analyze the organization's position with regard to business in other countries.
- Develop a set of standards within the organization that can be used as criteria when contracting with businesses abroad. The development process must include employees from all levels of the organization. There must be 100 percent commitment to the standards, so the company can find creative solutions to real-life problems without compromising their values.
- Review all corporate strategies that include global expansion and do a complete analysis of the impact on the host country.
- Review purchasing practices to identify products that might be purchased from developing communities.
- Analyze what the relationship will be with these communities prior to establishing a business agreement. The organization must be prepared to work within the communities to ensure the economic and social benefits for the individual populations.
- If a global business relationship is not part of the corporate strategy, seek out nonprofit organizations that present opportunities to give something to the global community. Keep employees, customers, and shareholders involved, from deciding what the nonprofit organization will be to how the company will support the cause.
- No contribution is too small. Pennies can add up to a big contribution when well spent.

Endnotes

1. www.the-body-shop.com/trade
2. Cohen, Ben and Jerry Greenfield, "Ice Cream Social," *Entrepreneur*, July 1997.
3. HRWire, Research Institute of America.
4. Mitchell, Russell, and Michael O'Neal, *Business Week*, August 1, 1994.
5. www.avon.com.
6. www.LensCrafters.com.

17

Environmental Awareness

"No business can be done on a dead planet. A company that is taking the long view must accept that it has a obligation to minimize its impact on the natural environment."

—Yvon Chouinard

T hat statement, written by the founder of Patagonia, an outdoor wear manufacturer in Ventura, California, was part of an essay that appeared in *Sacred Trusts, Essays on Stewardship and Responsibility.* The statement succinctly identifies corporate responsibility to the environment.

The time for choosing whether or not to be environmentally conscious is over. It is now an imperative for organizations to take responsibility for their impact on the world around them. Investors and stakeholders are holding industry accountable for environmental policies. Litigation for poor environmental practices is costly.

In addition, there is an upside to being environmentally responsible. Enlightened corporations are already aware of the positive effect "going green" can have on both customers and employees. Because employees want to feel good about the company they work for, the pride they develop from being associated with an environmentally conscious company can translate into motivation and loyalty. Customers, concerned about the world they live in, are increasingly willing to spend a little more to have a product that is environmentally sound or was manufactured by a company that cares about the environment.

As the world becomes more and more interconnected, every activity will ultimately have worldwide impact. The environment is affected by every decision to purchase, to repair or discard, to clean, to package, to sell, whether it's done on a mass or individual basis.

Meaningful companies will be increasingly aware and sensitive to their manufacturing processes, their packaging, and their energy use. These enlightened corporations will choose to clean up their own environmental houses. They will also take a leading role—both financially and with volunteer hours—to clean up, protect, and maintain the environment.

Changing the Way We Think about Consumption

This point about leading companies taking responsibility was brought home very clearly in a report from Yvon Chouinard, in the 1992 Patagonia catalogue, when he wrote about the environmental audit done by his company. The result of the audit indicated that everything they did polluted in some way, from the polyester that was made from petroleum to the cotton that was sprayed with pesticides to control boll weevils, ultimately making the fields barren.

In the face of these findings, Patagonia, one of the world's most environmentally conscious companies, decided to do a number of things. They discontinued all polyester products, used "organic" cotton, and purchased wool from temperate climates where the grazing of the sheep would not permanently destroy the vegetation.

Even more significant, however, was Chouinard's statement that they need to use fewer materials, and therefore would begin cutting the clothing line, with an ultimate goal of limiting or even halting growth altogether. Their policy is based on a belief that for the sake of the environment, consumers will need to think differently about clothing. The future of clothing manufacturing will be to create fewer pieces that will last a long time.

CrunchTime, a candy bar manufacturer, uses nuts from the rain forest and adds a direct educational component. The candy bar is not sold over the counter, but is sold to schools to use as a fund-raising project. Along with the candy, CrunchTime provides a video about the rain forest in Costa Rica so that students can understand the significance of the issue and learn about environmental stewardship. At the completion of a school fund-raising event, CrunchTime donates 35 percent of their own profits to "adopt" rain forest land in the name of the school.

Recycling Clothes at the Retail Store

Hanna Anderson, a company that manufactures high-quality children's clothing, also believes in Patagonia's concept of less is more. They go even further with the idea of long-lasting clothing by encouraging their customers to return used items to the store. Customers get a 20 percent credit toward their next purchase—and Hanna donates the used clothing to organizations that provide services for needy children.

Consumers Will Pay More
for Environmentally Friendly Products

Patagonia's idea may seem like a formula for corporate disaster, but environmentally conscious manufacturers may take the lead after all. The number of consumers who are willing to pay a little more in order to have an environmentally conscious product is increasing. A product that is both competitively priced and green will have a distinct advantage in the marketplace.

Even the government is beginning to make more "green" buying decisions. The federal government has purchased alternative-fuel vehicles, energy-saving computers, and paper with a recycled content.

Investors Rate Companies
on Environmental Records

Not only does a company's environmental record affect its customers' buying decisions, but also its investors. Citizens have the right to review any public company's environmental records and corporations must disclose their intent to transport toxic substances into local communities.

Moody's Investors Service includes companies' environmental records in rating whether a company is credit-worthy or not. This rating is a factor in the company's ability to offer stocks and bonds to the public to increase their cash flow. Fund managers who specialize in socially responsible companies analyze the quality of the environmental programs of a company before making investment decisions.

Balancing Growth and the Environment

Ecotrust is an organization that supports environmental projects and addresses them from a sound economic basis.

Co-founder and president Spencer Bebee believes that companies have an economic self-interest when protecting the environment. The problems come when the community doesn't have enough data to make sound environmental decisions. Given the right information, Bebe believes that loggers, fishermen, and landowners will see the connections that support their self-interest in protecting the environment.

Before starting any project, Bebe wants all the data that can be collected—everything from historical records to satellite imagery. With this information in-hand, he gathers local leaders together to share their ideas for the development of the project. By developing a coalition of stakeholders, he is able to create environmentally sound projects that also address the economic issues of the area.[1]

Energy Pollutes

Because we take energy for granted, except when a storm knocks everything out, we are unaware of the amount of pollution that is caused by our use of energy. For instance, 9 million tons of air pollution comes from energy production, as well as 60 percent of the greenhouse gasses. In the United States, carbon emissions that cause global climate changes are at an all-time high. If world energy consumption does not change, scientists predict that there will be a worldwide increase in carbon dioxide of 50 to 60 percent. In the case of energy consumption, downsizing is good.

By using more energy-efficient lighting, cooling, and heating and being more aware, organizations can reduce monthly expenses considerably. As you embark on this kind of strategy, inform your employees, customers, and suppliers. Advise them of your intentions and keep them apprised of your progress and achievements.

Energy Efficiency Saves Money and Can Increase Revenues

When Vic's Market, a small grocery store in Sacramento, California, decided to make some changes in their store, they looked at every aspect of the store, from lighting to refrigeration. In the end the energy savings were substantial. By changing the lighting in their store, they were able to increase light levels and decrease monthly expenses by $1,800. As a second phase, they changed the refrigeration units from open cases to closed cases. This improved equipment saved $1,600 more per month and they discovered that shoppers stayed longer in the frozen food aisles now that it wasn't so cold. The third phase was a change in the deli cases and freezers, resulting in additional $2,500 savings per month.

The upgrade in equipment and enhanced lighting brought in more customers, increasing sales 15 percent over the pre-facelift days. And the environment got a lift, because of the reduction in energy use. These dramatic results reflect just how cost-effective environmentally sound practices can be.

Recycle Everything

Recycling is a key element in any environmental program. Using and reusing helps sustain the resources we currently have. Home Depot has developed a recycling center for its customers called Recycling Depot. At these specially designated locations customers can drop off all kinds of things, from ordinary household recyclables to water heaters, copper wire, and home improvement scraps. Not only do customers have the opportunity to get rid of all the stuff they can't use, but Home Depot even pays for the recyclable items. If you are in the building trade, you can get a tidy sum for recyclable metals.

What happens to all this recycled stuff? Some of it might end up at a company called Deja Shoe, where company founder, Julie Lewis, turns plastic milk jugs, paper, old tires, old seat cushions, and other stuff into shoes. If you're curious about the ultimate recycled shoe, look at Nordstrom or Bloomindale's for a Deja Shoe style you like.

Recycling and construction are not often tied together, but John Picard, a Los Angeles-based environmental/ecological consultant, has taken recycling to a new level in the construction of the Environmental Resource Center (ERC) for the Southern California Gas Company. The gas company wanted the center to provide manufacturers with information about conserving energy and using resources more wisely. By applying the information from the ERC, businesses could meet the environmental regulations in Los Angeles instead of moving to another community.

Picard didn't waste anything in building the new facility. Sixty percent of the materials to build the new facility came from the building that was torn down. Confiscated guns from the LAPD, plus a decommissioned submarine, were melted down to be used as steel reinforcing bars. PVC pipe was pulverized and turned into walkways. Old U.S. currency was shredded and used for bulletin boards. The parquet floor was made from wood salvaged from a warehouse destroyed in the 1989 San Francisco earthquake.

Use of all those recycled materials is impressive, but the biggest idea is in the carpeting. The Environmental Resource Center *leases* its industrial carpeting from Interface, an ecology-minded carpet manufacturer. As parts of the carpet need replacing, Interface will do so, matching color, texture, and cleanliness. ERC can keep the facility looking its best and Interface enjoys a profitable, ongoing lease. Interface recycles the carpet and the environment is spared tons of carpet landfill that take about 20,000 years to decompose.[2]

Manufacture with Recycling in Mind

Tom's of Maine, a manufacturer of natural personal care products, is environmentally conscious as a matter of principle. Tom's products are made with natural ingredients and they are packaged with the environment in mind. The toothpaste tubes are made from aluminum with a thin plastic lining to keep the toothpaste from the metal and are 100 percent recyclable. Mouthwash bottles are a kind of plastic that is easily recycled and shampoo bottles are made of recycled milk bottles. Soy-based ink is used in all printing.

The manufacturing process is also environmentally sound with a special filtration system that removes 80 percent of the bio burden from the water. To decrease their impact on the local water system, the company uses saving methods that reduce water usage by 33 percent. Tom's donates 10 percent of pretax profits to nonprofit organizations in the community and to environmental causes. The company has also organized a community recycling program.

But just being concerned about their own manufacturing process is not enough for the folks at Tom's. They developed a radio program called E-Town to make people more aware of environmental issues through interviews, music, and special reports. With more information, listeners can make more informed decisions when buying products and may be motivated to take more active roles in protecting the environment. E-Town also gives out E-chievement Awards to people who have made an outstanding contribution to an environmental issue.

One interesting awardee is a flight attendant who organized a recycling program for airline flights. Through her efforts, 38 million cans were recycled and $165,000 in recycling money went to charity. Awardee Levi Strauss was saluted for a recycling program that uses scrap denim to produce office products, stationery, and corrugated boxes. This program by Levi saves trees and reduces landfill.[3]

The computer industry has used recycling for a long time, donating or exporting outmoded equipment. Apple now sends a prepaid return shipping label to use when the cartridge needs rebuilding. Furthermore, they donate one dollar to environmental organizations for every returned cartridge. Some manufacturers are making it easier to update rather than replace the machines when new technology comes along. General Electric has been experimenting with a refrigerator that can be disassembled so that parts can be recycled or reused. More good news—that design also makes it easier to assemble and thus more cost-effective.

Recycling Can Support Nonprofit Organizations

On the nonprofit side, New Directions, an organization that provides substance abuse treatment and job training for veterans in Los Angeles, California, is providing the recycling for a large veterans administration base that includes a hospital. The nonprofit uses the recycling process as part of its job training program for residents. Residents begin at the sorting level and increase their skills to become supervisors. The money generated by the recycling business helps support the New Directions program and increases the recycling efforts of the Veterans Administration by making the process very simple.

Whirlpool Corporation also helps the community by contracting to have their recyclables picked up by Gateway Sheltered Workshop, an organization that helps people find work. The program has created jobs for hard-to-employ individuals and enhanced the recycling efforts of Whirlpool. In the environmental arena, creativity gets high marks.

Incentives to Decrease Pollution

Often good environmental policies can benefit companies in both cost savings and employee satisfaction. The 3M company tackled pollution by creating its Pollution Prevention Plan (3P). Working on the concept that preventing pollution in the first place is better than cleaning it up after the fact, the company encourages employees to come up with suggestions. The criteria are that the project prevent or reduce a pollutant, reduce energy use or make more efficient use of resources, use technical innovation, and save money. If employee suggestions meet those criteria, they receive monetary awards.

Since the beginning of the program, 3M has saved $790 million and prevented 750,000 tons of pollution. One example of environmental changes developed through the program is the new equipment used for a resin spray. This new equipment eliminated excessive overspray and reduced the amount of resin needed, saving $125,000 on an investment of $45,000. The 3M program also developed a new product from a waste stream in the plant that can be used to contain and absorb hazardous waste spills. This new product not only cuts landfill costs and reduces waste, but serves as an additional revenue source.

The financial rewards are great incentives for both the employees who come up with the ideas and the company that saves money and gains new products. By encouraging employees on this level, 3M has a powerful environmental impact and employees have the opportunity to contribute to the company and protect the environment. The ability to have an impact through innovation is an important factor in recruiting and hiring good people, especially in a science-driven culture.[4]

Dow Chemical has a similar program to cut toxic emissions and waste. That program resulted in eliminating 13.4

million pounds of waste in 1990 for cost savings of $10.5 million. A number of other companies have organized aggressive programs to reduce emissions and waste.

Producing power is not an ecologically sound business, but at AES they take their responsibilities seriously. To off-set the projected 40-year emissions of a coal-fired power plant in Montville, Connecticut, AES planted 52 million trees in Guatemala. The oxygen produced by the trees would balance the carbon generated by the plant in Montville. AES extends its social responsibility to the peo-ple of the countries where it has facilities—funding medial care in Kazakhstan, organizing food banks in Argentina, and building schools in China.

Co-founders Dennis Bakke and Roger Sant have a strong sense of business values. Bakke applies his Christian ideals to the workplace and Sant, a active environmentalist, is active in the World Wildlife Fund and the Environment Defense Fund. Bakke says, "This isn't about maximizing profits. We do this because it maximizes our ability to have fun and make a difference."[5]

"Green" Hotels

In the hotel business, facilities can save as much as 5 per-cent for good housekeeping measures and 10 percent for low-cost measures. Things as simple as replacing regular bulbs with energy saver bulbs and maintaining moderate temperatures in unoccupied rooms lower energy costs. To motivate employees to recycle cardboard, plastic, and glass, give 50 percent of the recycling proceeds to employees.

John Picard (Environmental Resource Center) and his colleague, Ray Anderson of Interface (the carpet leasing company), are working together to test some interesting environmental ideas. They were to conduct a week-long comprehensive environmental test at the Grand Wailea Hotel

on the island of Maui in Hawaii. Here's what they planned:
- turning off the air conditioning and opening windows for natural ventilation
- turning off the decorative fountains that are run on imported diesel fuel
- changing bed sheets every three days
- reducing the number of towels to two bath and two hand towels
- using sugar-based cleansers; eliminating pesticides on the grounds
- using local food for banquets rather than importing the usual 90 percent from the mainland
- composting hotel restaurant wastes; and making guests take their garbage home (remember, the island is very small, with little space for garbage).

The results aren't in yet as this book goes to press, but the ideas have application to hotels and restaurants around the world.[6]

Resort hotels that rely on a beautiful location have much to lose if the environment becomes polluted. It is definitely to their benefit to use environmentally friendly cleaning products and to do business with vendors who share these views. Making these measures public will increase the loyalty of customers who appreciate the hotel's willingness to protect the environment.

The Green Hotels Association has developed a questionnaire to identify how "green" a hotel or resort facility is. The questions address issues of recycling that include food and beverage, meeting materials, guest room amenities, water, and energy. To encourage hotels to be environmentally aware, the Green Hotels Association provides the questionnaire to meeting planners and suggests that they fax it to sites as part of the selection process.

Recycling Ideas to Start Today

Recycling is one of the easiest ways to impact the environment. Whether you are a large or a small business, your recycling efforts can have an impact. Paper is the first item that comes to mind. How much paper do we all waste? Printing out multiple drafts of projects; sending copies to the entire world; using a new file folder when an old one can be relabeled; using a full sheet for a fax cover—the list goes on and on. Here are some recycling tips that you can easily implement:

- Save and reuse boxes and packing materials you receive from suppliers.
- Reuse rubber bands and paper clips from mail items.
- Save money and protect the environment by using toner cartridges that can be remanufactured.
- Recycle plastic milk and soda bottles with a 1 or 2 on the bottom, as well as aluminum soda cans and glass containers.
- Use a plain paper fax, since thermal fax paper does not recycle well.
- Use e-mail instead of memos.
- Print and copy on both sides of the paper.
- Use a smaller print size when printing drafts so that fewer sheets of paper are used.
- Use a Post-it type note for a fax routing rather than a full-page cover sheet.

Look around your workplace for other possibilities. Enlist employees in finding ways to save. Their participation in the process can increase the sense of teamwork and involvement in the organization. The cost savings can be shared with employees to sweeten the pot.

Stewardship for Our Natural Environment

Stewardship not only protects the environment, but also helps manage and maintain an endangered or fragile ecology. L.L. Bean, the world's leading mail-order business for quality outdoor wear and equipment, is active in conservation issues. They support organizations that seek to protect the environment and maintain it for the enjoyment of future generations. One project they support through grants and employee hours is the maintenance of the Appalachian Trail. A $20,000 grant by L.L. Bean to the Appalachian Trail Conference, a nonprofit group in Harper's Ferry, West Virginia, will help support local clubs along the 2,100-mile trail that stretches from Georgia to Maine.

Employees at L.L. Bean do their part, too. They volunteer to help maintain the 23.6 miles of the trail in Maine and in 1994 gave 1,721 hours to blaze 17 miles of the trail, clip 10 miles, clear blowdowns along 18 miles, build 15 waterbars, build a 15-foot bridge and 500 feet of bog bridge.[7]

Plant a Tree

The Tree People, an environmental group in Los Angeles, suggests that you plant a tree in honor of someone or something special. More trees not only create a more beautiful environment, but also help increase the amount of oxygen in the air. Your company may want to plant a tree in the name of the employee of the month, the person who submits the best recycling idea, or other employee award program. Local communities can benefit from landscaping around commercial areas or street medians. Get together with a local nursery or hardware store to do a "beautification" project. Maybe the high school senior class can maintain the landscaping on an ongoing basis.

There are many ways your company can start "going green." As you begin to put environmentally responsible policies in place, be sure your employees, shareholders, stakeholders, and customers hear about it. A key factor in the success of any environmentally conscious program like this is to enlist as many supporters as possible. News of your environmental efforts will spread and others will be encouraged to do the same.

As others have discovered, being environmentally responsible can save your company money and increase your market share. Involvement in environmental issues can also strengthen the sense of teamwork as employees work together on projects outside the workplace. Your reputation as an environmentally responsible company will also work in your favor to attract and keep the best employees.

KEY CONCEPTS

▶ Everything we do has an environmental impact.
▶ There are opportunities everywhere to make an environmental difference.
▶ Environment awareness is usually profitable.
▶ Recycle, recycle, recycle.
▶ Preventing pollution is easier than cleaning it up.
▶ Be a steward for the world around us.

ACTION PLAN

• Do an environmental audit of your organization, including energy costs, paper, plastic and aluminum can usage, pollution from manufacturing, heating and air conditioning costs, and emissions.

- If you are in a manufacturing environment, enlist the support of the scientists and engineers to develop environmentally sound processes.
- For basic business operations, involve employees in creating recycling and energy-saving activities. Consider using incentives, such as sharing the savings of recycling or energy cost savings with all participating employees.
- Find a way to participate in the preservation of some part of the natural world.
- Start today!

Endnotes

1. Roberts, Paul, "Ecotrust Stirs Up a New Shade of Green," *Fast Company*, April/May 1997.
2. Weisman, Alan, *Los Angeles Times Magazine*, January 11, 1998.
3. toms-of-maine.com.
4. 3m.com.
5. Markels, Alex, "Power to the People," *Fast Company*, February/March 1998.
6. Weisman, Alan, *Los Angeles Times Magazine*, January 11, 1998.
7. llbean.com.

18

Spirituality

"Most of us have jobs that are
too small for our spirits."
                                        —Studs Terkel

In fact, the pressures of the workplace, including the
struggle to survive under downsizing and constant
organizational change, have created a kind of burnout that
reaches the very soul of individuals. The International
Workplace Values Survey indicated that 69 percent of the
respondents would be interested in being part of a formal
organization that sought to further humanistic values in the
workplace.

Forward-thinking companies are evolving into providing
more humanistic environments and opening lines of communication that allow employees to voice and explore spiritual

issues. The results are remarkable. Rather than just attending work, employees are more cooperative, function better in teams, demonstrate an attitude of ownership, and are more productive.

This so-called *spiritual* view is not about imposing a particular religious belief. Instead, it defines spirituality in a broader scope to include values, ethics, communication, honesty, trust, cooperation—concepts that are common among many religions. The expression of that spirituality is as individual as the employees themselves. Wise employers are finding many ways to create an environment that encourages employees to express their spiritual sides, from exploring spiritual thought, to meditation, to the "Joy Gang" (a standing committee at Ben & Jerry's). However the companies express their respect for spirituality in the workplace, the results are a more committed, productive, and involved workforce.

Learning about Spirituality

Once a week some of the employees of the World Bank in Washington, D.C., get together at lunch to discuss a broad range of spiritual topics. It's part of a group call the Spiritual Unfoldment Society established by executive Richard Barrett to help open up the workplace for spiritual topics. In the beginning Barrett called together some co-workers to give him feedback on a book he'd written called *A Guide to Liberating Your Soul*. Other employees became interested in exploring spiritual topics as what started out as six brown bag lunches turned into the Spiritual Unfoldment Society.

They developed a mission statement that focuses on personal transformation through knowledge and awareness. The organization provides a safe place for the exchange of beliefs and ideas, with the ultimate goal of having an impact on the internal and external interactions of the Bank. Barrett looks to the business community to bring values back to society.

When employees are no longer afraid to speak up about

their personal values in the workplace, they will be able to create an atmosphere of cooperation. Creating an environment free of fear will allow individuals to be at their creative best. This absence of fear is also what will make it possible for employees to feel like owners of the organization.

Building Trust

If often not acknowledged, spiritual expression has always been evident in people's decisions and interpersonal relationships. But belief systems have usually been kept private, sometimes to the detriment of the organization. For instance, it is well known that a key element in the effectiveness of teams is trust. Trust is developed through common values and mutual respect. Values are part of our spiritual side. Open expression of that aspect of ourselves can strengthen the bonds of trust in teams and increase their success.

When teams fail to find a common value structure, they are unlikely to succeed because they cannot generate the trust level necessary to work together. It is at cross-purposes to ask people to enter into groups that require a great deal of trust in an environment that does not support the open discussion of individual values.

Building a Value System

World Vision is a nonprofit organization that provides food, shelter, and educational opportunities to people around the world. Besides helping people in developing countries, the organization believes in helping employees expand their spiritual lives.

Although Christian principles play an important role in World Vision's spiritual development program, the model they use can be applied to any organization. They use a values-based, spiritual development approach that was developed by Brian Hall, a professor at Santa Clara University.

Hall's key elements are: values are a part of behavior and can be identified and measured; values can be described in words; values develop in stages; and values may change based on circumstances.[1]

Using Hall's model, employees at World Vision actively seek a higher level of spirituality. The Human Resources Department created the Office of Spiritual Information to support employees along this path. The spiritual awareness process includes chapel meetings, devotions, group retreats, and individual conferences. As a result of this spiritual support, employees are more energetic, creative, and healthy, both emotionally and physically.

If your corporate culture is open enough to consider it, this kind of spiritual approach to work can be explored more fully. There is an increasing understanding that work must mean more than just a paycheck, that it is tied to an individual's sense of meaning and purpose. Because workers are spending more and more time at work, this need for purpose is becoming increasingly important. Matthew Fox is a well-known Episcopal priest who believes that there must also be joy in work. For Fox, "A job is making money to pay your bills, but work is putting your heart in the world."[2]

Religious Commitment

Many people express their spirituality through commitment and involvement in a defined faith. They belong to churches, synagogues, temples, communities, or other congregations comprised of people of similar religious beliefs. The adherence to religious principles and morals is generally seen as a positive thing in our culture. While selecting employees on the basis of religious beliefs might be considered discriminatory, some employers do place emphasis on some sort of involvement with religious organizations.

Putting heart and faith into the business world is the basis for the culture at Mennonite Mutual Insurance Company.

Christian principles provide the foundation for this organization. While the company is actively involved in the Mennonite community, their employee selection is not limited to those of the Mennonite faith. What they do require is that employees be actively involved and committed to their church.

David Lehman, president of the insurance company, said that hiring people with similar values eliminates conflicts of ethics and facilitates communication and decision making. The spiritual principles overflow into the way individuals and the organization conduct their daily business, define their standards, and make basic management decisions. Lehman sees a subtle trend in other industries toward understanding, identifying, and exploring core values.

Senior-level managers are beginning to take a look at the spiritual side of management.

There are, however, some universal values that transcend individual religious beliefs. The alignment of these core values of the individuals and the organization is a critical factor in the relationship between the employee and the employer. As Mennonite Mutual demonstrates, having a clear understanding and expression of the corporate core values and using this understanding as a framework for hiring can create a environment that is more compatible and effective.

Meditation

Other companies are finding ways to give employees a "spiritual" break in the workplace. Some companies are now sponsoring meditation classes at work. The concept behind meditation is that the process builds serenity, an inner peace that helps people focus more positively and comfortably on the work before them.

At Management Associates, a technical search firm in Santa Clara, all but the new employees meditate *at work* for about two hours a week. Employees who are not meditating can take a break or walk around the grounds. Val Baldwin, co-owner of the firm, has seen a number of improvements since meditation has been an option. Employees have been more productive, increasing revenues and logging more billable hours. And the relationship between Baldwin and his partner has also improved. They are able to work together more effectively in making strategic decisions for the company. Baldwin asks employees to pay $250 toward the $1,000 meditation class. The financial commitment on both sides makes the process more effective.

At Superior Foods, fewer employees take advantage of the opportunity to mediate at work, but there are benefits even for those who choose not to participate. The relationships between employees are improved and during meditation time the office is quiet so nonparticipants can get more done. The benefit to the organization comes as a result of the benefit to the individual.

For Alex Rodriguez, the president and general manager for a sanitation and storage company, meditation has enabled him to be a much better manager. Now instead of micromanaging his employees, he is able to give them more latitude in decision making. Not to mention that he's also less emotional in his management style. Rodriguez started by meditating himself and now plans to extend the opportunity to all his employees. He sees the benefit in the way employees can relate to each other with more honesty. For Rodriguez, the potential for increased productivity is secondary.[3]

Meditation can help employees find peace within themselves and as a result be more secure in times of change. Employees who meditate seem to be able to focus more clearly on tasks and worry less. When introducing a concept like meditation, be sure that employees do not feel pressure to participate. Keep the expense and time to a minimum so that those who do not participate do not feel slighted. In the particular case of meditation, it is especially important that no religious connotation be attached to this exercise in self-awareness.

Music Soothes the Soul

Donato's Pizza in Ohio contracted with Creative Learning Technologies to create a "sound machine" where employees could go to have a moment to collect their thoughts or take a stress break. This place is called N.E.S.T., which stands for Naturally Enhanced Sound Transmission. Employees can sit in the N.E.S.T. and listen to music, read, or just close their eyes for a moment. Having this designated place to "get away from it all" helps employees be more productive and creative.[4]

The Beauty of Nature

To create a peaceful setting conducive to work and environmental comfort, many companies have built their facilities in park-like settings. A pond, trees, landscaping, and other features create a place people want to go.

The buildings on MasterCard's campus in Purchase, New York, have large windows that practically bring in the beauty of surrounding Westchester County. The headquarters of the McDonald's Corporation in Oak Brook, Illinois, are beautifully landscaped and decorated with attractive sculpture and unique artwork.

The conference room on the 14th floor of Peoples Bank in Bridgeport, Connecticut is an excellent place for observing the sunset. Each day, employees gather there informally, each in his own private meditation or observation of the sunset. For some it may be a spiritual activity, for others simply a way to decompress between work and home. The important thing is that the culture of the bank is open to accommodate this quiet and very personal expression of individual spirituality. These moments of introspection can be time well spent.[5]

Time to Reflect

In the world of long working hours, increasing family responsibility and rapid change, people seldom take the time to reflect on experiences, to integrate the wisdom collected along life's journey. People are having a hard time putting it all together. Organizations are becoming increasingly aware of the need to give people the time they need *away from the workplace* to rekindle their souls and to open their minds to new possibilities.

If workers are to be sharp and focused, they need time to refresh their minds and spirits. It is important to help employees open up to their potential. Only when individuals have opportunities to explore their driving interests or pursue their talents, will they find a sense of fulfillment and satisfaction. Companies that support and encourage this search will not only have more enlightened and empowered employees, but will be able to attract the very best in their industry.

Leaves of Absence

Vacation time is the most common kind of leave offered by companies. The amount of time given each year is beginning to increase for employees who stay with a company. The two- and three-week vacations, given after one year and five to seven years respectively, are quite typical, but in 37 percent of companies surveyed by Romac International employees receive four weeks after seven to ten years. For about 14 percent of the companies, employees have five weeks of vacation after ten to fifteen years. It's an incentive for people to stay, but it also lets employees know that the organization recognizes their need to invest time giving to themselves.

Traditional leaves, or sabbaticals, constitute paid time off for the employee to pursue any activity he chooses. Personal leaves can be paid or unpaid and often involve an activity that has a direct benefit to the company as well as the employee. Social services leaves are paid time off for the purpose of community outreach. Extended personal leaves are unpaid time off with a guaranteed return to work and are often given to employees with young children. Voluntary leaves are unpaid and are in lieu of being laid off. Beyond this framework for employee leaves, companies are doing some very creative things to help workers keep their energy and creativity flowing.

Sabbaticals

Sabbaticals are one of the ways companies are helping their employees regenerate and refresh their minds and spirits. Much longer than the traditional vacation, sabbaticals are commonplace in the high-tech industry, with most of the major corporations offering some form of extended time off with pay. Intel was the first to offer a sabbatical program back in 1969, when the company was founded. The program remains in place today and serves a dual purpose: employees on sabbaticals have the opportunity to revitalize their energy and creativity; and, employees who remain at work have an opportunity they might not otherwise have to take on new challenges.

Companies that provide sabbaticals view them in different ways. For some they are a benefit, with the award based on the number of years of service. For others, like Microsoft, they are considered a reward for key employees. Microsoft employees must have seven years of service, meet certain job standards, and have the approval of the employees' vice president before they can take a sabbatical. Once approved, they may choose several ways to "spend" the time: the traditional way—time off with pay, an assignment in another part of the company, or a cash stipend added to their pay.

Team-Learning Sabbaticals

Hallmark has also taken the sabbatical, or what they refer to as "rotations," to a new level. They have two kinds of rotations. The first type is purely creative. Groups of up to ten people spend four months working on a new creative skill—full-time. The kinds of creative activities could be glass-blowing, papermaking, engraving, or any number of other unique activities.

The second kind of rotation is for small teams of three or four. These groups last six months and are designed to focus on a social trend. Issues run the gamut from "the meaning of masculinity" to "a study of angels." These teams travel and do extensive research and then return to build prototypes based on their work. A recent rotation centered on death and dying in the 1990s. The result of their research was a 20-minute video and a new product line. The new product line addresses the difficult issue of what is appropriate to send to someone who is dying of AIDS, a situation where the get well card is totally inadequate. Because of the intensity of the rotations, the participants themselves feel transformed, having gained new perspectives of both themselves and others.[6]

Mini-Sabbaticals

Regardless of the size of your company, you can provide "sabbaticals." You may not be able to have people out for months, but you can give them some special time to pursue something that is important to them. At Administrative Resource Options (ARO), a small outsourcing company in Minneapolis/St. Paul, that provides on-site office support and facilities management, full-time employees may request a paid leave to volunteer with a charity for up to five days. Employees at ARO have actively supported the program, with 40 percent of them donating time to local charities in the Twin Cities.

Here are some of the sabbatical options companies are making available to their employees:

- American Express allows employees to take a year of paid leave for community service after 10 years of service.
- Dupont employees can take a year of unpaid leave, but keep their health benefits.
- McDonalds offers 8 weeks of paid leave to full-time workers after 10 years.
- Senior-level employees at Microsoft can take eight weeks of paid leave, if they meet certain requirements.

Sabbaticals as Recruitment Tools

For companies in high tech, sabbaticals have become one of the significant tools in recruiting and retaining good employees. Because of the high level of training and knowledge that employees have in this industry, the loss of an employee to a competitor after two or three years is very costly. Tying the sabbatical program to years of service encourages employees to stay, as they near the time when they will be eligible, assuming all other factors, such as work environment, compensation, and other benefits are equal.

Recruiters in the industry use sabbaticals as a trading issue when pursuing a hot prospect. Clever recruiters will even offer to pay out the pending sabbatical time to encourage the prospect to make an immediate job change. In this industry, sabbaticals are more than just an opportunity for employees to get a creative break. They are a strategic requirement for companies to remain competitive.

In the same way quality of life policies must be backed by the corporate culture, so must companies have the supporting culture to make sabbaticals serve their purpose. Because of the competition in the high-tech industry, employees may feel that by taking a sabbatical they will return to a downgraded position or no position at all.

If the corporate culture does not support the policy of holding positions for employees on sabbaticals, employees will not take advantage of these opportunities to expand their personal horizons. Enlightened companies are creating an environment where employees can work as a team to allow individuals to take time off to enhance their creativity and spirit.

Time and Space for Creativity

Creativity and innovation are tremendously powerful for growth and success in many companies, yet the environment is not conducive to creative thinking. Enlightened employers provide physical environments—space and time for people to think, expand their minds, and generate valuable ideas.

Hallmark is a company that has developed a broad range of rejuvenation opportunities for workers. They have actually created two spaces, one a large warehouse facility next to their corporate offices and another called Kearney Farm, a Victorian farm house complete with a barn, where employees can go to get a creative break.

The warehouse space has places to do a number of crafts, from quilt making to leather tooling. It also can support a small-scope manufacturing operation. Out at Kearney Farm, there are artists' studios in the house, while the barn can be used for woodworking, blacksmithing, and crafting other products. Employees can spend all day or just an afternoon at either facility doing something completely unrelated to their work that allows them to expand their creativity.

Creating Joy

Laughter brings joy into the workplace and is good for the soul. Companies, both large and small, are learning how laughter and fun can create a highly motivated and loyal workforce.

Southwest Airlines, one of the top 100 companies to work for in America, is renowned for the unorthodox management style of its CEO, Herb Kelleher. He's been known to walk down the aisle of an airplane dressed in an Easter bunny suit; sing "Tea for Two" wearing bloomers and a bonnet; and sing a rap song with people in Teenage Mutant Ninja Turtle costumes. Humor is so much a part of the corporate culture at Southwest that interviewees are asked how they used humor at work or to diffuse a difficult situation. Southwest even goes so far as to have a Vice President of Fun.

The bunny suit may not be your style, but the idea of not taking yourself too seriously can have a very positive effect. Humor is one of the elements that creates a sense of teamwork for the hard-working, loyal employees of Southwest.

Motivation and Fun

Another CEO who walks on the outrageous side is Frank Spontelli, the owner of Business Stationery, Inc. in Cleveland, Ohio. In early Spring some high goals were set. To motivate the troops, the managers struck a deal with Spontelli. If they met the goals, he would serve breakfast to all the employees on Good Friday. If they surpassed the goals, he would also wear a bunny suit. Spontelli looked adorable in his bunny outfit as he applied his early career talent as a grill cook to preparing a full breakfast. Employees on all three shifts enjoyed his eggs, potatoes, and sausage— and the wonderful experience of having them cooked by Bunny, CEO. How often do you see the boss in a bunny suit?

Does your company have a Joy Gang? Or a Minister of Joy? These are official jobs at Ben & Jerry's. The folks at Ben & Jerry's have celebrated Elvis Day and Barry Manilow Day. The head of the Joy Gang has rented roller skates to be used in the hallways. Music and pantomime often accompany the packing of ice cream. The humor can be outrageous, but never hurtful. As with Southwest, the underlying principles of the lighthearted atmosphere are respect and genuine concern for employees.

Take an Unexpected Break for Fun

The benefits of a lighthearted corporate culture can extend beyond the employees and have an impact on the customer base. People want to do business with a company that looks like it's having fun. The high energy that good humor creates will be reflected in all the interactions your employees have with clients and prospects.

Laughter also releases stress and improves creativity. Have you ever been struggling with a problem or a deadline and the more you struggled the less active your brain became? The stress keeps blocking the creativity you need for a solution. The change of pace that a burst of laughter creates can release the stress gridlock and let the creativity come through. A workplace with a lower stress level will encourage creativity and productivity. In fact, humor is also related to flexibility. In today's economy all companies need to be both creative and flexible to compete in the rapidly changing and highly competitive marketplace.

One busy Thursday afternoon at Cornoyer Hedrick, a design firm in Phoenix, Arizona, an air horn went off. People weren't sure what was happening, but thought it might be a fire drill. To their surprise, it was really a yogurt drill. The principals of the firm had the local yogurt shop cater in frozen yogurt for all the employees. After this unexpected break, employees went back to work, refreshed and ready to complete the projects they were working on.

With a day or two notice, employees of HA-LO Industries, Inc., Chicago, take an extended lunch hour—an hour or two— to enjoy some delicious food and socialize with each other. The company sponsors vendors to come on-site to prepare ice cream sundaes or some other kind of food. The mid-day par-

ties are a welcome break, and they also build deeper friendships among the long-time employees of this busy company.

In these companies, as well as many others who include
fun as part of the workplace, there is a highly productive and
loyal workforce. That loyalty translates into fewer sick days
and lower turnover, two significant factors in profitability.
Having fun together is a terrific team builder. As people laugh
together, they break down barriers and create stronger bonds
that make it easier to find solutions when problems occur.

Visit a Comedy Club

If you have a comedy club in your city, see if you can
make arrangements for special mini-shows at your place of
work. The cost for the in-demand professionals might be too
high for a brown-bag lunch event, but there are plenty of ama-
teurs who would welcome the opportunity to practice before
live audiences. Be sure the comics avoid profanity and behaviors that may offend any of your employees.

As an added bonus, buy passes to comedy club perfor-
mances at a discount to distribute to interested employees.
Or stage a company event at a comedy club. Business
Stationery, Inc. of Cleveland, Ohio, had their annual end-of-
the-year party at a nice restaurant, then walked to a nearby
comedy club to enjoy a show together. The comedians knew
they were there, knew about the company and some key people, and wove that knowledge into their humor. The result—
lots of fun and some enjoyable bonding and sharing.

This concept doesn't mean that work should be a trip to a
comedy club, but that humor is accepted and encouraged in
the workplace. As Southwest Airlines and Ben & Jerry's
demonstrate, humor actually increases productivity and dedication to the job. Humor doesn't have to be in the form of
jokes. Needless to say, there are very few of us who can
deliver the punch line like Bill Cosby or Jerry Seinfeld. Yet
we can find humor in many things—most often in our own

foibles. And humor can also be a simple lightheartedness in the culture, an acceptance of silly.

The beauty of adding humor to the workplace is that it can be done with very little money, so don't let budgets get in the way of fun. The productivity of your employees will more than compensate for the cost. So take a moment now, send that adult in you somewhere else, and let the kid in you be creative. Use the following ideas as a springboard for creating ways to bring fun into your workplace.

"Fun" Ideas

There are all sorts of things you can do for fun in the workplace. Consider some of the things that humor consultants recommend:

How about small wind up toys, the kind you might get at a penny arcade, for employees' desks? How about plush bears that giggle when you push on their paws? It may be "canned" laughter, but it is impossible not to get caught up in it. Post a cartoon for the week in the employee lunchroom. Keep a mental health file of favorite cartoons. Change some of the art in the office to more whimsical or cartoon art. Celebrate some outrageous holiday or celebrity day. Almost every day has something attached to it.

Hand out something silly at the next staff meeting that has some bearing on the topics for discussion. Silly Putty and Slinkies are always fun for big kids.

Wear a hat to work day—anything from a baseball hat with a saying on it to the beach hat that got crushed on the plane would work. For the night shift, you might have everyone come to the staff meeting in pajamas. General Motors had an ugly tie day.

One company has an inflatable banana that has taken on a character of its own. Post baby pictures of everyone. They're cute as the dickens and remind everyone that we all started out the same. During tax season, many accounting firms provide stress release kits filled with snacks to help staff get through the long hours. Personalized fortune cookies can be ordered for as little as $2.00 for 25. Put messages in them that apply specifically to the people or an event at your company.

The foundation for this lighthearted approach to the workplace is a genuine concern for employees and the desire to make the workplace a more pleasant, productive place to be.

Videos at Lunch

The special days and toys can be "ice breakers" in the organization and create a less stressful daily environment, but fun can also have a purpose. At Rosenbluth, a large travel agency, they not only have fun, but it has meaning to the organization. For instance, they have a video day at corporate headquarters in the "Thought Theater." Employees bring their lunch and enjoy a video. The benefit is that each movie has a theme that the employees can discuss and relate to their job situation.

Goodie Bags for New Employees

To help make new employees comfortable, Rosenbluth Travel prepares a "goodie bag" that has lunch coupons, lists of employees' names, and information about where to get supplies along with a gag gift. It is a way to welcome new employees and let them know that they are part of the team. This small investment translates into happier employees, who are able to acclimate to the team much easier.

Employees want to be recognized as individuals with feelings, dreams, and desires to contribute something of value. This uniqueness is the spirituality that is the core of human beings. Ultimately the relationship of the organization and the employees is created at this deep level. Enlightened companies are finding ways to encourage and support employees in expressing their values, creativity, and sense of joy. As employers forge this new relationship with employees, they are creating a workplace where trust, commitment, and productivity come together for the benefit of all.

While many people are keenly sensitive to issues we group under the broad category of spirituality, more concrete rewards are also important to them. Let's explore tangible and intangible compensation ideas in the next chapter.

KEY CONCEPTS

▶ Enlightened companies value the spiritual side of employees.

▶ Spirituality can be expressed in many ways, but stems from the core values of the individual.

▶ Employees need the opportunity to explore their spiritual side, to have time to reflect on life experiences in order for work to be truly meaningful.

▶ Creating time, space, and an environment where individuals can express their spiritual side in the workplace results in a more creative, productive, and effective workforce.

ACTION PLAN

- Examine your leave policies. Consider ways to give employees time to pursue personal interests or to take a new point of view within the organization.
- Consider opportunities to interject humor into the organization. Not everyone can wear a bunny suit, but there are many ways to lighten up the atmosphere that are easy to implement.

- If your company culture is open to spiritual concepts, consider offering learning opportunities on core values such as honesty, ethics, trust, and communication.
- Determine the core values of both individuals and the organization. How compatible are the values of the employees and the company? If there is a significant gap, consider engaging a consultant to help facilitate a dialogue to align the value structures.
- When the exploration of spirituality moves beyond sabbaticals and humor, it can be a very delicate and highly personal issue. Go slowly and encourage spiritual expression by creating a safe environment where people can begin to share this important aspect of their individuality.

Endnotes

1. Laabs, Jennifer, "Balancing Spirituality at Work," *Personnel Journal*, September 1995.
2. O'Connor, Colleen, "Being Joyfully Employed is Latest Self-help Trend," *The Dallas Morning News*, February 23, 1997.
3. Quinn, Michelle, "Meditation Provides Mantras Amid the Mania," *San Jose Mercury News*, August 6, 1996.
4. Laabs, Jennifer, "Balancing Spirituality at Work," *Personnel Journal*, September 1995. (p. 293)
5. Ibid. (p. 294)
6. Fishman, Charles, "At Hallmark, Sabbaticals Are Serious Business," *Fast Company*, October/November 1996.

19

Meaningful Rewards

As companies evolve and redefine their relationship with employees, they will redefine their methods of compensation. They will challenge assumptions about what employees are worth to the organization in terms of money. They will become more sensitive to the value of their contributions in terms of overall profitability.

Enlightened companies already know that the collective knowledge of their employees drives corporate success. Those companies that share their profitability with their employees will continue to be successful. When financial rewards are connected to employee performance, the linkage underscores the significance of employee contributions to the success of the organization. This connection is a second key element in making work meaningful. Not only do employees need to see their ideas and suggestions implemented, but they also need to be acknowledged for their contributions.

Variable Pay

In the past, an annual salary increase was considered to be all that was necessary to keep employees satisfied and productive. In turn, the employees were expected to produce a certain amount of work as directed by the organization. Relationships are changing. The marketplace of the future will demand much more from companies and employees.

Hewitt Associates found in a survey of 1,681 companies that salary increases were not motivating employees to perform. The failure of salary increases to motivate employees is due in part to the fact that increases have been low, averaging only 3.9 percent in 1996. More important, the absence of a strong link of salaries and performance exacerbates the problem.

The difference between high and low performers is often only a percent or two of income increase. From an employee's point of view, there is no need to put in 110 percent, if the guy down the hall can put in 60 percent and receive almost the same increase.

More effective, according to the Hewitt survey, is the use of variable pay or incentives. On average, companies now allot 7.5 percent of their payroll budgets to variable pay programs, up from 6.4 percent in 1994 and 5.9 percent in 1993. Hewitt found that 61 percent of the organizations surveyed have some kind of variable pay program.

Variable pay rewards individuals, teams, or entire organizations based on their reaching specific goals. Variable pay can come in the form of rewards or incentives, which are usually small cash incentives, travel, or merchandise. Other more sophisticated methods of variable pay can be profit sharing, gain sharing, or stock options.

More companies find that customizing incentives to

reflect corporate goals results in greater improvements on the bottom line. Tying corporate goals to individual goals allows employees to see how their contributions have a direct impact on the overall success of the company.[1]

When a company has a clear operational mission, that is, corporate goals backed up by individual incentives for achievement, the whole organization is focused and can move in the same direction. Once focused, an organization and its employees have a much greater chance for success. Enlightened companies understand the significance of the contributions made by employees and reward those contributions by sharing the financial rewards of success.

Pay for Performance

Would you like to enhance financial compensation for your people? Adding to their paychecks through raises increases your overhead. An alternative is to emphasize pay for performance, paying bonuses for specific, measurable achievements that influence the company's bottom line. The funding for this approach comes from cost savings and increased profits, rather than adding to overhead.

This system of rewards helps to keep workers focused and motivated. Individuals or teams can be rewarded for accomplishments in a number of areas, such as reduction in expenses, technical innovations, or improvements in customer service, safety, quality, deliveries, or environmental protection. The variable pay for achieving these specific goals can bring compensation up to or above industry standards. Using this form of compensation, organizations and employees work *with* each other for the benefit of both.

Incentives for Quality

Quality improvement is a key factor in the ongoing success of every company, but implementing quality programs can be daunting. Incentives can motivate employees to expend the effort required to meet new quality standards. To be effective, the incentives must be directly related to the goals and be significant to the employees.

In order to be more competitive in the marketplace, Varian X-Ray Tube Products in Salt Lake City wanted to establish a 100 percent quality program. The company designed an incentive program to reward high quality and penalize poor quality: it contributed $125 to a special fund for every good tube, deducted $500 for every bad one, and deducted $600 for every customer return. Under the plan, employees who were responsible for the quality of the tubes would share in the profits at the end of the quarter. Not only that, but the pool would replace annual merit raises.

The workers were a little edgy at first. It was difficult to give up individual merit pay and rely on the contributions of a team. When the results were in, there was no need for concern. The dividends from the pool averaged 13 percent, where merit raises had averaged only 3 percent.

The company reaped benefits, too. It gained market share.[2] There is a twofold benefit here: first, this type of compensation program reinforces the significance the individual has in the corporation and second, it improves the services and products of the company.

Sharing Corporate Profits

Gain sharing is a particular type of variable pay that rewards employees when the company profits as a direct result of their efforts. As opposed to a particular division or department goal, gain sharing rewards employees for the overall profitability of the entire company. Not only does gain sharing increase involvement in the work process, but it can also be an effective tool in reinforcing teamwork. This kind of pay is especially effective in manufacturing environments where the connections between employees' efforts and profit are very clear.

The connection between effort and profit is very clear to the employees at Ford Motor Company. Their success in the U.S. truck business resulted in a $4.4 *billion* payback. As a result of the increase in sales of trucks, the 163,000 hourly and eligible salaried employees received checks averaging $1,800. Ford has been using gain sharing successfully for a number of years. Employees who have been with the company since 1984 have earned around $22,000 in profit and gain sharing.[3]

Bonuses for Meeting Specific Goals

Issuing bonuses for reaching specific goals gives employees both financial rewards and a sense of accomplishment. For employees who have worked hard to reach a goal, bonuses are direct and immediate acknowledgments of jobs well done. Positive reinforcement for desired results is always a powerful motivator.

Struggling at the bottom of the competitive airline business in 1994, Continental Airlines had to do something to get back on its feet. When new management took over, they took the opportunity to change the corporate culture. Most of the employees had experienced the airline's downward spiral. The challenge was to get them working together and committed to the company's goal of running an on-time, effective airline. They needed to prove their performance to attract and hold customers. Among many other changes, the airline started giving bonuses to employees every time a specific goal was met.

Every time Continental was in the Department of Transportation's list of top five on-time airlines, every employee received a $65 bonus. The airline made the list nine times in one year. Then the company upped the ante to

$100 for every time Continental was number one on the list and $65 for second and third place. For poorer performance than third place, no bonus was awarded.

The incentive program worked so well that Continental is consistently on top in on-time rankings. The company has proudly increased its ranking in handling baggage and lowering customer complaints as well.[4] Continental continues to be on time and profitable, while its stock continues to increase in value.

Employee Stock Ownership

Many companies are finding that employee ownership is the key to retaining good employees and maintaining a productive, motivated workforce. These Employee Stock Ownership Plans (ESOPs) either give or allow employees to purchase stock in the company and thus, become actual owners.

In some companies ESOPs are designed as benefits, ways to increase retirement income. On the other hand, enlightened companies are using this tool as a vehicle to truly transfer some *ownership* to employees. A big part of making employee ownership successful is creating a culture where information and decision making are shared—just like the democracy at Semco we discussed in Chapter 6. It is the sense of *true ownership* that gives meaning to work, turning employees from hired hands to businesspeople who are invested in the success of the enterprise.

Not unlike Continental, United Airlines had to do something to keep the company in the air. They opted for employee ownership. United Airlines' employees now own 55 percent of the company. They have developed a team approach to address and implement their long-term growth plan. Teams representing all areas of the company address general corporate problems, while local teams handle specific profitability and performance issues.

In Los Angeles, a United team solved a missing baggage

problem and saved the company $1 million. The kind of commitment this team demonstrated is important to the success of all companies. If the team hadn't acted to solve the problem, the company would have lost the $1 million, and the negative word of mouth would have cost them customers.

For United, employee ownership has been a good solution for a troubled company in a competitive market. The value of the stock has more than doubled over the past two years and costs due to absenteeism and workers' compensation have dropped dramatically.

Another company that has an ESOP is IHS Helpdesk Service, headquartered in New York City. All employees become vested in IHS's ESOP after only three years of service. Employees are automatically enrolled during specified periods twice per year. Employees enjoy receiving periodic dividend checks and knowing that their equity continues to grow with their efforts and longevity of employment.[5]

In general, companies that have employee owners are doing better than industry averages. A Rutgers University School of Management study of 54 companies indicated that companies with ESOPs had a 4 percent increase in productivity as compared to the average 1.5 percent for other companies. In addition, the annual growth rate for companies that have employee owners is 8 to 11 percent higher than others.[6]

Stock Options

Due to the shortage of workers in high-tech industries, stock options are offered often as incentives to prospective employees. In fact, these stock options have created a large number of very young millionaires. In the future, like many organizations in these fast-moving, rapidly changing industries, companies in other industries will consider this alternative for attracting and retaining top talent.

Microsoft, a leader in many areas of corporate culture,

has made it a practice to reward its employees in this way. Actually, the decision to go public was designed to establish a monetary stock value so that employees could be rewarded in stock. This compensation alternative provides a way to recognize the workers' contributions to the bottom line. If the company does well, everybody shares the wealth. That's just what happened at Microsoft: a number of employees, who joined the company in its infancy, became millionaires with its public offering.

At Science Applications International Corp. (SAIC) in San Diego, 90 percent of the 25,000 employees are stockholders. But unlike other companies that are publicly traded, SAIC shares are traded only among their own employees, consultants, and directors—and only one day per quarter.

When the founder and CEO, Robert Beyster, first started SAIC, he wanted to offer stock to employees. The problem was that the company was too small for outside broker-dealers. So SAIC established their own, in-house, registered broker-dealer to handle the company's stock transactions. As a result, their stock is less affected by market fluctuations, which helps it hold the value over the long term. Fortunately for the employees, the stock has been a good investment— with returns of 34 percent for the fiscal year ending in January 1997.

Stock ownership is a key value at this high-technology and engineering firm and, as such, has created a culture of owners. There are four ways to get SAIC stock. First, there is the standard ESOP plan that applies to everyone. Second, for employees who bring in new contracts, there are opportunities to buy additional shares equal to the dollar amount of the contracts. In these two instances, employees write personal checks to increase their stock holdings, as opposed to other stock option plans where stocks go automatically into a retirement plan without specific action taken by employees. Actually buying the stock increases the employees' sense of involvement and increases the incentive of employees to help the company perform.[7]

Third, in the 401(k) plan, employees can choose between various funds and SAIC stock, and the company matches contributions with stock. Fourth, for up-and-coming leaders in the organization, there is an additional $25,000 in stock that vests over seven years. This additional stock acts as an encouragement for key talent to stay at SAIC, since this stock is forfeited if they leave prior to vesting.

In a survey of employees, Beyster found that being a stockholder had a significant relationship with turnover rates. Stockholders in the company had a turnover rate of only 5 percent, while those who had not invested in the company had a turnover rate of 12 percent. This enlightened leader believes that it is imperative that every employee feels like an owner.

This concept is so important to him that in 1986 Beyster set up a nonprofit organization called the California Foundation for Enterprise Development. This organization works with private companies to design and implement employee ownership programs. Sharing the wealth of the company has certainly worked for Beyster. SAIC is a $3.4 billion company, and Beyster, with 1.5 percent ownership, is worth about $27 million. He could have kept it all as a 100 percent owner, but he says, "How much money can you spend anyway?"[8]

Starbucks is a coffee importer and retailer headquartered in Seattle. Starbucks, sprouting stores all over the country, offers all employees "bean stock." CEO Howard Schultz wanted to find a way to link shareholder value with long-term rewards for his employees—almost unheard of in retail and privately held companies

His plan was not just for top performers or senior-level people. Everyone at Starbucks, from the baristas (counter workers) to the top level of management, is awarded a percentage of their annual base pay in stock options. Schultz knew that if all the employees were partners in the business, they would have reasons to give their best performance. Even before employees knew whether the bean stock would be worth anything, they started looking for ways to cut costs, to increase value, to sell more. Just the idea that the company was willing to share any profits with the employees had an influence on performance and attitude.

Since the company has been successful, the percentage of stock options to base pay has risen from 12 percent to 14 percent. For example, a Starbuck's employee earning $20,000 a year in 1991 could cash in stock options worth $50,000 only five years later.[9] Employees who are "invested," both personally and financially, care and do more. Their actions have a direct connection with the organization and with their personal, financial well-being. Their work has meaning for the organization and, in return, the stock options demonstrate the company's appreciation of its employees.

Instead of stock, employees at Bloomberg Financial Markets, a New York-based financial information company, receive certificates each year. The goal of Bloomberg employees is to lease information terminals to investment companies and well-heeled individual investors. The value of the certificates is dependent upon the number of terminals placed in the *subsequent* two years. This certificate method of revenue sharing supports the reinvestment of money back into the company, rather than a desire for dividends to be paid out.[10] Bloomberg certificates provide unique "golden handcuffs" that bond good employees to the firm.

Watson Wyatt World Wide is a human resource consulting firm in Bethesda, Maryland, with revenues of $672 million. When the original owner died 50 years ago, the five employees bought the stock from his widow. Employee ownership has been part of the corporate culture ever since. Now, employees who are with the firm for one year are given the chance to buy shares of stock. The company will help finance the purchase, but when employees leave the company they must sell their stock back. In this way, the stock pool is maintained for future employees. Currently about 75 percent of Watson's 5,000 employees are also stockholders.[11]

Compaq Computer employees believe in their company. They're motivated, in part, by a significant return on their personal investment. Through the company's 401(k) plan, all employees have an opportunity to purchase company stock. In 1997, the value of that stock increased 90 percent.

Company-wide Bonuses

Robert Haas, Chairman of Levi Strauss, dissolved the stock option plan because he felt it was unfair to nonmanagement and overseas employees who could not participate. In its place he rolled out a remarkable incentive reward program called Global Success Sharing. The amount of the distribution and the global scope of the involvement make this program unique. When the company meets its goals of $7.6 billion in revenues by 2001, Levi Strauss anticipates that $750 million will be distributed among eligible employees. There are approximately 37,000 eligible employees, ranging from hourly workers to senior executives.[12]

This incentive is considered to be a focal point for a shared objective among employees. Haas and Levi Strauss have a history of acknowledging the contributions of workers through financial rewards. This egalitarian approach invests workers in the overall success of the organization and reinforces their worldwide connection.

Incentive "Credit" Cards

Credit cards, issued for a specific amount, are another way to provide incentives for employee performance. This kind of incentive uses standard credit cards like MasterCard and Visa to give employees flexibility in choosing the reward that is most meaningful to them. This plan can even work well in a company that has a broad range of employees because it affords a wide range of options.

If you are thinking about using this kind of incentive program, contact schools and churches in your community, because these affinity cards are an increasingly popular way to raise funds. There are also companies that provide a credit card-type program. One such company is Card Express, Inc. in Newport Beach, California. With their program an employee can specify an amount to be applied to the card and employees can use the card at any location that accepts MasterCard. Employers may authorize the card for a one-time-only usage, for a specific amount, or unlimited-time usage. The card can have the amount recharged or increased as employees earn additional incentives.

Incentive Ideas for Companies of All Sizes

Financial rewards through profit participation are an effective way to engage employees in the success of the company. But rewards do not always need to be large or financial to demonstrate to employees that the company values their contributions. Regardless of the size of the company, there are many creative ways to acknowledge the effort and importance of the work employees do.

Tying incentives or rewards to a specific goal or result is the key factor in making the program successful. The following examples show how some companies have increased employee involvement in the organization and reinforced the link between employee performance and profitability. If you are a small company where stock options do not apply, consider some of these ways to get employees involved and link employee performance and profitability.

Games
Games involve people in the organization and increase

awareness of opportunities to contribute to company profitability. Creating a game or friendly competition between departments to increase sales, decrease expenses, or lower absenteeism can achieve the desired result by making the process fun. The added benefit is that the games also increase the sense of teamwork within the department.

One multi-office insurance and brokerage house created the postage game. Postage costs were tracked monthly, based on the expenses the previous year. Fifty percent of the savings were placed in an incentive pool and paid out at the end of the quarter. The other 50 percent went to the company's bottom line. In this case the employees won there, too, because they have an ESOP. Articles in the company newsletter with postage-saving ideas supported the program. That way, everyone could see, use, and add to the ideas of the other employees.

The process created a synergy around the goal. Managers in each department were actively involved in the support of the program to keep everyone on track and motivated. Obviously, saving postage means other methods of communication are being used, so the company added one more element, the phone bill. As tasks are added, employees learn about the interdependency of different aspects of business and how they can directly drive profitability through cost savings.

"Fun" Rewards

Rewards or incentives don't necessarily need to be monetary. They can be parties, paid time off, or the chance to just have some fun. At one manufacturing plant, the goal was to improve safety. The management team offered that if the staff worked 500,000 hours without losing any time due to an accident, the managers would dance through the plant in dresses. Well, you guessed it, the management team looked just darling, and the staff enjoyed it so much that they are aiming for one million accident-free hours to get an encore.

Games can bring attention to any measurable aspect of a business and can be used a problem-solving method. By having the participants themselves devise the game based on a specific goal, employees become "invested" in the process, and the company benefits from the collective knowledge.

While incentives are customarily used to reward increased sales or cost-cutting ideas, they can be used to reinforce behavioral goals as well. In a previous chapter, we discussed the significant changes the Black and White Film Manufacturing (BWFM) division of Eastman Kodak needed to make to ensure its profitability and success. When the group undertook a radical cultural change, incentives contributed to the success of the process.

In any change effort there are many components. One aspect of the change at BWFM was to encourage employees to "play to win." That new attitude required some risk on the part of employees as they changed how they worked together and shared information. Although Eastman Kodak had a formal incentive program, the BWFM group developed their own informal ways to acknowledge employees who had gone beyond the norm.

Lead by a group of 15, as previously mentioned, they adopted the name "Team Zebra." The colors were right—black and white—and the name also incorporated the idea that each zebra is unique, yet part of the herd. Imagine the experience of receiving awards like Zorba the Zebra, an inflatable zebra, or Stinky the Skunk, a stuffed skunk.

Zorba the Zebra was awarded to employees who were innovative or who exerted exceptional effort. Stinky was given to people who stepped out of their comfort zone and tried something new. As a winner, you were responsible for presenting the award to the next recipient. Sometimes, the presentation was a simple transfer of Zebra or Skunk; other times, it was in conjunction with a full-blown presentation in recognition of a winning effort.

As silly as it sounds, the two awards not only put some

fun into the culture at this stressful time, but also reinforced behavior changes through peer acknowledgment. Positive reinforcement by peers was a key factor in the culture change at BWFM, but peer pressure worked in a different way through the R-plus Award.

The Team Zebra process required that all employees make a list of things that made them happy. Employees then shared their lists with everyone else, so that they could give each other positive reinforcement for new behaviors. For people who didn't provide the list, there was a default reinforcer—a yellow Kodak raincoat poncho. The desire to avoid this R-plus Award was a powerful motivator to preparing the list![13]

Noncash Incentives

Incentives play a big part in the success of Dolphin Data, a small database management and mail personalization firm in El Monte California. With only 35 employees, owner Audrey Martinez has used ideas from big companies to support the growth of her small company. Martinez and her leadership team developed an incentive program based on points that are exchanged for scrip. The scrip is redeemable for a wide variety of goods and services, including groceries, department store merchandise, books, home improvements, sporting goods, electronics, toys, airline tickets, restaurant certificates, drug store purchases, and gasoline.

The incentive program is designed to encourage participation by employees in sales, safety, quality control, absenteeism, and developing new ideas. In some cases, the awards are based on votes from fellow employees. In other cases, the managers make the decision. Martinez and Renee Bean, the employee who introduced the idea, kept the program under wraps until they were ready to launch it.

It was a complete surprise when Martinez and Bean called a meeting and started handing out balloons containing incentive points and cash, Dolphin Data T-shirts, and a bound book containing all the information about the program. A key factor in this program is that incentive points are equally attainable for plant workers as office managers. Martinez started everyone off with 50 points to get the program rolling.

The Golden Dolphin, the highest award, is nominated and voted on by the production meeting members. Winners have gone way beyond the call of duty and the company has benefited significantly from their actions. A plaque is awarded, as well as a dinner certificate for $100 and 1,000 incentive points.

"Crack the Whip" is awarded to employees who figure out how to do a job faster, cheaper, or better. Winners received a large wooden plaque with a removable riding crop. Employees enjoy having the whip in their offices and receiving 500 points.

Employees can nominate co-workers for the "Spark Plug" award. You guessed it: a spark plug attached to a plaque. This award is given to employees who display a "winning attitude," or who "make it happen" through their extra efforts. The winner must receive a 50% vote of all the employees and approval of the department manager.

Team awards go to departments that are error-free—winning department team members get 50 points each. An accident-free month nets all employees 75 points; individuals who have no absences in a month receive 50 points.

The "Brilliant Idea" Award encourages employees to make suggestions. If the idea gets used, it's worth 250 points. For bringing in a new client or providing a lead to the sales department that results in new business, employees receive incentive points equal to the dollar amount of the first job. Referring an applicant for a job opening can bring 500 points, if the referral is hired and successfully completes the first 30 days on the job. And just for fun—employees can nominate each other for the privilege of parking in the VIP parking spot in front of the building.

Department managers can use the incentive point programs to support a particular program or project. The telemarketing manager can use additional incentive points to reward an outstanding telemarketer or grant a team bonus for reaching a goal. In the mailroom, completing a rush job or improving turnaround without increasing errors can also be supported with incentive points.

Employees are already benefiting from the program. One employee leveraged her incentive points to help outfit her young children for school. Other employees have been able to take their families out to dinner at restaurants that normally would be beyond their budget. Because the workforce is so diverse, ranging from high-tech computer staff to plant workers, to mailroom employees, the incentive program has to be applicable to a broad range of people. The scrip from a variety of merchants makes the program valuable to employees at every level in the organization. The design of the program also makes it possible for every employee to participate since each receives some points for perfect attendance. Team awards help people work together to accomplish goals that have high value for the organization, such as being error-free and accident-free.

Dolphin Data's program has an extra benefit beyond incentives for employees. The scrip is sold through a local elementary school as a fund-raising project. Every time an employee at Dolphin Data redeems incentive points, the local school makes money. In this way, the company can accomplish three things at once: provide employees incentives to contribute to the organization; utilize the intellectual capital of employees and enlist them in activities that benefit the company; and provide funds to support education in the community. Employees enjoy the rewards for their accomplishments and see the benefits to the community.

The program takes only about four hours per month to administer and the benefits for the company are readily apparent. Most employees have zero absences, the safety record is improving, and employees are all involved in the success of the company. The scrip is redeemed at a rate of $1 for 10 points. While the dollar amount is not extremely high, the impact on the workplace is significant. Workers at all levels see an immediate benefit for actions that have a positive impact on the organization.

For Martinez, the incentive program is also a way to recruit and retain good employees. She wants Dolphin Data to be the *best* place to work and this program sets her company apart from her competition. She also knows that the best way to grow a company is to have good employees who are involved in making the company better.

More Recognition Ideas

People like to be appreciated for who they are and what they do. Recognition is important. As the adage goes, "Praise publicly. Criticize privately." When someone deserved to be recognized, give the valued employee something tangible and stage a celebration . . . even if it's a small one. Be sure to put an account of the recognition in the employee's personnel file as a permanent record.

Holsum Bakery, Phoenix, Arizona, has a variety of recognition activities for its associates (the term they use for the people who work there). The incentive and inspiration of these awards contributes to the company's earning customer loyalty . . . and achievements like the Arizona Governor's Pioneer Award for Quality (a state award that parallels the Malcolm Baldrige program on the national level).

The associates, themselves, are involved in saluting each other's performance. Tell-a-grams and Caught-Ya cards, sent associate-to-associate, are written to appreciate someone doing something over and beyond his normal job responsibility. These awards are used to collect Holsum "dough," which can be exchanged for merchandise from the company store. Associates can nominate another associate or a team for a Golden Gram. This recognition is written and present-ed by the company president to honor outstanding accomplishment. Team Grams recognize team performance. Each team member receives two movie tickets and a copy of the Team Gram.

Here are some other awards used in Holsum's comprehensive recognition program:

Humanitarian Award	Act of Heroism	Certificate, Guardian, and Angel Pin name added to plaque in Hall of Fame
Community Service Award	Work in a Community Project	Certificate and name added to plaque in Hall of fame
Safety Program	Milestones in lost-time work due to accidents	Luncheon and earned points exchanged for merchandise
Service Award	Milestones in service —5-year increments	Personal note from president & gift selected from catalog
Perfect Attendance	No unauthorized absences/ tardies	Brunch with Team Leader and gift certificate ($50 —yr 1, $10 each additional consecutive year)
Safe Miles Award	Per each million safe miles	$100 gift certificate each million safe miles
Quality Graduation	Completion of quality education program	Diploma, clock, quality pin
INVEST	Per each 25 hrs. of lessons	Coffee mug & certificate
Board of Recognition	Years of Service	Display—Photo with years of service
Holsum Hall of Fame	Holsum activities	Plaques, certificates, awards, etc. received by Holsum
Retirement	Retirement after 10+ years & 55 yrs. of age	Engraved watch, plaque, luncheon/dinner

Wall of Fame

Publicly recognizing employees for innovation and service can often be relatively inexpensive. For the minimal cost of plaques or picture frames, companies can earn respect, appreciation, and loyalty from the employees.

The reception area at Kayser-Roth Direct in Greensboro, North Carolina, has what we call a "Wall of Fame." When the entire Kayser-Roth corporation initiated a total quality process, this division wanted to develop its own system of meaningful recognition for its valued employees. The wall dedicated to recognition is covered with an impressive display of plaques awarded to individuals and teams for innovative ideas that improved customer service or found better ways to exceed customer expectations.

Peer recognition makes this system work. People enjoy having their names and pictures posted on the Wall of Fame and mentioned in the company's newsletter.[14] Although there is no direct monetary compensation, the rewards chosen by management have a high-perceived value to the employees, so they are motivated to work toward winning.

Another organization with a Wall of Fame is IHS Helpdesk Service. Their Wall of Fame consists of individually framed e-mail messages and letters from clients acknowledging IHS' analysts for outstanding peformance. Each framed communication contains the analyst's name in large letters along with the company's congratulations.[15]

Holsum Bakery has a Team Wall located near the company's training room. Team Grams, framed certificates, and team photos are displayed to recognize and reward teams.

Imagine the message these walls send to applicants arriving for initial interviews. The message that comes across loud and clear is, "We acknowledge our employees! Join our team, excel and we'll acknowledge you, too!" That's powerful!

Designing an Incentive Compensation Program

To keep employees motivated and productive, they also need to know that their work has a direct connection to the success of the organization. The methods and formats for this kind of compensation are as varied as companies themselves.

You'll want to examine your company for the best way to compensate your employees for their contributions.

Go slowly and establish trust.

If your company is in the process of moving toward a team-based culture or if you are considering a change to team-based compensation, it is a good idea to go slowly. A strong trust level among employees is vital to the success of a team-based culture.

Involve people at all levels.

As we emphasize in our consulting work, "People support what they help to create." When you are ready to make changes in compensation, involve people from all levels of the organization. If a new compensation program is attempted without input from every level, it is likely to be met with resistance.

The idea that an individual's compensation is now tied to other people's performance can be a radical, frightening thought. By including people at all levels in the process, they will have a chance to make their concerns known and be part of the solution. With employee participation in the design of the compensation program, management will enjoy easier buy-in from employees when the new plan is launched.

Benchmark other programs, rely on experts.

You may want to research other companies that have already implemented team-based compensation, but this kind of plan does not come in a one-size-fits-all format. You may borrow ideas, but your company will need to design a plan that is custom-tailored to your organization. Because the method of compensation is such a critical factor in every business, consult with experts in designing team compensation programs.

There are many ways that organizations can reward employees for their contributions. Enlightened organizations are reinvesting in their employees, their human assets, through variable pay, gain sharing, employee stock owner-ship, and other incentives. Employees are acknowledged and rewarded for their contributions more directly than ever before, and organizations, in turn, are rewarded with moti-vated and involved employees—vital to company success. The result is a partnership between the organization and the employees that provides benefits to both.

We've covered a great deal of material in the preceding chapters. Now, its time for you to look into your own organ-ization and . . . get started with Chapter 20.

KEY CONCEPTS

▶ Compensation is an effective motivator when it is connected to performance.

▶ Variable pay rewards teams or individuals for accom-plishing specific goals that enhance company prof-itability.

▶ Gain sharing rewards employees based on overall corporate profit.

▶ Employee ownership (ESOP) gives people a stake in the success of the company.

▶ Stock options give employees an opportunity to be and feel invested in the organization.

▶ Incentives of any kind can be valuable in gaining the commitment of the employees to achieve a goal or to make continuous improvements.

▶ Compensation plans should be customized to the individual organizations to provide the most meaning for employees.

ACTION PLAN

- Review your current compensation structure. Does it reward and motivate, or does it maintain the status quo?
- Identify and quantify a corporate goal and establish a reward/incentive for goal achievement.
- Involve employees in the methods and solutions for reaching the goal. This involvement reinforces the connection between work and compensation while acknowledging the value each individual can have.
- Support the process with education.
- Enlist the advice of financial and legal professionals if you are considering employee ownership.

Endnotes

1. Hein, Kenneth, "Raises Fail, but Incentives Save the Day," *Incentive*, November 1996.
2. Clark, Kathryn, "Nobody Gets Soaked in Workers' Pool," *Human Resource Executive*, August 1997.
3. Adler, Alan, *Detroit Free Press*, Knight-Ridder/Tribune Business News, 1997.
4. Flynn, Gillian, "Continental's People Lift It to New Heights," *Workforce*, February 1997.
5. Conversation with Eric Rabinowitz, IHS Helpdesk Service, February 20, 1998.
6. Bencivenga, "Dominic, Employee Owners Help Bolster the Bottom Line," *HRMagazine*, February 1997.
7. Matson, Eric, "Own It, Grow It, Trade It," *Fast Company*, June/July 1997.
8. Geer, Carolyn, "Sharing the Wealth, Capitalist-style" *Forbes*, December 1, 1997.
9. "Starbucks: Making Values Pay, *Fortune*, September 29, 1997, pp. 261–272.
10. Geer, Carolyn, "Sharing the Wealth, Capitalist-style" *Forbes*, December 1, 1997.
11. Ibid.
12. levistrauss.com/hr_benefits (page 317)
13. Anfuso, Dawn, "Kodak Employees Bring a Department into the Black," *Personnel Journal,* September 1994. (p. 321)
14. Conversation with Carol Burke, Kayser-Roth Direct, March 9, 1998.
15. Conversation with Eric Rabinowitz, IHS Helpdesk Service, February 20, 1998

20

Getting Started

We've certainly covered a lot of territory together in this book. When you think about all the wonderful, innovative things that employers are doing today, it's almost overwhelming!

Don't be intimidated by the volume and variety of what you've read. Be excited about the possibilities of what you can do in your organization, regardless of your starting point.

Remember, by applying the principles promoted in this book, you'll be changing your organization's culture. Corporate cultures do not appear overnight; they evolve over a period of time. Your company's transformation will be gradual, regardless of how fast you move to institute new ideas.

Approach the journey to improving your position eagerly, but methodically as well. We encourage you to do these activities in concert with others—at least a team of senior executives. The job to be done is substantial and will require tangible and tacit support of numerous key people. Get them on board at the start—people support what they help to create. Here are some steps and considerations for you to think about.

Step 1. Diagnose your current situation.

Step 2. Evaluate the effect and consequences of your current situation.

Step 3. Establish criteria for your company's leanness and meaningfulness.

Step 4. Develop goals—based on the results, the outcomes, you desire.

Step 5. Explore alternative strategies and tactics.

Step 6. Involve people from all aspects of your organization—get ideas, feedback, and support.

Step 7: Determine which plans you want to implement, considering priorities, budgets, and effects on the way you do business.

Step 8. Implement selected strategies and tactics.

Step 9. Assess and analyze results of implementation.

Step 10. Repeat the procedure to plan the next phase of your improvement. Becoming more lean and meaningful is a process, an evolution, not just a one-time experience.

Depending on the size of your organization, the talent you already have on board, and time available to work on these issues, you can manage most—if not all—of this work in-house. The alternative is to engage outside consultant(s) to assist with the process.

If you manage your metamorphosis internally, consider two alternatives. One approach is to assign the responsibility to a task force; another strategy is to place the challenge in the hands of all employees. The best idea is probably to combine the two approaches. Get everyone involved—under the coordinated leadership of a team of employees who can serve as the champions of change.

Inspiration, encouragement, and support from the top executive(s) are essential for success in this process. Strong statements, backed by congruent action, will make it clear that changes will occur. This kind of overt engagement will help overcome the natural inertia, the innate resistance to any kind of change.

Many organizations will find it more appropriate to engage outside counselors to facilitate transformation to a more lean and meaningful culture. The top executive(s) must still be highly involved, regardless of who is charged with the role of guiding the process. An objective outsider can be a great asset, particularly if employees are very active with heavy workloads or if there are disparate groups that have to be gradually brought into the fold.

Recognizing the importance of having highly competent, trustworthy, experienced advisors, we recommend favoring Certified Management Consultants. Their proven credentials and adherence to a strict Code of Ethics will be a source of comfort and confidence as you build your relationship with outside professionals who can help you change your organization to better compete in this fast-moving world.[1]

Our experience in working with our client organizations is that some are eager to move into a new way of operating. Others are reluctant, more difficult to work with because of long-standing traditions, power-hungry managers, suspicious employees, or other factors. In most cases, people will be watching very carefully to see if the transformation efforts are genuine . . . or just another management trick to get people to work harder. Move deliberately, assuring that each step is one you really want to take. If you do something as an experiment, be very clear about that and set an ending date for the trial.

For more ideas or advice, you're invited to visit the web site (www.leanandmeaningful.com) or give the authors a call.

Endnote

1. The Institute of Management Consultants offers a free referral service to organizations interested in engaging Certified Management Consultants. Contact them at 521 Fifth Avenue, 35th Floor, New York, New York 10175-3598. (212) 697-8262. Internet: www.imcusa.org.

Recommended Reading

Billings-Harris, Lenora. *The Diversity Advantage*. Oakhill Press, North Carolina,1998.

Case, John. *Open Book Management*. Harperbusiness, 1996.

Conger, Jay A. & Associates. *Spirit at Work*. Jossey Bass, California, 1994.

Danzig, Robert. *The Leader Within You*. Lifetime Books, 1998.

Edelston, Martin, and Buhagier, Marion. *I-Power*. Barricade Books, New Jersey, 1992.

Goldblatt, Eliahu. *The Goal*. North River Press, New York, 1986.

Herman, Roger E. *Keeping Good People*. Oakhill Press, North Carolina, 1998.

Klein, Eric, and Izzo, John B., Ph.D. *Awakening Corporate Soul*. Fair Winds Press, Canada, 1997.

Nelson, Bob. *1001 Ways to Reward Employees*. Workman Publishing, New York,1994.

Russell, Chuck. *Right Person, Right Job*. Johnson & James, Georgia, 1996.

Semler, Ricardo. *Maverick*. Warner Books, New York, 1993.

Weinstein, Matt. *Managing to Have Fun at Work*. Simon & Schuster, New York, 1996.

Weiss, Alan J. *Our Emperors Have No Clothes*. Career Press, New Jersey, 1995.

Womack, James P., and Jones Daniel T. *Lean Thinking: Banish Waste and Create Wealth in Your Corporation*. Simon & Schuster, New York, 1996.

Zoltners, Andris A., Sinha, Prabha K., and Murphy, Stuart J. *The Fat Firm*. McGraw-Hill, New York, 1997.

Resources

This list of resources is provided to support your movement toward becoming more lean and meaningful. It is by no means a complete list. Most of the resources listed here were mentioned somewhere in the book. We've added a few more for you.

As you learn of other resources that may be valuable for companies to know about and to use, please let us know. We'll post the information on our

www.leanandmeaningful.com
web site.

Responsible Investing

Resource Conservation Capital Group
www.greenmoney.com
801 Compass Way, Suite 216
Annapolis, MD 21401
410-212-7557

Social Venture Network
www.svn.org
PO Box 29221
San Francisco, CA 914129-0221
415-561-6501
nonprofit association of businesses and social entrepreneurs
"changing the way business is done"

Domini Social Investments
www.domini.com
PO Box 959
New York, NY 10159-0959
1-800-762-6814

Certified Management Consultants

Institute of Management Consultants
35th Floor
521 Fifth Avenue
New York, New York 10175-3598
(212) 697-8262

Child and Elder Care

Family Care Services
www.familycareconsultants.com
1025 Silas Deane Highway
Wetherfield, Connecticut 06109
860-563-6901
Provides companies with referral sources for child and elder care

National Association of Child Care Professionals
www.naccp.org
304-A Roanoke Street
Christiansburg, Virginia 24073
540-382-5819
Regional resources for child care

CareGuide
www.careguide.net
1160 Battery Street
4th Floor
San Francisco, CA 94111
415-474-1278

Children of Aging Parents
Links through www.careguide.net
1609 Woodbourne Road,
Suite 304-A
Levittown, Pennsylvania 19057
800-227-7294

Elder Care
1160 Battery Street
4th Floor
San Francisco, CA 94111
415-474-1278

LaPetite
www.lapetite.com
14 Corporate Woods
8717 West 110th Street
Suite 300
Overland Park, Kansas 66210
913-345-1250

National Council for Adoption
www.ncfa-usa.org
1930 Seventeenth Street NW
Washington, DC 20009-6207
202-328-1200
fax 202-332-0935

Community Service

Carnegie Library of Pittsburgh
4400 Forbes Avenue
Pittsburgh, PA 15213
662-3114
www.clpgh.org
Lists of nonprofit organizations and links to their homepages

Institute for Global Communication
Presidio Building 1012, First Floor
Torney Avenue, PO Box 29904
San Francisco, CA 94129-0904
415-561-6100 fax 415-561-6101
www.igc.org.
Directory of nonprofit organizations

Americas Charities
12701 Fair Lake Circle
Suite 370
Fairfax, VA 22033
1-800-458-9505
www.charities.org
Resource for employers to set up giving programs

Action Without Borders
www.idealist.org
350 Fifth Avenue, Suite 6614
New York, NY 10118
212-843-3973
Links people with community services opportunities.

America's Promise
909 North Washington Street
Suite 400
Alexandria, VA 22314-1556
www.americaspromise.org
Information on becoming a community of promise and calendar of events 800-365-0153 Ext. 160

Environment

Environmental Protection Agency
National Center of Environmental Publications and Information (NCEPI)
PO Box 42419
Cincinnati, OH 45242
1-800-490-9198 fax 513-489-8695
www.epa.gov
Includes industry partnerships, projects for Business and Industry

Green Lodging Establishments
Green Hotels Association
Email: info@greenhotels.com
713-789-8889
fax 713-789-9786
www.greenhotels.com

Disabled Workers

The President's Committee on the Employment of People
with Disabilities.
www.pcepd.gov
1331 F Street, NW
Suite 300
Washington, DC 20004
202-376-6200
fax 202-376-6219
TDD 202-376-6205
They maintain a database of 1,100 job candidates that have
been prescreened in personal interviews. The database
includes information about the workers' skill levels and
qualifications.

Job Accommodation Network
Links from www.pcepd.gov
West Virginia University
PO Box 6080
Morgantown, West Virginia 26506-6080
800-526-7234

Welfare to Work

The Welfare to Work Partnership
www.welfaretowork.org
1250 Connecticut Avenue, NW, Suite 610
Washington, DC 20036-2603
202-955-3005

The Partnership offers publications, a toll free number for information, and a web page(www.welfaretowork.org). There are no dues or requirements to belong, but participants are asked to "have hired or pledge to hire at least one person off public assistance without displacing existing workers."

Take Your Community To Work
Operation Education
212-439-4671

Education and Training

NAM/National Association of Manufacturers
www.nam.org
1331 Pennsylvania Avenue, NW
Washington, DC 20004-1790
800-248-6NAM
Helping companies educate and train workers for the future

Unique Employee Benefits

Elite Concierges
www.leconcierge.com
5777 W. Century Blvd., Suite 1640
Los Angeles, California 90045
310-568-2777

Alternative Work Arrangement

New Ways to Work
www.nww.org
785 Market St., Suite 950
San Francisco, CA 94103-2016
415-995-9860

Catalyst for Women Inc.
Information Center
250 Park Ave. S., 5th Floor
New York, NY 10003-1459
212-777-8900

More Resources

Incentives

Card Express, Inc.
www.cardex.com
4665 MacArthur Ct., Suite 250
Newport Beach, CA 92660
714-955-2121

Local/Minority Businesses

American Association of Minority Businesses, Inc.
www.aamb.com
222 S. Church Street
Charlotte, North Carolina 28202
704-376-2262

National Minority Supplier Development Council
Email: webmaster@mbnet.com
www.mbnet.com
Provides resources and links to minority businesses

Ecology

Ecotrust
www.ecotrust.org
1200 NW Front Avenue, Suite 470
Portland, OR 97209

Child Care

Child Care Systems of America, Inc.
1008 Moreland Blvd
Brentwood, TN 37027
www.childcaresystems.com
800-377-6959
Provides child care program management services

ParentNet, Inc.
www.kindercom.com
888-522-6123

Professional Organizers

National Association of Professional Organizers (NAPO)
e-mail: NAPO@assnmgmt.com
1033 La Posada, Suite 220
Austin, Texas 78752
512-206-0151

Training

American Society of Training and Development
www.astd.org
1640 King Street, Box 1443
Alexandria, VA 22313-2043
703-683-8100

Wage and Salary Surveys

Online Career Center
Email: webmaster@occ.com
www.occ.com
2780 Waterfront Parkway E Drive
Suite 100
Indianapolis, IN 46209-1439

Spirituality/Social Responsibility

World Vision
www.worldvision.org
34834 Weyerhaeuser Way South
PO Box 9716
Federal Way, Washington 98063-9716
888-511-6598 (general information)

Community Service/Social Responsibility

Starlight Foundation
www.starlight.org
website lists local chapters

National Capital Area Expansion Committee
4301 N. Fairfax Drive, Suite 1119
Arlington, VA 22203
703-908-1878

Make-A-Wish Foundation
www.wish.org
100 W. Clarendon, Suite 2200
Phoenix, Arizona 85013
800-722-WISH(9474)

Operation Smile
www.operationsmile.org
220 Boush Street
Norfolk, VA 23510
757-625-0375
1-888-OPSMILE

Habitat for Humanity
www.habitat.org
121 Habitat Street
Americus, GA 31709
912-924-6935

I-POWER Kit
Greenwich Institute for American Education
55 Railroad Avenue
Greenwich, CT 06830
$99.00

International Telework Association
204 E. Street NE
Washington, DC 20002
202-547-6157
fax 202-546-3289

American Telecommuting Association
1220 "L" Street NW
Suite 100
Washington, DC 20005
800-ATA-4-YOU
fax 818-224-4343

Commentaries

As futurists, we study trends and forecast what we see coming. As consultants, we observe and report what we see happening in organizations. As consulting futurists, we project corporate trends and advise business leaders on appropriate strategies.

Even with all this insight and influence, we are clear that we are not the people who actually lead the companies that make a difference for their employees. Humbly, we expect that readers who do run organizations may be a bit skeptical about what they read in *Lean & Meaningful*. Are these words simply consultants talking? What do my counterparts—the people who really make things happen—have to say?

Appreciating a desire to hear from peers, we invited a number of thought-leaders and innovators to share their perspectives with you through brief commentaries. Some wanted to contribute much more, but we held them to one page for consistency and fairness. These people do have a lot to say to us—some of their message is contained in the following pages; even more is communicated by their actions described in the pages of this book.

Listen carefully as they share their thoughts about the relationship between meaningfulness and the bottom line. Listen to the "why" of this new direction in corporate culture.

I didn't start out as a florist—far from it. My first vocation was as a social worker, running a home for troubled boys in Queens, New York. In a lot of ways, it was nothing like the flower business. But in many respects, what I learned as an administrator at the St. John's Home for Boys was more important in making 1-800-FLOWERS the world's largest florist than learning the difference between roses and tulips.

At St. John's, I was faced with a group of hostile, unenthusiastic young men. Getting them to go to school was a challenge; building relationships with them seemed impossible. But I did. I learned how to get them to open up, to build loyalty with trust and reward. I found that motivation works best when you have common goals. "Go to school and we will go camping," I'd say. No one missed a day.

At 1-800-FLOWERS, things aren't all that different. I'm not dealing with poverty, drugs and abuse anymore, but my challenges as a motivator are still the same: build relationships and loyalty, create a fun atmosphere, reward achievement. We do all sorts of things to have fun and recognize achievement.

Make work fun, I've learned, and it's not really so much like work. Make people care about what they do and they tend to do it a lot better. Build lasting friendships and they will remain loyal. Care about your employees and they'll care about you—and in turn, your company.

Jim McCann, CEO
1-800-FLOWERS

At Ben & Jerry's, we live what *Lean & Meaningful*'s authors describe as "building more meaningfulness into work." From the very beginning 20 years ago, Ben and Jerry wanted to run the company in a way they described as "doing good by doing good." We manage our company with concern for the community in our day–to-day business practices.

This was the genesis of our 3-part mission:

Product Mission: to make, distribute, and sell the finest-quality product

Social Mission: to operate the company in a way that actively recognizes the central role that business plays in society, by initiating innovative ways to improve the quality of life in the local, national, and international communities

Economic Mission: to operate the company on a sound fiscal basis of profitable growth

Our philosophy means committing 7 1/2 percent of our pre-tax profits to employee-led philanthropy, partnering with nonprofits in our franchising, sourcing some of our ingredients in ways that achieve sound societal and environmental gains, and being the first public company to sign the CERES environmental principles. All our sites have Community Action Teams that plan community projects.

We take care of our people. We provide what we regard as a livable wage at the bottom of our pay scale, based on what it really costs to live in Vermont, supplemented by excellent benefits. In an informal workplace, we have pay equity, good representation of women in management positions, and an employee stock purchase plan.

Reaching out to our communities helps us build within.

Perry D. Odak
President and CEO
Ben & Jerry's

Eight years ago, we invented a system that has made Boardroom Inc., just about the most productive company in America. A simple measure of productivity is dollar sales per employee. With well over $100 million in sales—and only 90 employees—we're right up there. When we started, sales were under $25 million/yr.

This system did great things for profits, too. It has also cut absenteeism . . . just about eliminated personnel turnover . . . done amazing things for teamwork . . . increased morale. It even seems—believe it or not—to eliminate divorce. We've had no divorces here since we began our program.

All of this came about accidentally. We started by following a simple suggestion from Peter Drucker. To make our meetings more interesting, have each person contribute two ideas on how they—or the company—could work more effectively. Just stitching those meetings together very lightly produced this business miracle.

What we call I-POWER is similar to *Kaizen*, the system that pushed Japanese companies to their incredible performance levels. Our suggestion system is a very, very effective alternative to the standard military model. And, we all have some idea about how many people it takes to get just one to fire a gun.

What is this I-POWER system? We just ask our people to give us, in writing, two suggestions each week on how they or the company can operate more effectively. It works. The people grow . . . and the company grows.

We've produced a very useful kit kit to help others get started. It incorporates all that we have learned. It's available from the Greenwich Institute for American Education, 55 Railroad Ave., Greenwich, CT 06830, for only $99.

Sincerely,
Marty Edelston
CEO
Boardroom, Inc.

As a small firm, our people factor has been intense. Each team member in our firm indeed brings his own set of values into the workplace, but one of our core values is the importance of family. Our team players welcome children for a day at the office with movies and snacks and, of course, computer games. As we expand our facilities, we plan to make a safe kids camp area and include sports/entertainment events for the entire family.

Certainly my management style will change over the years, as our team will itself evolve. Interestingly, we have maintained a large percentage of our staff over five years. I have seen our team self-monitor and weed out those who are not pulling their share. It's our corporate value system that says who we are to ourselves, teammates, customers, and most important—to our competitors. I believe it is our value-advantage.

After the initial launch of our team incentive program, we reaped the benefits as a company within the first 30 days. The program did not simply produce short-lived results, but created a vital new outlook in our people that will have long-reaching effects for our company.

For my firm, this program truly was win-win and I heartily encourage you to try the various systems in this book. As millennium leaders, we must be the guides to drive our firms' management teams to meaningful growth, not profit-driven growth without meaning.

Audrey H. Martinez
President/CEO
Dolphin Data

The foundation for Great American Cookies' relationship with its employees is its mission of "Share the Fun of Cookies." This is a mission in which we believe passionately. Sharing the Fun of Cookies encompasses sharing the fun of this exciting business with our employees, with our franchisees, and with our customers.

Our customers buy approximately 80 million cookies per year from us. They do not buy them from us because they need to buy them, but because they want to buy them. As a result, their experience with us needs to be fun. We cannot ask our employees to facilitate a fun experience for our customers, if we have not created a fun and enjoyable workplace for our employees.

This philosophy of caring for our employees so that they provide for our customers has produced results. In the past two years, turnover of Company store management and employees has declined. Comparable store sales have increased at twice our historical average. The profitably of our stores, even with these additional costs, has improved over 10 percent a year.

To us, the above is very logical. By developing a mission for everyone to believe in, by fostering teamwork, and by committing ourselves to actions, we have been able to improve our business. By taking care of our employees, our employees are able to take care of our customers.

David Barr, CEO
Great American Cookies

The greatest asset we have as leaders of organizations is the talents of the people we employ. Our role is to build and maintain the high standards of performance that will inspire top people to join and support the proud quality we produce.

Large organizations require a lot of managers to keep in touch with what's happening. Each and every one of those managers must understand the critical importance of working closely with their people. Their job is to bring out the unique qualities that enable each of those people to maximize personal and professional contributions to the organization's success. Managers' tasks include honoring the potential of each person, and encouraging growth and fulfillment. When people perform well, they should be strongly appreciated and recognized by their superiors.

When people really demonstrate their talent by doing special things, gaining internal or external recognition, or making a difference, it's important that they be recognized by the senior executive as well as their own manager. A call, a note, a small gift from the person at the top can have a wonderful positive impact. That connection with someone important who may seem distant has a powerful effect. People with talent like to be noticed, in ways that are comfortable for them. The congratulatory communication can be rewarding, inspiring, and motivational—for them and people around them at home and at work.

Bob Danzig
Chief Executive Officer
Hearst Newspapers

We are a lean company and have been for years—long before it was fashionable. We do well over a $1 billion in sales with approximately 287 people. That's almost $5 million per employee. No other company in our industry even comes close to that productivity!

My philosophy is fewer people, but better people. I don't believe in layers of management. Retailers like doing business with us because they get answers promptly; that's what they need in this highly competitive market.

I believe in the three P's: People, Product, and Promotion. And our people always come first. Without our good people, we wouldn't be in business. What's worked well for us is to create a family feeling.

We often refer to our organization as "the JVC Family," and you'll find that attitude in all we do. Like in a real family, everybody supports each other to get the job done. At JVC we never hear, "Not my job." It's challenging to operate with so few people—and our people meet that challenge very well.

As a Japanese company in America, we have Japanese and Americans working side by side. Each division has a Japanese manager and an American counterpart with appropriate responsibilities. We support our American workers with an American human resources person and our Japanese employees have their own Japanese personnel manager as well.

The payoffs are high productivity and very low turnover. In a nutshell, we take care of our people, and they take care of us.

Harry Elias
Chief Operating Officer and Executive Vice President
JVC Company of America

Forty-seven years ago, I was an expectant mother with $2,000 dollars to gamble on a new idea. Now, Lillian Vernon posts sales of over $250 million dollars. Our success is largely due to our fusing the entrepreneur with the professional manager. To me, it's a marriage made in heaven.

If I've learned anything, it is the importance of drawing the best qualities from both the internal entrepreneur and the professional manager. These are the left and right sides of the business brain; they must harmonize in a healthy corporation. Both sides learn from the other and grow as individuals.

Lillian Vernon's operating environment is very entrepreneurial. And although our business has multiplied in recent years, I've kept our management team lean. We are probably one of the few organizations our size to operate with senior staff of a president and fifteen vice presidents.

But if Lillian Vernon has marched to the beat of an entrepreneurial heart, I know that a managerial head must temper it for continued growth. My managers are as important to me as my customer list. They have the expertise I lack and provide invaluable advice and information. They are priceless.

In addition to valuing our entrepreneurs and professional managers, we also value our front-line employees. We demonstrate that appreciation by showing an interest in their personal lives in our employee newsletters and their physical health with our health fairs. At Lillian Vernon, we know that *all* of our human resources are our most important assets.

Lillian Vernon, CEO
Lillian Vernon Corporation
Author, *An Eye for Winners*

The focus today is on choices and change, especially with high-tech companies in California. The new emphasis is on working conditions, equitable benefits that improve the quality of life for all employees, and a corporate culture that lets employees craft policies for themselves. Improving an employee's quality of life, health, and outlook has tangible benefits to a corporation. Today's challenge is to affect desired changes to an employee's well being while taking into account the changing role of family and lifestyle. Focusing benefits on one type of employee does not accomplish this goal. It causes others to feel left out and does not foster team spirit. People left out of the traditional equation may leave, depriving the company of resources and talent, leading to a homogeneous versus a diverse and heterogeneous workforce.

A company's goal in crafting a benefit package cannot be a social one like improving child care or the quality of life for a husband, wife, 2.5 children, and a dog "nuclear" family. The purpose is to directly benefit the company by developing a program that attracts and retains high-quality human assets, enabling them to be more productive. In a secondary way, this is also very beneficial to the employee. A win-win situation results. Small, innovative companies like Motek lead the way in this area because people are our most important asset. We must foster an environment that ultimately benefits all our employees because our corporate well-being, profitability, and future depend on it.

Ann S. Price
President and CEO
Motek

We are employed because of the satisfaction of our investors and business partners—without them we have no business. To maintain a quality relationship with our customers we know we must attract, hire, and retain the best staff to grow this franchise.

Employees must be dedicated and well trained in order to offer the best service to our customers, so we work with them from day one to provide the right tools, guidance, and training to do their jobs effectively.

While offering employees such tangibles as a fitness center, an on-site stamp machine, and ATM, we believe it is more important that job content be satisfying and challenging. People want to be motivated by their work. They need opportunities to learn, grow, and find better approaches to accomplish their work.

We've embarked on a new project to put all components of a customer's transaction within the control of a single staff member from beginning to end. This gives the employees not only the satisfaction of accomplishment, but an opportunity to earn more money as their skills and knowledge base grow.

The financial services industry—like so many other areas of business—is constantly changing and growing. We ask a lot of our employees. They need to be flexible. They need to understand the changes in the business. They need to offer outstanding customer service. We want to reward our employees for all of their efforts. We want them to know we appreciate their hard work and innovations.

Barbara Hennigar, President and CEO
Oppenheimer Funds Services

Our culture is an indivisible part of our success. It is comprised of the six Core Values that we call FASPAC:

Focus
Accountability
Superiority
PAPA (**P**eople **A**re **P**riority #1 **A**lways)
Attitude
Constant Improvement

At Papa Johns, People Are Priority #1 Always. Team Members are the heart of our Papa John's family. Nothing demonstrates this more clearly than the compassion and support we show one another and the way we are expected to live our Core Values, breathing life into the words. This commitment touches the families of our Team Members, who are influenced by our actions, and indeed, to all those around us.

We are proud of who we are and what we do. Papa John's not only makes a difference internally—in the lives of thousands of Team Members—but also externally in the lives of the customers and in the communities we serve. What we do is rewarding. We feed people, we unite friends, and we bring families closer together. Each and every day, we have the good fortune to provide joy and nourishment to the customers we serve. Our Core Values allow us to be successful and achieve our goals within this framework of work, family and community.

Team Members who live the Core Values are extremely successful at their particular disciplines. Our Core Values work; they are resilient; they have stood the test of time. That's why our core values are non-negotiable. They are the foundation upon which all our success must be built.

John H. Schnatter
Founder and CEO
Papa John's International

I believe the key value for the future of business is the golden rule. Not a geometrically growing bottom line; not annihilating the competition (though these thing occur naturally when you follow the golden rule). I'm talking about running your company in the spirit of friendship—treating employees, clients, and suppliers like you would want to be treated. It might sound idealistic or simplistic, but it is neither. It is difficult to do in the real world, yet the only lasting recipe for preeminence.

In my first book, ***The Customer Comes Second***, I talked about the importance of focusing on employees first. In my latest book, ***Good Company: Caring as Fiercely as You Compete,*** I talk about how important it is to hold fast to core values (like an employee focus) but at the same time be able to change swiftly yet gracefully–a requirement for survival today. And it can only be done in companies that care about their people.

People are the only sustainable competitive advantage a company can have. In the end, they are all that separates one company from another. To reach their full potential, their brilliance must be matched by their dedication, and that only happens when they are appreciated, cared for, provided the finest tools, nurtured in an extraordinary culture, and treated like friends. The golden rule is worth more than its weight in gold.

Hal F. Rosenbluth
CEO, Rosenbluth International
Co-author, ***Good Company: Caring as Fiercely as You Compete***

Our philosophy is simple: if you care about me, I'll care about you. This attitude has resulted in superior quality and almost no employee turnover.

We believe in running a lean operation. Our organizational chart is very shallow. As president, I'm much more involved in being with our people than I am in sitting in my office. We're all this way; we're a team of equals, each with valuable skills to get our jobs done.

Since founding our company in 1989, we've reached out to serve our people in special ways. To make it easier for them to get to work, we provide door-to-door transportation. The city provides the bus; the company provides the driver. To give employees more time with their families after work, we offer on-site laundry service. Workers bring their laundry with them in the morning. The clothes are washed, dried, and folded while they work. This service is provided at cost . . . no company mark-up.

Since many of our employees are working parents, we offer a childcare resource and referral service, coupled with a childcare subsidy. The company pays $15 per week for every child in licensed care or $1 0 for children in part-time and after-school care. Checks are payable to the caregivers. The subsidy program enables parents to find better care than they might otherwise afford.

We stay close enough to our people to understand their needs, then we fulfill as many as we can. Through sincere caring, we make a difference for each other.

Witon Conner, CEO
Wilton Conner Packaging

Organizations Cited
in
Lean & Meaningful

The following list includes all the companies and government agencies that are used as examples in this book. Each of them is involved in some aspect of meaningfulness that we felt worth sharing with you.

Our use of their efforts should not be interpreted as an unqualified endorsement of everything the organization does. We make this statement purely from a disclaimer perspective, not because we have any problem or concern about any of these organizations.

This list should not be construed to be a complete list of enlightened and involved meaningful organizations. There are many more. As we learn more about their activities, we'll post them illustratively on the book's web site, www.leanandmeaningful.com. You're invited to visit the site frequently to stay current.

3M
1-800-FLOWERS
A & M Records
Administrative Resource Options
Advanced Duplication Services
Advanced Micro Devices
Advanced Technology Staffing
Advantage Rent-A-Car
AES
Aetna Insurance Company
Air Mauritius
Aladdin Knowledge Systems
Alamco
Allstate Insurance

AMD
America West Airlines
American Airlines
American Booksellers
    Association
American Express
Amoco
Anderson and Associates
Arthur Andersen
Apple Computer
Arizona Mail Order
Armstrong World Industries
AT&T Wireless
Autodesk
Avon Products, Inc.
Baldor Electric Company
Bank of America
Bank of Montreal
Bell South
Ben & Jerry's, Inc.
B. F. Goodrich
Bloomberg Financial Markets
Boardroom Inc.
Brayton International, division of
    Steelcase
Business Stationery, Inc.
Brink's Home Security
Cadillac Division, General Motors
California Public Employees
    Retirement System
Calvert Group
Campbell Soup Company
Cardinal Meat Specialists
Carolina Biological Supply
Chase Manhattan Bank
Chez Panisse

Citibank, N. A.
Citizens Bank, Rhode Island
City of Phoenix, Arizona
Coca-Cola Bottling Company
Compaq Computers
Computer Associates
Continental Airlines
Cornoyer Hedrick
Crown Honda
CrunchTime
Dana Corporation
Deja Shoe
Digital Equipment Corporation
Dolphin Data
Donato's Pizza
Donnelly Corporation
Dow Corning
Dreyfus Third Century Fund
Duluth, Minnesota, Police
    Department
Dupont Nylon North America
Dupont Merck
Eastman Kodak
Ecotrust
Eddie Bauer
Ellis Memorial Hospital
Donald English, Esq.
Farm Fresh Bakery
Federated Department Stores
First Tennessee Bank
Ford Motor Company
Forsyth County, North Carolina
Fox, Inc.
Gateway 2000
GE Fanuc Automation North
    America, Inc.

General Mills
Grand Wailea Hotel
Great American Cookie Company
Greystone Brownies
GTE
Habitat for Humanity
Hallmark
HA-LO Industries, Inc.
Hanna Andersson
Harley Davidson
Healthtrax
Hearst Newspapers
Hewlett Packard
Hoechst Celanese
Holsum Bakery
Home Depot
Honeywell, Inc.
IBM
I H S Helpdesk Service
Incentive Magazine
Intel
J.W. Pepper & Son
James River Paper Company
John Hancock Financial Services
Johnson & Johnson
Just Desserts
JVC Company of America
Kimberly Clark Corporation
Kinetix Division of Autodesk
Kingston Technologies
Klosterman's Bakery
KPMG Peat Marwick
Land's End
La Soul Bakery
Leisure Craft/USA Display
LensCrafters

Levi Strauss
Lillian Vernon
L. L. Bean
Los Angeles Department of Water
   and Power
Lotus Development
Magic Johnson Theaters
Malden Mills
Management Associates
Manpower, Inc.
Marriott Corporation
MasterCard International
McDonald's Corporation
McGunn Safe Company
McNeil Laboratories
Memphis Light, Gas & Water
Mennonite Mutual Insurance
   Company
Merrill Lynch
Metropolitan Life Insurance
Microsoft
Monsanto
Moody's Investors Services
Motek
Motorola
National Football League
National Semiconductor
New Directions, Inc.
New York Eye and Ear Infirmary
NFL Football Players Association
North Dakota State Attorney
   General
Northwest Airlines
NOVA Corporation
Office of Personnel Management,
   US Government

Index

Symbols

A

D

F

H

I

Ireland, 80

J

J.W. Pepper & Son, 82–83
James River Paper Company, 146–147
job(s), enrolling, 67
    rotation, 146–147, 177
    sharing, 149–150, 210
    summer, 245, 250
Job Training Partnership Act, 244
John Hancock Financial Services, 112–113
Johnson & Johnson, 264–265
Johnson, Magic, 237–238
Jordan, Michael, 192
"Joy Gang" at Ben & Jerry's, 288, 299
Just Desserts, 230–231
JVC Company of America, 353

K

Kazakhstan, 80
Kelleher, Herb, 299
Kids-To-Go, 112–113
Kimberly Clark Corporation, 221
Kinetix Division of Autodesk, 152
KPMG Peat Marwick, 221
Kodak, Eastman, 167–168, 320
Kuapa Kokoo, Ltd., 260

L

L.L. Bean, 284
La Soul Bakery, 235, 238
Lambert, Robert, 149
Land's End, 67
LaPetite, 111
Latin America, 17
leadership, 13–16
    old-style, 13–14

S

U

About the Authors

Roger E. Herman

Roger E. Herman is Chief Executive Officer of The Herman Group, a management consulting, speaking, and training firm he founded in 1980.

After serving as a Counterintelligence Special Agent during the Vietnam era, he held a variety of management and sales positions in manufacturing, retail, distribution, and direct sales. He has also served as a City Manager. A graduate of Hiram College, Roger holds a master's from The Ohio State University in the field of Public Administration.

As a sought-after speaker, Roger earned the coveted Certified Speaking Professional designation from the National Speakers Association. He is also a Certified Management Consul-tant—one of only 14 people in the world to hold both the CSP and CMC.

A Strategic Business Futurist concentrating on workforce and workplace trends, Rogers forecasts are consistently on-target and his commentaries about trends are penetrating and provocative.

Roger has published over 500 articles, writes a column that is carried by a number of trade magazines, and frequently appears on radio and television talk shows. He is Contributing Editor on workforce and workplace trends for *The Futurist* Magazine.

Joyce L. Gioia

Joyce L. Gioia is President of The Herman Group, based in Greensboro, North Carolina.

At the age of 28, she became the youngest magazine publisher in the country. Her diverse background includes experience in hard and soft goods, wholesale, retail, personnel recruiting, and direct marketing.

A Specialist in Adding Value, for 11 years Joyce was president of her own consulting firm, where she created groundbreaking value-added programs for her diverse clients. There, she also arranged strategic alliances for some of the top Fortune 100 companies.

A frequent speaker for corporate and association audiences, Joyce is a Professional Member of the National Speakers Association.

A graduate of the University of Denver, Joyce holds an MBA from Fordham University and master's degrees in counseling and theology from The New Seminary. Joyce is a Certified Management Consultant and has taught at the university level. Joyce has published and been quoted in numerous articles in trade, consumer, and business magazines.

Oakhill Press

Oakhill Press is an independent publisher of business and self-help books. Our team of professionals assures that our products uphold our standards for high quality, readability, and usefulness. We are dedicated to helping leaders do a better job—in their business and in their personal lives.

Since the inception of Oakhill Press in 1988, we have endeavored to bring well-written books by knowledgeable people to readers who can benefit from them. The information and insight shared in our books is the result of years of experience combined with appropriate research. We value highly the letters, calls, and e-mail we receive praising our books.

Our authors are all management consultants and/or professional speakers. They are on the leading edge of their fields of expertise, strengthened by continual interaction with clients and audiences. Their thinking, speaking, and writing are stimulating, educational, and practical. We are pleased to serve as a vehicle for them to convey their thoughts to the world.

For further information on Oakhill Press publications, you are invited to visit our web site, www.oakhillpress.com. And, of course, you can give us a call at (800) 32-BOOKS. Thanks for giving us an opportunity to make a difference in your life.